Visionary Compacts

The Wisconsin Project on American Writers

A series edited by Frank Lentricchia

In Defense of Winters: An Introduction to the Poetry and Prose
of Yvor Winters
　　　　by Terry Comito

A Poetry of Presence: The Writing of William Carlos Williams
　　　　by Bernard Duffey

Visionary Compacts: American Renaissance Writings in Cultural Context
　　　　by Donald E. Pease

"A White Heron" and the Question of Minor Literature
　　　　by Louis A. Renza

The Theoretical Dimensions of Henry James
　　　　by John Carlos Rowe

Specifying: Black Women Writing the American Experience
　　　　by Susan Willis

Visionary Compacts
American Renaissance Writings
in Cultural Context

Donald E. Pease

The University of Wisconsin Press

Published 1987

The University of Wisconsin Press
114 North Murray Street
Madison, Wisconsin 53715

The University of Wisconsin Press, Ltd.
1 Gower Street
London WC1E 6HA, England

First printing

Printed in the United States of America

For LC CIP information see the colophon

ISBN 0-299-11000-1

Jacket illustration: Asher B. Durand's *Kindred Spirits*. Courtesy of Arts, Prints and Photography Division, The New York Public Library, Astor, Lenox, and Tilden Foundations

For Patricia McKee

And they conversed together in Visionary
  forms dramatic, which bright
Redounded from their Tongues in thunderous
  Majesty, in Visions,
In new Expanses, creating exemplars of Memory
  and of Intellect.
                                    —*William Blake*

Contents

Preface

Like many others, this book began with an entirely different subject. When I first started work on this project over eight years ago I became interested in those moments within American Renaissance writings when characters' actions seemed out of keeping with their motives, when their cultural identity seemed opposed to their previous experiences and their utterances resistant to the thematic structures designed to organize them into coherence. Eight years ago I was convinced that the dominant paradigm explaining American Renaissance writing, proposed by Matthiessen and Chase and Bewley and refined on in different ways by Richard Poirier, Quentin Anderson, and, more recently, Joseph Riddel, John Carlos Rowe, and John Irwin, was an appropriate framework to explain American Renaissance writings. According to these critics, inconsistencies in character, theme, and cultural action participated in a much greater cultural contradiction, the permanent opposition between the culture's past and present demanded by the Revolutionary mythos, the dominant structuring principle for all American culture.

Eight years ago I hoped to produce a work able to explain American Renaissance writings in terms of the crisis in self-legitimation the Revolutionary mythos produced. But now I think this crisis in legitimation more applicable to post–World War II American culture than to pre–Civil War America. Prior to the Civil War, Hawthorne, Whitman, Emerson, and in very different ways Melville and Poe searched for forms of cultural agreement more lasting than the mere opposition to a past sanctioned by the Revolutionary mythos. The Revolutionary mythos produced citizens who believed in nothing but opposition—to family, environment, cultural antecedents, and even their former selves. Their relationships with others were no more lasting than the time it took to prove superiority to another. Such associations may have been valuable as a way of weaning Americans from their roots in the East and turning them toward the western territories, since the western territories needed settlers who depended on their own wits more than the company of others. But in the troubled years preceding the Civil War, the issues of union, expansionism, and slavery turned the

United States itself into the equivalent of a British tyrant for some states and territories. The threat of secession proved to be one of the consequences when the Revolutionary mythos was turned into a means of cultural association, and made it necessary for Americans to reflect upon cultural principles they could agree upon.

During this period the writers comprising what we refer to as our American Renaissance did not adhere to the Revolutionary mythos but devised in their writing what I call visionary compacts. The Revolutionary mythos sanctioned a notion of negative freedom keeping the nation's individuals separate from one another. Visionary compacts sanctioned terms of agreement from the nation's past—capable of bringing together the nation's citizens in the present. Instead of corroborating the Revolutionary mythos which would have justified a civil war, they restored the terms constitutive of the nation's civil covenant, terms of agreement every American citizen could acknowledge as binding. At a time in which many Americans used the Revolutionary mythos to guarantee self-interest, these writers returned to the nation's grounding compact in order to reflect on what was in the general interest of the nation.

A nation of self-interested individuals was a nation devoid of civic relations. Civic relations could appear only when individuals put the nation's general interest—what political scientists call the general will—before self-interest. In the absence of civic relations, mid-nineteenth-century Americans confronted the possibility of a civil war.

American Renaissance writers, I claim, wished to avoid a civil war by returning America to agreed-upon relations, thereby restoring to America a common life all Americans could share. Restoring these relations meant reminding Americans of the agreements that made them possible, which meant reminding nineteenth-century Americans of the hopes, ideals, and purposes they shared with their ancestors. It meant restoring their relationship with the nation's past, and involved an acknowledgment of a living tradition of cultural ideals, begun in the past but demanding realization and renewal by subsequent generations. Such a collective memory would remind individuals of the memorable life they shared with everyone else in the community. Moreover, a commemorative attitude, insofar as it demanded that an individual come to terms with separation through the connective tissue of memory, would replace the superficial bonds of self-interest and restore an interest in the general weal at a time in which secession threatened the nation.

In turning the visionary compacts reestablished in nineteenth-century literature into the subject of this book, my intention is not to isolate them within that time period but to suggest that these compacts await renewal as a way of liberating us from the general crisis in cultural legitimation ruling the days of our present lives.

Acknowledgments

And so it was I entered the broken world
To trace the visionary company of love.
  —Hart Crane

If the line of thought holding together the ideas in this book were traced, it would reach back into my undergraduate years and would include in its lineage many teachers, students, and friends. Professor Warren G. French and Professor James E. Miller, Jr., started me on the way to this understanding of America. My first teaching experience at Dartmouth, in a class I taught with James M. Cox, led me to rethink many of the received ideas about American literature. And discussions with Cox, Lou Renza, Blanche Gelfant, Noel Perrin, Horace Porter, and Ivy Schweitzer, all colleagues in American Literature at Dartmouth, led me to refine my ideas.

In postgraduate seminars with Paul de Man and with Edward W. Said I engaged some theoretical questions at work in my project. The critical community responsible for *boundary 2,* a group comprising William Spanos, Paul Bové, Daniel O'Hara, and Jonathan Arac, provided me with the best kind of intellectual environment. Individually and as a group, these critics challenged my ideas of visionary compact, tradition, and collective memory, giving me the resistance needed to refine and in many cases reevaluate my ideas.

I found in Allen Grossman's notion of cultural personhood and in Frank Lentricchia's critique of modern social change discriminations essential to the completion of my project. Kate Nicholson forced me to think critically about the notion of transition. For much of my understanding of the binding work of mourning as a cultural process and the cultural value of associations I am indebted to Paco Garcia. I also owe thanks to David McLaughlin, President of Dartmouth, who challenged me to put some of these notions about community into practice when he appointed me Chairman of the Committee on Student Life at Dartmouth.

Richard Poirier, James Cox, Lou Renza, and Jonathan Arac generously gave sections of the manuscript readings critical enough to demand crucial revisions. Allen Fitchen and Frank Lentricchia believed in it from the first draft and were extremely helpful editors. And Susan Tarcov gave me a much-valued writing lesson in her copyediting of the manuscript.

But this book would never have been completed had Patricia McKee not taught me the difference between visionary compacts and a genuine human bond. The entire book is an acknowledgment of that difference.

Hanover, New Hampshire
November 26, 1985

Visionary Compacts

Chapter One

Visionary Compacts and the Cold War Consensus

If interest relates men, it is never more than some few moments. It can create only an external link between them . . . where interest is the only ruling force each individual finds himself in a state of war with every other . . . nothing is less constant than interest . . . it can only give rise to transient relations and passing associations.

—*Emile Durkheim*

Men are free when they belong to a living, organic, believing community, active in fulfilling some unfulfilled, perhaps unrealized purpose. Not when they are escaping to some wild west. The most unfree souls go West and shout of freedom . . . The shout is a rattling of chains, always was.

—*D. H. Lawrence*

In the aftermath of World War I, D. H. Lawrence traveled to America, whose "spirit of place" he hoped would revivify the root idea of the Western world. Lawrence turned to America because he believed that the great passional life of Europe, what he called its "spirit," had already migrated to America. While in Europe, this great westering spirit had resulted in great artistic and cultural achievements; but they belonged to Europe's past. To interpret the achievements of American culture as a branch or province of European culture Lawrence considered a betrayal of the living spirit of European culture. And to betray the spirit is to lose the opportunity to be remade in its image. So instead of experiencing American life as if it were an unsuccessful effort to remember Europe's past achievements, Lawrence described Europe as a dying civilization in need of America's spirit for cultural renewal.

> And it is this change in the way of experience, a change in being, which we should now study in American books. We have thought and spoken

till now in terms of likeness and oneness. Now we must learn to think in
terms of difference and otherness . . . The knowledge that we are no
longer one, that there is this unconceivable difference in *being* between
us, the difference of an epoch, is difficult and painful to acquiesce in. Yet
our only hope of freedom lies in acquiescing. The change has taken
place in reality. And unless it takes place also in our consciousness, we
maintain ourselves all the time in a state of confusion. We must get clear
of the old oneness that imprisons our real divergence.[1]

Lawrence's words are inspiriting. He meant them as a mandate, a cultural imperative directed to all of his fellow Europeans, asking them to
come to terms with the fundamental challenge of modern culture. It was in
coming to terms with America, Lawrence believed, that Europeans first
encountered the great challenge of modern existence. It was in America
that the gulf between change and the unquestioned authority of Europe's
past—what Lawrence elsewhere referred to as its tradition—first became
visible. "There is an unthinkable gulf between us and America," Lawrence
writes in "The Spirit of Place," and across this gulf "we see, not our own
folk signalling to us, but strangers, incomprehensible beings, simulacra,
perhaps of ourselves, but *other,* creatures from an other-world. The connection [between Europe and America] holds good historically for the past.
In the pure present and in futurity it is not valid. The present reality is
a reality of untranslatable otherness, parallel to that which lay between
St. Augustine and an orthodox senator of the same day. The oneness is
historic only."[2]

The historical association with which Lawrence closes this moving passage carries all the force of his vision. By drawing a parallel between Saint
Augustine's relation to a Roman senator and an American's to a European
Lawrence preserves an image of the progress of Western culture. The
"idea" of Europe began, Lawrence believed, in the elaboration of differences between African saints like Augustine and the senators in Rome.
These saints were not Romans, but "the prelude to a new era." In these
saints Lawrence felt the same mystic passion, generative of a new life out of
old decadence, that he finds in America.

In its difference from Europe, America's spirit reminds Lawrence of the
origins of Europe. By migrating to America Lawrence is only following in
the steps of the great spirit of Western civilization itself, as it progressed
from Rome to Europe then to America. By studying the classics in American literature, Lawrence aspired to embody the spirit of Europe's past in

its living form. Lawrence did not separate himself from the great works achieved in Europe's past but renewed his relation with a living form of the same westering spirit that gave rise to them. His wish was not to recall what Europe had already achieved but to realize, for his age, what had been envisioned for it in the past but not yet fulfilled. So instead of emigrating to the Old World of Europe's past, as did his contemporaries Eliot and Pound, he migrated to a new world, the America that Europe had dreamed of in the past when her spirit needed revival but that had not yet been turned into a living reality.

Lawrence turned his face away from the realm of memory, where everything endured the way statues do, and toward what remained to be made of the stuff of memory, a new life in the "pure present." This world in the pure present was not the America Pound and Eliot had left but the world Lawrence would envision by writing *Studies in Classic American Literature.* In writing that work, Lawrence came into consciousness of another enabling difference. Not this time the difference between African saints and Roman senators, but a related one: the difference between the world the founders of American culture envisioned and present-day America. By experiencing this difference between the original vision of America and its present reality, Lawrence entered into renewed relation with the unrealized purposes and ideals—what he calls the spirit—of American culture. He needed to tap the reservoir of this culture's living spirit from the past because he believed that America was the last resting place of the spirit of the Western tradition. And after the deadening effect of World War I, Europe needed a renewal of its spirit, or it, like Rome, would fall of its own weight.

D. H. Lawrence's Visionary Compact

In situating Lawrence's study of American literature in this context, I wish to draw attention to the cultural duties to which he assigned his *Studies.* As the essay introducing that work—"The Spirit of Place"—indicates, Lawrence needed to write this book. And his need was not merely a personal one but was related to the needs of his culture. Like Lawrence, Western culture needed to be replenished by vitalizing sources of life. To let the spirit of the culture's founders become active in him, Lawrence had to let their spirit replace the life that had become decadent in him—which meant that he had to address their classic visions in terms of modern America's loss of that vision. Only a writer who put himself in present relation with the living ideas of the true America from the past could make the present America vanish like a bad dream.

In writing his book on America's classic writers Lawrence renewed their commitments and underwent their struggles. He forged a visionary compact with the continuing goals, purposes, and aspirations of these figures from America's past. I call the compact Lawrence established visionary for two reasons. The term "visionary" is consonant with Lawrence's key term "spirit" and emphasizes the demand implicit in both terms to make visible what has not yet been realized from a past. When joined with "compact," "visionary" calls attention to what is most vital about America's civic covenant, its basis in the spirit all of its members share.

At the time Lawrence wrote, the notion of a civic covenant had suffered the same fate as his belief in a "spirit of place." Modern liberalism, the ruling ideology in Lawrence's culture and our own, emphasizes an individual's struggles against the conformity demanded by his fellows, thereby demoting civic covenants to the status of contracts and the "spirit of place" to a cultural superstition. But Lawrence believed modern liberalism to be a form of negative freedom, the desire merely to be free *from* a variety of constraints, whether of European tyrants, constrictive legislation, or, more pervasively, the past itself. In "The Spirit of Place" Lawrence carefully distinguishes negative freedom from what freedom meant in America's classics. "It is never freedom," Lawrence writes, "till you find something you really want to be." "Men are free," he continues,

> when they are in a living homeland, not when they are straying and
> breaking away. Men are free when they are obeying some deep inward
> voice . . . Obeying from within. Men are free when they belong to
> a living, organic, believing community, active in fulfilling some un-
> fulfilled, perhaps unrealized purpose. Not when they are escaping
> to some wild west. The most unfree souls go West and shout of free-
> dom . . . The shout is a rattling of chains, always was.[3]

Lawrence's rationale for distinguishing the "classic" vision of American freedom from the merely negative freedom is related to his purpose in writing *Studies in Classic American Literature*. He turned to America as a cultural locus for a tradition of freedom compatible with the westering spirit that had given rise to the classic work in Europe's culture. He believed that in America the cultural contradiction of modern existence—the gulf between change and tradition—could be resolved as a transmission of freedom.

In studying the classics of American literature, Lawrence attempted to make a cultural reentry into the modern world. Whereas Eliot and Pound turned away from modern America for traditional, Old World values alienated from it, Lawrence returned to modern America with his vision of the living tradition from America's premodern past. The founders of America's tradition, Lawrence believed, had already found a way to transform the purely negative freedom at work in a modern existence into a more enduring form of liberty. In recalling what remains to be made of the vision of her classics, Lawrence felt himself called to an alternative experience of the modern world.

Studies in Classic American Literature constituted Lawrence's symbolic "naturalization" as a citizen of an American Republic of Letters. Only through this symbolic transfer of citizenship could Lawrence recover what he called "true liberty" as a culturally transmissible, collectively inherited commonwealth of freedom.

Modernism, Crisis, and Negative Freedom

Unlike Lawrence, who saw the American classics as an antidote to the negative freedom at work in modern existence, most modern interpreters of the American canon have transposed that canon itself into an example of negative freedom. Underlying most modern readings of the American canon is a common wish. These interpreters need to assign value to the independence of a present moment from past moments because they identify this independence with the cultural motion of modernity. Their commentaries assign value to the passing moment, the sheer appearance of the new, by associating it with the Revolutionary moment in America's past. In so doing they reinstate the authority of a negative freedom as well as the cultural contradictions it produces.

The greatest difficulty confronting any advocate of negative freedom is cultural legitimation.[4] Cultural legitimation becomes a problem when citizens base their personal identity as well as their nation's identity on a refusal to acknowledge the authority of institutions inherited from the nation's past. Without a past to inform their present lives, individuals have no basis for present identity. Many citizens in Revolutionary America experienced this crisis in legitimation when they refused to acknowledge their pre-Revolutionary past. They based this refusal on the same grounds as do many modern commentators on the American Renaissance, that is, the Revolution: an event from the nation's past that has been subsequently elevated into a mythos, a political fiction capable of organizing the lives of many Americans. The Revolution had indeed secured the nation's freedom from an oppressive past. The mythic associations accruing to this historic event subsequently made freedom synonymous with liberation from an oppressor. And this negative freedom granted cultural authority to a variety of breaks from an equally variable series of oppressors.[5]

Now, as long as the British tradition along with all its coercive laws, customs, and regulations remained a presence in America, the authority invested in our liberation from its oppression remained unchallenged. But by the middle of the nineteenth century, when most of America's classics were written, the presence of an oppressive British past had all but disappeared, leaving Americans with a problem in self-legitimation. Without a British tyrant and his Old World customs to oppose, Americans had to discover a basis for the nation's identity in something other than a break from Britain's past.

Trouble attended any new discovery because that definitive break had already turned into a dominant way of producing an American culture. The mythos of the Revolution, and the negative freedom supporting it, encouraged many Americans to turn liberation into a daily ritual. Long after the historical conditions supporting the Revolution had disappeared, revolution in the attenuated form of oppositions to received institutions remained the rule of the day. Opposition to the established, whether in the form of received ideas, practices, or institutions, based its authority on the patriot's break from an old world. But it also generalized that mythical event until it became a defining trait in the nation's character.

American authors turned this oppositional model into an advantage, modern commentators have argued, by insisting on their difference from Europe's tradition. But this model also posed an obstacle to any effort to begin a vital tradition of American letters. At its most radical level (and the model supported radical interpretations of its implications) this model supported an intolerance of anything past, whether that past be measured in centuries, decades, or, in the case of newspaper dailies, days. Without any past to carry forward, the nation's authors found themselves without a cultural context, and without a context they could depend upon no consistent set of purposes and had no legitimate tradition to carry forward.

Unlike Lawrence, the regnant tradition of American critics has argued that American writers turned even their cultural dislocation to an advantage. Their very separation from a tradition, according to these modern commentators, afforded these writers a unique relation to both literary forms and cultural institutions. Exempt from submission to these structures, American writers were free to take artistic possession of them, and, through an investment of inventive energies greatly exceeding the endurance of existing cultural structures, work themselves free of them.

Such critics as Richard Chase, Richard Poirier, and Harold Bloom have claimed that America's classic authors turned the crisis in cultural authority into the defining principle of their art. They did not feel culturally deprived by the loss of context; rather, any context capable of assimilating their vision they wrote out of existence. Consequently when writers, like Melville in *Moby-Dick,* released into their narratives rhetorical energies, visionary perspectives, and multiply dimensioned characters vastly superior to the power of any organizing principle to control them, theme went the way of context—as did characters, plots, structure, anything able to claim control. What took the place of control, in the canonical modernist view, was the negation of any form capable of restraining visionary forces. And without the need for validation, these writers invested illegitimacy itself with great cultural value.

But this argument, along with the tradition of criticism it sustains, rationalizes an oppositional model more compatible with modern than premodern America. In the "Renaissance" moment in our literature, this oppositional model, as well as the Revolutionary mythos supporting it, did not sustain but threatened the nation's identity. And many Americans looked to the pre-Revolutionary past with the urgency Lawrence would display three generations later. They too needed a renewed sense of a living past to sustain their present lives.

Many Americans put "Union" in the place of the oppressor, and their subsequent threat to secede turned negative freedom into a negation of the nation's identity. More than at any other time in the nation's history, Americans now looked for a non-Revolutionary context to define the nation's purposes. Instead of appearing as a definitive break from a past, the Revolutionary moment was redefined by such writers as Whitman and

Emerson in terms compatible with Lawrence's, as an unfulfilled promise for the future, an as yet unrealized vision, with principles awaiting answering deeds, motives in demand of present enactment. Instead of remaining an oppressive burden to be opposed by the present age, the nation's pre-Revolutionary past underwent a similar elevation in value.

Mid-nineteenth-century Americans confronted in the issue of slavery unfinished cultural business from the Revolutionary past. And the ensuing debate over liberty led many Americans to challenge the value of negative freedom sanctioned by the Revolutionary mythos. For freedom negatively defined freed an individual not only from oppressive institutions but from his neighbors, his family, his past, and in many cases from his principles. In the arguments over the divisive issue of slavery, the nation's orators emphasized the positive value of liberty.

There were other issues—expansionism, free trade, national conscription, to name the most divisive—demanding the attention of American citizens. There were also many unprincipled ways of addressing these issues, compromises arrived at by opportunistic legislators, and Supreme Court decisions protecting special interests. Melville carried his dispute with his father-in-law, Justice Lemuel Shaw, over the Fugitive Slave Law over into his narratives. Nathaniel Hawthorne preserved his disgust with the corruption of partisan politics in the preface to *The Scarlet Letter*. Throughout the antebellum period, not just Melville and Hawthorne but many American writers tried to recover a social context. They did not need to write themselves free of existing structures. The nation's divisiveness over its fundamental principles had already produced a surplus of negative freedom these writers found threatening rather than enabling.[6]

A Twentieth-Century Consensus

But in the twentieth-century commentary on American Renaissance literature, these divisive political questions, as well as the pre–Civil War cultural context, tend to drop out of sight. They are supplanted by more rarefied struggles: what Richard Chase has designated the artist's quest for an open form in defiance of constricting structures, what R. W. B. Lewis has called the American's need to sustain radical Adamic innocence in the face of familial and social responsibilities, what Charles Feidelson has described as the American's effort to return all things—facts, characters, places—

to unity in the organicist activity of language. Such characterizations, or variations of them, presently accompany the classics of the American Renaissance.

Part of the reason for the elision of context is historical. Writers immediately after the Civil War, like Mark Twain and Henry James, also separated antebellum letters from an ideological context. The Civil War, in its bloody resolution of the nation's political issues, caused Twain to treat even the issue of slavery as a pretext for practical jokes and burlesque. After that war, Twain along with the rest of the nation needed to believe himself forever free from divisive contexts. Disagreement had, after all, led people to give up their lives for political principles. Following the war, Twain reduced political beliefs to the status of tall tales, occasions for pleasure in taking someone in rather than taking someone's life. Those who took lives rather than jokes, like the Shepherdsons and Grangerfords, were what Twain's humor put behind us.

Not just Twain but most Americans needed to believe that the Civil War had put an end to ideology, if only so that they never again would need to confront the troubling questions leading the nation to war. After the Civil War, the mythos of the Revolution returned: to claim the Civil War as its definitive reenactment.

Critics whose politics were as different as F. O. Matthiessen's and Charles Feidelson's could not claim the Civil War as the basis for their elimination of the pre–Civil War context. But these critics did share a predisposition with Americans who wrote immediately after the Civil War. They too needed to believe in an end to ideology in America. Writing in the years immediately preceding World War II, Matthiessen needed to put aside internal disputes over ideology, the better to defeat the totalitarian powers Germany and Japan. And in the Cold War that followed World War II, Feidelson had reason to dissolve all signs of literary dissent into an organicist process. His book *Symbolism and American Literature* uses the literary term "symbolism" to separate America's literature from any merely local or national identity so that it can the better enter the modern world.

Here "symbolism" becomes indistinguishable from the process of change and the activity of modernization. Like symbolism these two processes include every determinate form—whether it be a character, a theme, or their setting—in an open-ended process, capable of dissolving their objective structure into its movements. Feidelson sets up an opposition between this organicist, utterly free process and forms of closure intent on containing the freedom of this process within structures; the parallel with the Cold War is obvious. A Cold War consensus on the question of liberty opposes the freedom of an open-ended process to the totalitarianism of closed systems.

In the final chapter of this book I will discuss the relationship between the Cold War and the American canon more fully. Now I would only point out that Feidelson's study uses symbolism and its organicist processes to draw together writers who lived at a time when the nation's symbolic apparatus was breaking apart. Feidelson's attention to symbolism elevated the value of studies in American literature, putting the classics in American literature on an equal footing with studies of more prestigious figures in the modern tradition. In doing so, however, *Symbolism and American Literature* also made visible a relationship modernism shared with a certain aspect of premodern American culture.[7]

To explain how, I need to return to the discussion of the mythos of the Revolution. Earlier I suggested that the Revolutionary mythos identified a break from an oppressive past with true freedom. So does modernism. Like the mythos of the Revolution, modernism is definable out of its denial of historical continuity. And critics who write from within a modernist moment often reclaim works from the past for a modern tradition by finding evidences of breaks and discontinuities in them. Later I will distinguish the cultural function of the Revolutionary mythos from the cultural work performed by modernism. Now I will only call attention to the work these two quite different cultural forms accomplish for each other. When put into service together, modernism and the Revolutionary mythos effectively dissever American literature from any historical context other than the one foreordained by the mythos of the Revolution.

To return that literature to its context, we need to remind ourselves of the ways in which nineteenth-century writers found the mythos inapplicable to their situation. Since modern critics of American literature have made the mythos of the Revolution seemingly the only applicable context, I will return to a nineteenth-century context by way of a modern critic who has used the Revolutionary mythos to replace it.

A Pre-Revolutionary America

Washington Irving's "Rip Van Winkle" is an ideal focus for any discussion of the relationship between different time periods. It was, after all, the anxiety-filled years of the Revolutionary War that Rip chose to sleep through. For many commentators on this fable, Rip's liberation from a difficult wife and troubling family responsibilities indicate a crucial effect of the Revolution—it freed American men from a past filled with responsibilities, anxiety, and in some cases domestic as well as political tyranny.

In elaborating the implications of Rip's character for American culture, Leslie Fiedler writes that "the myth of Rip is much more than just another example among the jollier fables of masculine protest; it is the definition, made once and for all . . . of a fundamental American archetype. In some ways, it seems astonishingly prophetic: a forecast of today's fishing trip with the boys, tomorrow's escape to the ball park or the poker game. Henpecked and misunderstood at home, the natural man whistles for his dog, Wolf, picks up his gun and leaves the village for Nature—seeking in a day's outing what a long life at home has failed to provide him. It is hard to tell whether he is taking a vacation or making a revolution, whether his gesture is one of evasion or subversion."[8]

Fiedler manages this set of assertions about Rip by first positing him as an American archetype rather than a character located in a specific locale and confronted with a peculiar historical dilemma. Rip in Fiedler's version no longer shares the plight of the other Dutch settlers around Tarrytown. They were faced with a new leader (George Washington instead of George III) to honor, and a new form of government (democratic rule as opposed to a monarchy) to negotiate. They also had undergone a change in cultural and national identity. No longer Dutch settlers, they had to become citizens of the United States. Among them in the village were figures who had once identified with the Tories rather than the patriots, and many others who, although they had opposed British rule, still sympathized with older village ways, inevitably associated with British rule.

Rip's village, in other words, was filled with many individuals who were as confused about the effects of transition from colonial to postcolonial America as was Rip. Fiedler's elevation of Rip into a universal American archetype exempts him from any complicating transactions with his native village as effectually as did Rip's twenty-year sleep. Indeed Fiedler might be considered a twentieth-century analogue of the Hendrick Hudson figure from the tale, for in elevating Rip into the lofty position of cultural archetype, Fiedler enables him to remain untouched by his village context, just as Hudson's flagon of spirits protected him from the effects of war.

In a sense Hudson and Fiedler share a common rationale for their treatment of Rip. Hendrick Hudson as the presiding "spirit of place" needed

Rip's mind free of the complications of the war in order to preserve the memory of Tarrytown's pre-Revolutionary past. Leslie Fiedler, as a Cold War American critic, needs Rip to domesticate revolutionary impulses. Turning these otherwise political energies homeward, Fiedler turns Revolutionary independence into freedom from a termagant wife, wearisome family responsibilities, and a settled past. In the cultural uses to which Fiedler puts Rip, it is no wonder he cannot distinguish Rip's revolution from an "evasion." It *is* an evasion.

In fact Rip's sleep had nothing in common with a revolution, then or now. Fiedler silently equates revolution with Rip's freedom from a variety of confining contexts in order the better to associate freedom with a form of twentieth-century liberalism that Fiedler and many of his generation adopted after World War II. Liberals confine revolutionary freedom to quite a narrow context, defining it as a freedom from a variety of constraints. They also celebrate its consequences as if they could be described in terms of a continual furlough, with plenty of rest and recreation for soldiers who need not distinguish the war of freedom they waged against Nazi totalitarianism from the domestic struggle they will wage when they return home—against inevitably dominant wives and confining home lives.

While the archetypal Rip may seem to fill in the details for the portrait of American life proposed by a liberal-minded post–World War II critic, he bears little resemblance to the character in Irving's tale. There, unlike the other villagers, Rip does indeed have a difficult domestic situation. But Irving attends to Rip's need for freedom from his wife only to reduce the implications of American liberty to a manageable domestic context. When Rip awoke, he found himself free from his wife, but he found himself free from every other defining context as well. And as a consequence of this freedom, he found it difficult to find himself at all.

Without his dog, his family, his former village friends, and confronted with a set of faces, buildings, outfits, and village manners he had never before encountered, Rip experienced America's freedom as a loss of character. Upon awakening from a twenty-year sleep, Rip initially recognized no one, and no one recognized him. Without the possibility for mutual recognition he found himself unable to distinguish the negative freedom Fiedler celebrates so jovially from a terrifying sense of estrangement. As well he should; for he was from a pre-Revolutionary Tarrytown the Revolution had left behind.

Or was supposed to have left behind. While apologists for the Revolution may have claimed that it liberated America from her past, that liberation was more easily managed in their abstractions than in the lives of many Americans. As a figure in transition from a town life before the war, Rip enabled the townspeople to elaborate upon the changes the war made in their lives. When he appeared from out of the "nowhere" that once was Tarrytown, he made it necessary for the rest of the townspeople to do what the Revolutionary pundits claimed they should never do: that is, remember the conditions, cultural attitudes, and characters in the village life before the war. To give Rip back his identity they had to identify themselves with what the Revolution had forcibly cut them off from.

Coming to terms with Rip's lost identity made it necessary for them to explain their present village life to a figure from its past. In explaining their culture to Rip, they implicitly accommodated their present world to their broken past, thereby recovering connection with what the Revolution had disconnected them from. Their assimilation to the past also made it possible for them to assimilate formerly alienated characters from the Revolutionary past: loyalists to the British cause, Dutch settlers who still followed the "Old World" ways in Tarrytown, and even Rip's ne'er-do-well son, who found in his father a historical precedent and excuse for his laziness. Rip turned the pre-Revolutionary past into a presence in their village. Since he had slept through the Revolutionary War years, Rip, unlike other townspeople whose years bridged the gap between pre- and post-Revolutionary America, did not feel compelled to change himself into a post-Revolutionary American. Because it took place while he slept and thus never happened as an event in his life, the Revolution made no drastic change in Rip's life. He enabled the rest of the village to drop it out of their lives as well, and recover relation to the town's past, their personal pasts, and the locale's history.

Unlike Fiedler, Irving did not exploit Rip's revolutionary potential but used his status as a transitional figure to do the work a transitional object does for an infant. Rip enabled the villagers to give up their need for an exclusive attachment to one historical period and make it continuous with others. Irving did not write about Fiedler's modern culture. His America did not need to define freedom in terms of a set of cultural constraints it confirmed by opposing. But the villagers in the upper New York towns he traveled through were undergoing crises in their identities akin to Rip's. Like Rip they needed a way to make their present cultural lives continuous with rather than disconnected from their past.

In the story's linking up the two separated Americas, much more was at stake culturally than finding the lost identity of Rip Van Winkle. Without a firm belief in the purposes it carried forward from a past, a nineteenth-century American village lacked any coherent sense of cultural purpose. Like Rip Van Winkle, its purposes were too quickly elevated into the realm of abstract and universal archetypes and too quickly separated from the daily lives, cultural situation, and local contexts of its citizens. In the nine-teenth century the political myth of manifest destiny became, for those who found themselves uprooted by the turmoil following the Revolution and for the many others—recent immigrants, the poor, the homeless—who had no roots at all, an archetypal catchall term enabling them to inter-pret cultural alienation as part of the nation's polity. But while the already alienated may have had little difficulty in situating their placeless lives within a mythical archetype, many more Americans felt threatened rather than exhilarated by a politically brand-new world.

In response to the threat of cultural anomie, many writers turned post-Revolutionary America into a haunted landscape. Unlike the writers of Gothic romances which surged up in post-Revolutionary Europe, writers of the supernatural in America did not find in their country the ruins of lost traditions and devastated aristocratic lineages from Europe's past. If anything, post-Revolutionary America was insufficiently haunted. It lacked what a revolutionary culture needs in order to flourish—the rem-nants of an old tradition to continue to oppose. Without such ruins from an older world, Americans confronted difficulty in experiencing their his-torical situation at all. To restore time to America's places, writers looked for ways to haunt them with an archaic past, as Irving did in "The Legend of Sleepy Hollow."

In this tale, the tree from which Major André, an American traitor, was hanged and the horse a Hessian soldier rode figured prominently. The tree, having lived through the Revolution, shared a trait in common with Major André who was hanged from it: both were possessed of dual sympathies, with a British past and an American present. After the war Americans were asked to get rid of memories from their personal pasts because sympathetic memories of British rule may have been stored in the personal memory as well. But many Americans needed their memories as well as their past in order to lead significant cultural lives. And they were willing to tell ghost stories about such figures as Major André, who died because of his divided loyalties, to keep these memories vivid.

The legend surrounding Major André's hanging tree enabled those who exchanged it to come to terms with the self-division in their own characters and translate their personal self-division into a way of characterizing their locale. By converting the need for a local past into a haunting ghost tale, these post-Revolutionary Americans could both satisfy their wish to recover a past and simultaneously deny that past—as the work of an ineradicable, alien, even un-American presence. Like Rip Van Winkle, the ghost of Major André was a transitional figure who enabled many Americans to affirm their past through the presence of his ghost yet deny it in their acknowledgment of his disloyalty.

After the village locals produced their haunts, they could use them on figures like Ichabod Crane. An uprooted, upwardly mobile American from somewhere else, Ichabod Crane would have felt quite at home with the universal locale made available in Fiedler's archetypes and the politicians' myths. He would have been at home with them because he could call no place his home. Thus, unlike the village locals, Crane feared the spirits who insisted on "possessing" places, because they implicitly identified him as trespassing upon other people's worlds and thereby threatened him with retribution.

There was another reason for haunting tales. Ghost tales not only inhabited American places with memories from the past but also heightened the sense of place. Without the headless horseman haunting the spots he rode through, these local places would not have demanded much more than merely passing acknowledgment. Haunting these local regions added those mysterious dimensions of time and space necessary for the development of a unique local identity. Crane's fear of the headless horseman enables him to recognize Tarrytown's peculiar character. Unlike other towns he might have passed through, Tarrytown was not a uniform, featureless terrain but a culture with customs, manners, and tacit rules of behavior. Ichabod Crane's faith in mobility, progress, and other generalized qualities resulting in a uniform American character made him a stranger in a world with specific, historically situated characteristics and clearly defined local types. By terrifying Crane with their legends, such inhabitants as Brom Bones were able to identify themselves with the spirit of this place rather than with Crane's progress through it.

Conversion and Self-Division

In calling attention to the hunger for continuity at work in nineteenth-century Americans, I have indicated a need they shared with D. H.

Lawrence, but I have considered only in passing the major cultural barrier to any belief in cultural continuity they shared with modernist commentators—that is, the change in identity the Revolution was believed to have made possible. The Revolutionary War did, of course, change the political and cultural identity of America, but many Americans had great difficulty in matching up the Revolutionary change in the nation's identity with changes in their own lives. Many Americans were unable to complete their conversion from one identity to another. Instead, many Americans experienced divisions within their identities, in which the British loyalist coexisted with the American patriot, the local inhabitant with the national citizen, the immigrant with the settler.

Often these self-divisions required radical cultural strategies for accommodation. We have already considered how in "Rip Van Winkle" Washington Irving invented a transition figure able to heal the divisions at work in Tarrytown. In his Gothic romance *Wieland,* Charles Brockden Brown invented a set of characters who felt unable to meet the demands America made on their personal identities. Brown peoples this novel with the descendants of a German visionary who felt called to America but was unable to answer the call. Answering the call meant giving up his German identity and becoming someone remade in an image compatible with the call.

The older Wieland's dilemma is one with which many European immigrants could identify. They found it necessary to change their manners, their past, their language, and sometimes their personal identities to answer this call to become citizens in a new culture. Most immigrants did not associate the call with a religious destiny. But Wieland did, and, when he could not live up to this high calling, his body, instead of undergoing a conversion experience, underwent spontaneous combustion. Wieland experienced the need to change his identity as an impossible demand. And he died instead of changing. But his descendants in America underwent an even more uncanny experience. They heard voices within themselves urging them to perform actions with which they could not identify.

To understand this division between inner voice and identity, motive and deed, we must remember something else about nineteenth-century America. It was a culture of oratory. In the nation's past, great orators like Patrick Henry and Ethan Allen had matched Revolutionary deeds with inspiriting words. More contemporary orators like Daniel Webster and Henry Clay maintained Revolutionary passions in the pitch of their voices, creating a mode of speech invested with extraordinary cultural value. In listening to these orators, who claimed the right to speak for America's citizenry and to America's destiny, many Americans experienced a separation between the sheer motivating power in the orators' words and the actions urged by them. Whose deeds could match Webster's words, Emerson, for one, would wonder in his notebooks.

Whose person could embody the orator's motives, Charles Brockden Brown wondered through his characters. If they could change their persons into a form more compatible with the fiery quality of the orators' language, something like the spontaneous combustion of Grandfather Wieland might be the result. If they could not assimilate their characters to the conviction carried by these voices, they could become like Carwin, another character in *Wieland*. Unlike the elder Wieland, who tries to meet the demands of a voice, or the younger Wieland who believes he hears his grandfather's voice, Carwin simply impersonates other people's voices. Like an immigrant who would learn a new language but without bothering with the convictions and beliefs accompanying it, Carwin learns how Americans speak but he does not speak like them. He separates their passions from his voice, thereby increasing his mobility through regions with different dialects but decreasing the possibility of his ever identifying with the convictions the local inhabitants share.

Carwin can change places because his power to impersonate voices takes the place of a personal identity. He changes places but he never undergoes a change of identity. He does not have any identity to change. For the characters in *Wieland*, as well as many of its nineteenth-century readers, personal identity was indistinguishable from a voice of conviction. These inner voices had undergone the change of identity called for by the Revolution. But although they were honored like the nation's orators who were also possessed of Revolutionary identities, these voices had no influence over the everyday lives of the persons in whom they spoke. Brown's characters experienced themselves as split apart, undone, victimized, or quite literally burned up. His characters could not turn these voices into motives for personal actions because the scene of the Revolution able to make them meaningful had disappeared. The dissociation of the voice of passionate conviction from the everyday actions of most Americans created a favorable context for the unprincipled compromises the nation's orators would bargain into existence.

As we have seen, this dissociation of Revolutionary motives from local actions was of great sociological use. Elected representatives in Washington could exemplify a national identity, while in the towns and villages individuals could continue to construct their characters according to more local demands. The need for a national identity, in other words, led to the election of political representatives who could meet that demand, but at the expense of local identities, personal pasts, and vital group life.

The Frontiersman and the Loss of a Past

I have begun to point up the ways in which nineteenth-century Americans needed to recover a past. Now let me consider why they needed to abandon one.

The move west made it necessary for many individuals to pull up their roots; it also made cultural anomie, or the inability to designate oneself as part of any vital community, a common form of social malaise. The doctrine of manifest destiny was, on one level, intended to convert this anxiety accompanying cultural displacement into a national mission. And the figure of the frontiersman was intended to give this experience of uprootedness a heroic appearance. Here indeed the Revolutionary mythos resurfaces, in characters resembling Fiedler's archetypal American hero. This descendant of the "natural man" always in a state of transition between nature and culture also appears within a particular historical and political context. The elevation of the homeless American into a national archetype enabled Americans who looked westward to separate themselves from their local communities with a sense of heroic mission. But when frontiersmen like Davy Crockett and Daniel Boone were elected to national leadership, they brought the frontiersman's code to Washington, sanctioning policies that placed no limit to America's boundaries or the individual's drive to self-aggrandizement.

Unlike many Americans who were compelled to move west for reasons of impoverishment, such frontier heroes as Daniel Boone, Davy Crockett, and Cooper's Hawkeye chose to move west. By representing their relationship with the West as a heroic confrontation with the elements, the writers who popularized these figures made a western identity available nationally. The cultural identity these figures like Hawkeye represented was based on an individual's power to affirm his separation from any roots, a power that was a necessity for survival. Unlike the Easterners whom he leads through the western territories, Hawkeye has no attachments to anyone except the adventuring spirit itself.

To be in Hawkeye's company is to learn how to impersonate a variety of forest characters but to identify with none. Through this character, Americans could learn how to experience disconnection from a past, their families, and even one another—as Hawkeye is ready to do as he chooses the last of a dying Indian tribe for his companion—as an affirmation of identity.

Unlike Ichabod Crane, who experienced his difference from the others in Sleepy Hollow as a loss of a personal identity, so that he recognized himself in the headless horseman, Hawkeye celebrates his power to accommodate himself to different regions, languages, personalities, and even bodies (in his impersonations of Indians, soldiers, animals). Hawkeye asserts his freedom from a personal past or a local region in order to nationalize his identity. Cooper's insertion of the national character of Hawkeye within a frontier context permits him a certain necessary legal fiction. Hawkeye's relationship with the last of the Mohican tribe, who were, in Cooper's view of it, the last Indian nation truly worthy of the American landscape and whose purity of blood lineage established their clear entitlement to the land, put Hawkeye in line to receive America's frontier from them. In Hawkeye, in other words, Cooper invented a figure who was able to transform cultural dispossession—that of the Mohicans— into a form of self-possession. Cooper was also able to treat Hawkeye's act of taking possession of himself in the woods as a rationale for America's legal title to the frontier. And every time Hawkeye teaches one of the Yankee greenhorns the ways of the woods, he initiates them into the same cultural process.

In Hawkeye the contradictory demands made on America's citizens on the one hand by the nation's manifest destiny and on the other by local regions were resolved. In Cooper's *Leatherstocking Tales* Americans could find a set of characters confronting a characteristic dilemma of the time— the need to give up a past world for a completely new life out west—and find in Hawkeye a means of working through the dilemma. They could discover how to experience their otherwise painful separation from local roots as an opportunity to participate in the expansion of the national character. The tales were set in the years of the French and Indian Wars to find in those pre-Revolutionary years a historic precedent for national as opposed to local self-definition. By converting those pre-Revolutionary years into a historical period in which Americans were affiliated with the last of a noble Indian line, Cooper enabled Americans to imagine the American nation as the beginning of a new cultural line which included all Americans as its heirs.

Hawkeye and the General Will

If Cooper's Hawkeye indulged in the Revolutionary fantasy, he did so only in his permanent conflicts with Indian tribes. He equated them with Old World rule; their noble bearing, stringent traditions, and often oppressive rulers clearly had European equivalents. Although Cooper also distinguished the Indians from their European counterparts, he did so to maintain a Revolutionary opposition more appropriate to historical conditions at the time he was writing. Without a European tradition to oppose, Americans traveling west could treat the Indians as an appropriate substitute.

A difficulty arose, however, whenever the figures in Cooper's tales wished to settle down. In elevating Hawkeye's national identity above any local identity, Cooper made it difficult for any of his settlers to consider the life they shared within the settlement as something other than a loss of the frontiersman identity they shared with Hawkeye.

Outside the *Leatherstocking Tales,* however, the nation had a place for its Hawkeyes, and for any other Americans who could prove their power to act upon a seemingly permanent supply of Revolutionary motives. Andrew Jackson, General Tyler, and Davy Crockett were some of the figures whom the nation sent to Washington, as the only locale appropriate for their identities. Here their sometimes frightening acts of taking possession of their own characters at the expense of others' would be taken not as self-interest but as examples of heroic individualism.

If we put Hawkeye into relation with the characters in Brown's *Wieland,* we can begin to see another reason for Cooper's popularity. Hawkeye acted on those Revolutionary powers of voice Wieland found so terrifying. In Hawkeye we find a character who derives his power to lead a group not from his enactments of the group's mandates but rather from his separation from the general interest of the group. In finding a way to become like Hawkeye, the other Americans in Cooper's narratives find not only a way to separate themselves from their pasts but a way to separate themselves from each other—as, say, David Gamut and Major Heyward do in *Last of the Mochicans*.

In Hawkeye, in other words—as well as in Jackson, Crockett, and Boone—Americans found a way to separate from their local identities and to identify with a national character whose self-interest became the defining feature of his ability to lead. Americans characteristically identified a leader's ability to lead with the power of his personality, and they defined that power as the ability to transcend the limitations of a local past. In the same characters through whom they nationalized their identities, Americans learned how to give up their pasts, their local roots, as well as any vital group life. While these various forms of disaffiliation gave Americans increased possibilities for social mobility, multiple associations, and personal aggrandizement, they nevertheless threatened the cultural and political life of the country as well.

The pressure to develop a national as well as a local identity often led to an opposition between the two, and the opposition was sometimes resolved through a move west, in which the past was dissolved, or, less frequently, through a move into politics, whereby the past could be transcended as a gain in one's national identity. One gained, however, by losing vital relations with others. And this loss threatened civic life altogether.

In the nineteenth century, I am claiming, Americans underwent a crisis in their understanding of the duties owed the self and the group. The major cause for the crisis inhered in the notion of a national identity. Duing the Revolutionary War Americans did not need to confront a distinction between their persons and an interest greater than the personal. Everyone who fought in the war did so for the sake of national freedom. But after the war Americans had to invent an identity for the nation, and a national character to match it. When the mythos of the Revolution made it necessary for them to give up their personal pasts for the sake of the new nation, it left them with no sense of national interest other than this act of dispossession. Consequently, many Americans based their American identity on the inability to distinguish their personal identities from the national identity.

The national policies of westward expansion and manifest destiny provided a national motive within which individuals could establish their national identity. At the same time, however, the question of local as opposed to national self-definition reappeared. In the mid-nineteenth century, many Southern and western Americans considered the national Union itself to be a constraint on personal freedom. These Americans insisted that the individual's responsibilities to local conditions and community concerns were definitive. Secession, particularly when entangled with the issue of liberty, struck many Americans as the only recourse in order to recover local rights.

The secessionists, or at least their representatives in Washington, did not argue for local rights in terms of the allegiance they owed to local conditions. They borrowed terms from the Revolutionary mythos to argue for their freedom, as opposed to the tyranny of the Union. Clearly, something was missing from the terms of a debate on the relationship between the responsibility an individual owes on the one hand to local groups and on the other to national concerns, when both sides used the Revolutionary mythos as their means of pursuing that debate. Modern critics tend to leave this missing consideration out as well. There is a reason for this persistent omission. In the nineteenth century, local group interests had no way of articulating themselves in terms compatible with the national interests. The split between local interests and the national interests was mediated in Washington where politicians from different locales could be reborn as national characters who shared the common ability to rise above the shortcomings of a modest (often log-cabin) past and become national spokesmen.

What was missing from both the politicians' considerations and the nation's politics was any belief in what Rousseau called a general will and what nineteenth-century Americans called a general interest or public will.[9] But whereas in the nineteenth century not only Irving and Brown but in more complex ways Hawthorne and Melville were calling attention to the need for a recuperated public will, most twentieth-century commentators associate the general will with a form of despotic control. Fiedler, in the work I have cited, affiliated communal life in Rip's village with the domestic tyranny he suffered at home, claiming Rip rebelled against both when he went on his twenty-year jaunt with the boys. But Fiedler's version—and, I will soon argue, those of many post–World War II critics—equated any group interest with the demands of an oppressive power.

Most of the critics who developed what I will call the Cold War consensus about American literature did so in the years following the formation of two mass movements: World War II and totalitarianism. Many of them served during World War II and compensated for their submission to the control of the military by redefining freedom solely in personal terms on return home. Not just Rip, but all of America and all of America's culture were defined as freedom from an oppressive structure—whether in the form of an Old World tradition, an individual's past, family responsibility, or a group's interest. This negative definition of freedom was sustained by the continued presence of a totalitarian power in Europe as well as the constant threat of mass destruction by nuclear weapons. The prospect of sharing a mass grave, as Allen Grossman has pointed out, drives people to overvalue their individuality.[10]

While this purely negative definition of freedom does release a lively sense of personal autonomy, it does so at the expense of a vital public sphere. For individuals who conceive of the life they can share together as a threat to their personal freedom cannot organize any vital community at all. While the loss of group life was experienced by many post–World War II critics as a gain in personal freedom, it was experienced by many nineteenth-century Americans as a threat to personal freedom. One of the ways American writers expressed this threat was in the terms of what I earlier called the legitimation crisis, for without a community in which they could express their identities many Americans experienced their national identity as a form of personal illegitimacy.

When we consider this experience, we tend to impose upon it our twentieth-century notions of the elevation of personal over community freedom. Thus, in his sequel to *Inventing America,* a book that investigates the sources of political power in pre-Revolutionary America, a recent commentator, Garry Wills, has chosen the post-Revolutionary legend of George Washington as the locus for meditation.[11] The subject of his meditations can be reduced to a single question: having been, in Wills's term, "invented" through the actions of the charismatic founding fathers, how could America develop an orderly line of succession? In formulating a response to this question, Wills finds in Washington the figure who, as the legendary father of our country, deliberately promoted the nation's sense of a genealogical line of succession. To add force to the issue of legitimate succession, Wills separates the legendary materials surrounding Washington's life from their usual historical locations—his decision to command the Revolutionary army and his election as the first president—and brings them into relation with those two extraordinary occasions when the question of national succession and the related issues of national security and historical continuity seemed most urgent: the historically distinct but psychologically inseparable decisions to resign from military duty and from the office of the presidency.

Because they seemingly contradict a presupposition in the theory of secular charisma guiding Wills's discussion, these resignations from office fascinate Wills much more than do Washington's acceptances of power. According to the most fundamental tenet of that theory, a charismatic leader's resignation from office should result in the disruption of the orderly procedures of succession he alone could legitimately authorize. Washington's resignations differ significantly, in Wills's versions, from those of other charismatic leaders because they signal his willingness to give up the power he has agreed to exercise with reluctance. After emphasizing the relation between the willingness to resign power and the reluctance to assume it, Wills equates public reluctance with political pretense. Washington carefully staged these resignations, Wills argues, because within the context of Revolutionary America those who appeared least eager for power, those resigned to accept rather than eager to attain it, would be those most readily invested with power. What Wills calls Washington's carefully staged "acts" of resignation thus legitimize the theory of secular charisma informing Wills's book.

Wills gains historical legitimacy for this argument when he reminds us of the "historic" affiliation by artists, writers, and politicians of Washington with Cincinnatus, one of those legendary figures from world history our young nation used to come to terms with George Washington's unusual actions. The similarities make the comparison seem inevitable. Like Cincinnatus, Washington gave up the sword for the plow; like Cincinnatus Washington treated his military office not as a legitimate but as an "emergency power" granted by the nation's government at a time of national danger and to be handed back to that same government once the danger had passed.

But the one crucial dissimilarity should lead us to a qualification of Wills's argument. Unlike Cincinnatus, Washington did not as yet have a duly constituted government capable of accepting his resignation from command of the army. The separation from England, achieved by his command, had not as yet resulted in the agreement among the colonies, the social contract, that would convert them into the United States of America. Without such a government, Washington, unlike Cincinnatus, would find no legitimate power capable of accepting his resignation. When reconsidered within this context, Washington's resignation has a different significance for American history.

The unusual terms of resignation of military power were implicit in Washington's letter accepting it. In offering him the commission to serve, the New York legislature wrote: "America . . . may have sure pledges that he will faithfully perform the duties of his high office; and readily lay down his power when the general weal requires it." And Washington replied: "When we assumed the soldier we did not lay aside the citizen; and we shall most sincerely rejoice with you in that happy hour when the establishment of American liberty, upon the most firm and solid foundation, shall enable us to return to our Private Stations in the bosom of a free, peaceful, and Happy Country."[12] We can best ascertain the effect of Washington's decision to lay down arms when we consider the alternative. As commander-in-chief of a victorious army, he could have established, after the defeat of the British, a military government. Instead, Washington aligned himself with the foundations of what was to become the Constitution, and, as a representative of this as yet unwritten document, he actually persuaded General Gates and his party of militia away from the military takeover they thought the only valid form of government.

He did not resign from his military duties, then, so much as he used his prior office as commander-in-chief of the armed forces to authorize the validity of a not as yet formulated contractual agreement that would lead to the formation of the United States. If we correlate this unwritten document with one of the terms used in the empowerment of Washington, i.e., the "general weal," we discover an unusual turn of affairs. Washington did not resign when, as the New York legislature put it, "the general weal required it." The general weal did not yet exist. But in resigning, Washington acknowledged or rather affirmed the existence of a general weal capable of accepting his resignation. In his prior office as the commanding general of an army, Washington converted what otherwise could have been interpreted as the rash and impulsive demands of upstart colonies into the decisive powers of a nation that was about to be. In his surrender of military duty Washington indicated his faith in a general weal or commonwealth whose demands were greater than any personal interest. His resignation, in other words, constituted the preformation, as a scene in the life of a private citizen, of a pro tem government. In surrendering to a general will not yet constituted, Washington performed what the Constitution would later turn into part of a national agreement: the orderly transfer of power, as ensured by the "separation of powers."

What remains most uncanny about Washington's conversion of his personal action into the site of a transfer of national power, however, inheres not in the action itself but in its constitutive agencies. For Washington did not merely resign from his office of representative of a nation's military; he resigned to his office of representative of an as yet unwritten contract, the Constitution, which would resolve the conflicting interests of the colonies into the general weal of the United States of America. Washington, then, as a private person, never truly appeared at all. Or rather, the private person Washington appeared only long enough to preenact the acceptance of an as yet unwritten social compact which required the surrender of the self-interest of each private citizen to the general weal.

Put simply, Washington's resignation translated civic virtue, the sacrifice of self-interest for the general interest of the commonwealth, into an exemplary founding action. In his association of Washington with the mythic Cincinnatus, Wills effectually ignores what Washington was eager to emphasize: the implications of his actions for the commonwealth. As a post-Revolutionary nation, America needed to convert the fundamental impulse of will certain to motor a revolution—the urge to rebel against an authority—into a past action. And one of the ways in which the rebellious impulse was made to seem past was through its redesignation as a lower, primitive, or unevolved form of a higher or civilized will. Not the impulsive will of a single man, but the commanding design of a higher; or, borrowing the terms of Enlightenment philosohies, a more mature will, resulting when individuals surrendered the conflicting interests and warring impulses keeping them separate for the agreements bringing them together. When considered in this context, the image of Cincinnatus accrued power for Washington not by underscoring his reluctance to exercise it, but by supervising its orderly transfer. As the figure who oversaw from the past the resignation of the representative of rebel forces to the representative of a polis of mature citizens, Cincinnatus implicitly corroborated that the first responsibility of the new government was the need to get the Revolution behind them.

In designating his resignation from the Revolutionary army as a return to the liberty and peace of a private citizen, Washington, in his private person, established two claims prerequisite for a stable government—its ability to be permanent and to represent the will of the people. By resigning the rebel will to what would become the Constitution, Washington preconfirmed the government's power to represent the will of the people; by treating this governmental power as a form preexisting his entrance into the Revolutionary army, Washington gave that government a pre-Revolutionary form, or rather a historic form. In his resignation, then,

Washington did not, as Wills claims, conceal his private need for continued "Revolutionary" power through the public charade of a reluctance to accept it. By representing himself as the citizen of a pre-Revolutionary nation to which he could return after performing the extraordinary and unusual duties of revolution, he turned the Revolution not into the nation's founding moment but into that extraordinary episode in the nation's history where it became necessary for the nation to recover and secure an already existing past.

All of which is to say that Washington's public resignation turned out to be the occasion through which the nation could imagine a past for its social contract. And we can best ascertain the force of this transformation by resituating it within the authoritative political context of our own day. For in our day, the fiction of the social contract as the ongoing negotiation with the general will of the people has been replaced. No longer can the individual express freedom through a working relationship to a general will expressive, in turn, of varying agreements working through the continuing negotiations of the collective heterogeneity known as the people. Instead, the people have been turned into a collective homogeneity, the masses, and individuals more commonly express freedom as their separation from the masses than, as was the case in Washington's time, as their participation in the will of the people. An even more fundamental revisionary equation presently sustains this attitude. Consequent to the appearance of fascism and communism as political systems competitive with America's, the general will has been generalized into a totalitarian will to power, and this generalization has, in its turn, demanded a revision: of the formerly free will of the people into the tyranny of the masses.

In his modern book on Washington, Gary Wills clarifies the difficulty of getting the Revolutionary moment behind us. According to the logic of Wills's oppositional frame, the individual can express freedom not through associations with but only through independence from the will of others. And this fundamental separation of the individual from any group necessarily leads to and validates the notion of secular charisma guiding Wills's discussion, for it implies the inability of the general weal ever to arrive at a decision that will do otherwise than bind the individual to the distractions of the moment: a bondage that, in its turn, can be answered only by a superior, because individually rather than group-formulated, mode of decision making: that of the charismatic individual. The individual chooses alienation, in the decision to be free from the group, as both the legitima-

tion of power and the best way to exercise power. Which is why he is reduced to one of two positions: either to that of a passive spectator of unfree because group-associated forms of power (which, Wills suggests,
political life really is); or to that of a leader who accrues power by "staging," as in Wills's analysis of Washington's scenario of resignation, his independence of the group.

Will's analysis highlights the contradiction at work in this modern conception: the power of the charismatic political leader derives its only legitimacy in the eyes of the people from his independence from the group. But
he is not independent: his leadership depends upon his power, again and
again, to get the people to follow him. His assertions of independence are
therefore inauthentic or theatrical, and his power illegitimate. Put into the
simplest form, the will of the charismatic leader becomes indistinguishable
from the tyrannical will of the people.

Now I should like to reactivate our earlier qualification of Wills's theory
by suggesting that Washington was exercising a political virtue utterly
inimical to both the notion of charismatic power and the oppositional
frame underlying it. For Washington, as we have seen, did not stage a resignation but resigned himself, not as either an individual or a mass man but
as the mediation between them, to a general weal which his act of resignation lent palpable form. The reappearance of Washington's resignation in
popular legend as well as the classics in American literature only underscores its most fundamental quality: in resigning, Washington was not
staging but carrying out, as his newly won right, an action embodying all
the terms of the civic covenant[13]—the surrender of self-interest for the interests of the commonwealth.

We can say that Washington resigned from military duty in order to
fulfill the obligation of a prior contract. But in order to ascertain the force
of the obligations of this absolutely prior contract we might wonder what
might have happened had Washington taken an alternative course of action: what would have happened if Washington's resignation had been demanded rather than freely offered. Would we have had a smooth transfer of
power from military action to civil government, or would America have
found herself in an endless vacillation between rebellion against authority
and tyrannical assertion of authority, characteristic of, say, the aftermath of
the French Revolution? Or characteristic of, on the other hand, Wills's description of the relations between Washington and the American people
and Fiedler's description of Rip Van Winkle's relationship with his wife.

These descriptions are of a piece: while Fiedler's Rip had to get free of his wife, Wills's Washington had to be free of the American people. But they coincide in modern rather than historical contexts. And their concept of freedom, as that which can belong only to an individual and be expressed only negatively, is modern too.

In arguing for a different interpretation of Washington's resignation, I do not want to replace one idealization, that of the free individual, with another—of the American people. Instead, I want to call attention to an element missing from these modernist versions, but one very much present in the past. The best way to call attention to what was present then and missing now is to remember how the role George Washington plays in Washington Irving's "Legend of Sleepy Hollow" differs from the part he plays in Garry Wills's *Cincinnatus*. The legend of the headless horseman involves the Major André incident, and that incident concerns Washington's power to execute a decision on his own authority and his need for consultation with the general will of the people. Many of the American people sympathized with the division in Major André's sympathies because they shared them. And in continuing to feel haunted by the injustice of Washington's decision, the Americans who kept the incident alive by trading on versions of the legend established a council of their own on the matter, quite different from Washington's. Part of the reason the citizens of Sleepy Hollow kept alive the legend of Major André was to differentiate their local judgment from Washington's decision. Through such legends as this one, and such related activities as rumor, gossip, and regional tales, Americans in the nineteenth century came into collective relation with issues of national importance.

This communal and collective participation, with the particular, and now extraordinary, relations of individuals and groups it entailed, is difficult for us to identify, because for one thing, as I suggested earlier, local group interests tended not to be articulated in Washington by men interested in representing a national identity. Modern critics have had especial difficulty, given the modernist assumptions I have been considering here. Yet such collective participation is clearly active in the exchanges of rumor, gossip, and tales that function in Irving's *Sketches*, Brown's Gothic novels, and Hawthorne's historical romances.

By exchanging these forms of group discourse, communities took collective possession of historical facts and political persons. Legends, gossip, and local tales required interpretation, from within an otherwise undifferentiated group. Each individual within the group worked out his own attitude to an issue only in relation to those of the other members of the community. And the decision-making process included tale telling as an essential aspect of communal deliberations. Tales, legends, and gossip brought otherwise impersonal, abstract questions within terms compatible with community organization. Different local regions developed different legends about Washington. The different legends allowed each region to identify Washington as a participant in its processes. These legendary associations enabled local communities to participate collectively in national decisions.

Gossip is the more transitory of these communal forms. As an account of what a people would like to believe about a subject, it establishes a superficial relation between the subject and the community. The superficiality often proves to be the most beneficial trait. For instead of turning its subject into an object of contempt, gossip usually resulted in intimacy among those exchanging it. Through the exchange of gossip, a group experiences an intimacy more usually associated with individuals. Gossip offers a community the opportunity to form what we could call the private life of the people. In gossiping about someone whose personal affairs otherwise endanger a community's relations, the community finds a way to return that person to their terms.

Legends, on the other hand, are cherished accounts of what a people cannot help believing. The people of a region gather these accounts and hold onto them precisely because they cannot or will not be verified by history. Unassimilable to history yet indicative of the ways in which communities organize their acknowledgment of what continues to draw them together, legends are what remains unspoken about a people. Yet legends bear repeating precisely because they constitute the preconditions for a people's history. Legends are what history cannot accommodate because they outline the shadowy border between the fictions history has produced as its facts and the facts history must pass over as mere fictions.

Representations and Legends

Wills assumes an attitude toward Washington's identity as a leader much different from that of the citizens of Sleepy Hollow. But Wills's attitude is not only a modern anachronism. Following the Revolution, many Americans tried to invest the Revolutionary heroes with a surplus of cultural authority. Again, for quite specific political reasons.

In the political debate transacted in the Federalist Papers, American theorists with views as different as Jefferson's and Madison's tried to invent a governmental process able to balance out the very different political energies of economic interests released by the Revolution. The "balance of powers" theory of government resulting from these debates was designed to permit both newer and older versions of government to exist side by side. The relationship among the executive and legislative branches of government was founded in the hope of enabling a balanced exchange between national leadership and local interests, with the judiciary branch designated to sustain the balance.

The major difficulty confronting the designers of this theory was the issue of political representation. More specifically, they wondered how to represent the will of the American people. For the Federalists among them, the American people were indistinguishable from mobs, susceptible to the rabble-rousing rhetoric of counterrevolutionaries. To prevent a reactivation of volatile Revolutionary energies, they represented the Revolution as a permanent feature of American government. When described as a balance of power, the relationship between the executive and the legislative branches of government designated the power of the people not merely to represent themselves to their leader but to direct his will, through their legislation. Should the president fail to act properly, the Revolutionary imperative of the people could result in impeachment proceedings.

The Federalists wanted to contain the Revolutionary impulse within this representation of balanced powers. But they also wanted to assure that the people would have a represented, rather than a direct, relation to the federal government. In centralizing the quite diverse, multiply directed interests of the American people in their model government, the designers of the Constitution alienated the people's expression of their will from its representation. To sustain this alienation, they enhanced the value of the men chosen to represent the people's will, as well as their oratorical means of representing it.

We can best ascertain the consequences of this overidealizing of the political function of representation by considering the social role played by "founding fathers." In designing the political organization of a nation described as democratic, and which should have been free to revise that organization, these men had to devise a way to maintain it. As democratic men they were no different from their equals; but as founding fathers they were not men among equals: they were progenitors, who produced the equality and liberty the rest of the American people represented. Designated founding fathers, they could claim to *be* the freedom and equality other Americans could honor and thereby learn how to represent.

The idealization of the characters of the people's representatives, in other words, assumed the early form of a denial of their representative function and in effect reversed the relation between the leaders and the will they were to represent. They were what the American people should represent. With the people turned into representatives of the founding fathers, the founders could claim to be the most representative of the will of the people—by simply being themselves. The Adams family exploited the founders' monopoly over the representative function of government to establish a version of an American royal family each of whose members inherited the power to rule by being.[14]

In redressing this imbalance in representation, local groups removed the founders from their positions within national office and turned them into characters within their tales. Popular legends and tales about these officials literally subjected them to the renegotiation of their characters among sometimes quite brutal townsfolk. When the overidealized founders passed through tales told and retold by townspeople and villagers, they lost their social distance as well as their national identities. The extraordinary little boy in Weems's biography, who chopped down a cherry tree but never told a lie, grew up to father children by his slaves in popular legends, brutalize his troops, and aspire to monarchic rule.

Now, it could be argued that these local accounts only confirmed Washington's authority by "rounding out" the official biographies. Local accounts could be understood as ways of coming to terms with federal decisions by putting them into more local terms. They could be understood as such, that is, were they not associated by Thomas Jefferson during the decisive election of 1800 with the authority of the popular as opposed to the federal will. Jefferson encouraged the people to take possession of their representatives by subduing the representatives' self-interest to the public will. The people's tales compelled the nation's leaders to step down from the public stage that was more compatible with the self-representations of the Federalists.

The fundamental debate between the Federalists and the Republicans during the election of 1800 concerned the role of the public. The Feder-

alists dismissed the public's opinions as prejudice, unworthy of consideration when arriving at a political judgment, while Jefferson considered the
public will the fundamental value of political life. Without a public will,
there could be no civic virtue but only self-interest. The public will constituted the greater interest of a nation to which every citizen should become
subservient.

Jefferson of course recognized that the public will could dissolve into the
undifferentiated reaction formations of unruly mobs. He turned to interest
groups, vital regional communities, city clubs, and local guilds and associations of various kinds as examples of democratic organizations. He also
recognized the value of tales in organizing these collectives into individu-
ated groups and group-minded individuals. Through tales and romances,
Jefferson wrote, "the field of imagination is thus laid open to our use and
lessons may be formed to illustrate and carry home every point." Without
these tales, the group's power to make up its own mind on matters of
political importance would be countermanded by official accounts. The
tales, instead of being subservient to national accounts, permitted local
groups to accrue national value for their local associations. Tales put their
tellers into vital relation with otherwise alien national powers, and the different versions, additions, elisions, and other "telling" procedures these
groups engaged in when retelling an important political incident enabled
them to make it an event for their collective experience. This activity was
constitutive of a will of the American people suitable for representation in
Washington.

Unalienated Will

National leaders claimed a center stage, set upon the scene of the nation's
founding, with appropriate social actors (the founding fathers and their
line of charismatic succession) and appropriate roles for them to play. But
their claim to centrifugal political power was opposed by the competing
centripetal claims of the heterogeneous interest groups through the states.
Positioning, say, John Adams in a local tale rather than a White House
meant disclaiming his powers over the self-determination of a local group.
And these disclaimers, when coupled with the power to vote a politician in
or out of office, developed validity for an American public sphere.

What I cannot overemphasize is the role these protoliterary forms played in the formation of any American public sphere. Without legends, romances, and local gossip to countermand it, the Revolutionary mythos was possessed of extraordinary generalizing powers. We have already considered its power to abstract local places into its scene. It also provided a permanent backdrop for the national political stage, lending Revolutionary force to the actor's words. And as Sacvan Bercovitch has reminded us, this mythos lent typological force to the words and deeds even of conservative politicians. When invoked by an American politician, the rhetoric of Revolution could make the most conservative of political platforms sound prototypically American. Refusing to engage the politicians on the national scene, local groups developed other forms of self-representation invested with local associations rather than official memories.

Thomas Campbell emphasized the political function of village legends when in 1816 he described them as a version of countermemory making up for an "almost total deficiency in those local associations produced by history and moral fictions." In reflecting on the cultural value of his "sketches," Washington Irving explained in 1848 that they provided "imaginative associations which live like spells and charms." And many American writers with aspirations for an American republic shared Longfellow's wish that all of its locale would "one day be rich in associations."[15]

As all of these citations indicate, during the early nineteenth century writers needed to invest local regions with memories of their own, because the Revolutionary mythos threatened to translate all of American life into a compulsive reenactment of a single national event. As a reaction against the disconnective power of the nation's myths, these collective memories reestablished connections between local will and national events. They produced a form of political tranference, permitting the popular will to recover local relationship with the issues, purposes, and motives formerly reserved for national politicians, whose self-representations tended to become separated from the people's will. In these activities the people made the politicians servants of their will. Which is another way of saying that if the politicians would not serve the interests of the people, these forms of popular will made the politicians subservient. And in a way that would have been impossible in the official arena of discussion. As practical actors in the art of public persuasion, most politicians knew how to turn occasions for discussion into opportunities for dramatic display. As I make clear in the final chapter, politicians theatricalized the scene of public discussions, turning their speeches into spectacles to be witnessed rather than positions to be argued.

To reclaim vitality for a public sphere, local groups did not engage politicians on their own terms but established a different culture. Understanding this culture requires an attitude toward protoliterary forms as well as the public through which they circulated different from the one Fiedler and Wills adopt. For both of them, the collective life of the American people is a homogeneous, generalized mass formation. As an undifferentiated collection of anonymous persons, the masses are susceptible to control, both Fiedler and Wills would have it, by cultural forms that satisfy their demand for pleasurable distraction. Since they would define the masses as that which defies differentiation, the ideal form of mass culture would confirm the masses' undifferentiated status. According to this definition, public spectacle, as that which enables a leader to separate himself from an undifferentiated mass of spectators, would be an ideal form of mass culture. In public spectacles, large groups discover the uniform response they share with a multitude of strangers. The separation between the spectators and the spectacle controlled by the leader is felt not as a loss but as the precondition for enjoyment. On the politician's stage they can watch as an actor who appears larger than life at once claims to represent them yet separates his action from those who can only witness it from within the crowd.

In the nineteenth century the historic sites the American Revolution left behind provided the nation's politicians with appropriate scenes for mass spectacles. By speaking every ten years or so at the Bunker Hill Monument Daniel Webster would corroborate the powers of his person over any issue requiring national attention. And the gathered multitudes would surrender their need to participate any more deeply in the process than as spectators. When such a relation was given legendary form, however, both the personal appropriation of attention and the surrender of the public will were subject to revision.

In order to dissociate the politician's position from his dramatic persona, such writers as Hawthorne in *The Scarlet Letter* turned him into an allegorical presence. Allegory is a literary form with origins in a community rather than a private person. When claiming to represent an abstract principle like liberty, a dramatic speaker could make the representation appear adequate by investing it with the force of his presence. But in a community in which allegorical claims are made for the person, as in Puritan New Boston, every person is not only him- or herself but also whatever moral virtue he or she is trying to perfect. His or her confessional relation to the community turns the question of adequate representation from a private matter into a subject of group deliberation. Whether or not Arthur Dimmesdale represents piety or passion, for example, does not remain an issue for him personally to decide. As soon as he makes public his struggle with these abstract moral qualities, in a community for whom the embodiment of any moral quality is always a matter of struggle, his personal struggle turns into an occasion for collective debate.

All the protoliterary forms at work in the nineteenth-century public sphere had allegorical components. In working variations on the cherry-tree legend of George Washington, for example, participants in the communal narrative were interested not so much in his personal character as in the trust that his character was supposed to command. In impersonating the headless horseman, Brom Bones worked through his own irresponsible, reckless relationship with the community by finding such behavior indistinguishable from a Hessian mercenary's. In permitting him to alienate his character from the qualities of irresponsibility and recklessness, the allegorical figure of the headless horseman helped Brom Bones to find an identity more appropriate to his standing in Sleepy Hollow and allowed the community to acknowledge the change in his identity.

As these examples suggest, allegory played an important role in the formation of the collective life. Specifically, allegory denied the separation between the individual self-representation of universal principles and the community's power to make sense of those principles as well as of the individual. Since allegory turns principles represented in a person into subjects for communal consideration, it makes it impossible for an individual to claim merely personal relationship to them. The politicians claimed in the political arena a separate sphere for their representations of such national principles as liberty, equality, and justice. But allegory became a means of breaking down the distance between the political arena and the rest of the public sphere.

Instead of sustaining a homogeneity within a group, allegory separates an individual's response to a question from already established group judgment, thereby making room for further consideration. Allegory, like other vital forms in the public sphere, turns the group mind into an active participant in a deliberative process. An individual does not make up his own mind about the significance of a moral or political principle for his community, nor does he let a group make up his mind for him. Instead, the single individual and all other participants in a decision over allegorical significance consider its meaning not only for themselves but for the group.

The "good" of the group becomes a constitutive aspect of deliberation, as it mediates between individual discussants in their deliberations. The group life is not merely the outcome but an active participant.

To call attention to the collective life forwarded by his allegories, Hawthorne often referred to them as twice-told tales. For to repeat a story is to deny sole responsibility for its authority and to reveal its socializing power. The twice-told tale exists as a relation, involving the tellers in an ongoing deliberation over something that takes place, in the telling. A twice-told tale, by demanding another telling, expands and intensifies the collective life. Such a tale can enter into relation to everyone precisely because it is authored by no one in particular but invites participation by everyone. By releasing the energies of deliberation within a group, allegory eliminates the distinction between those who participate in a decision and those who watch them. In the nineteenth century, the sense Americans made of the global allegory called the United States removed them from a spectatorial to a more involved relationship with political life.

I have called specific attention to the value of allegory in the life of a collective in order to remove it from the dubious work it has been asked to perform in previous discussions of nineteenth-century American literature. In *The American Novel and Its Tradition,* for example, Richard Chase defines allegory as "a language of static signs and a set of truths to which they refer. In allegory the signs or symbols have little or no existence apart from their paraphrasable meaning. Allegory flourishes best, of course, when everyone agrees on what truth is, when literature is regarded as exposition, not as discovery."[16] Chase proceeds to contrast allegory with symbolic literature, which "responds to disagreements about the truth." Throughout his discussion of *The Scarlet Letter* he finds value in it only when it approaches the "symbolistic."

Chase's distinction between the allegorical and the symbolic has political overtones. For him allegory has its origins in the group's opinion rather than in an individual's judgment. Consequently he can find value only in the multiple, often contradictory meanings a sign can command. In basing his distinction between allegory and symbol on the difference between a group's agreement and individual disagreements, Chase joins the modernist consensus we have found represented in Fiedler and Wills. He too believes freedom resides only in separation from a collective life, predefined as homogeneous, uniform, and unfree. But Chase is more valuable for our discussion in the implicit connections he draws between the tradition of the novel and American political life more generally. Like cultural life, "the American novel tends to rest in contradictions and among extreme ranges of existence." Like a participant in American culture, a reader of an American novel "would have found that it lacked the sense of life as it is actually lived, that it did not establish the continuity between events and the characters' sense of events and that there was a general lack of that experience" which Chase defines as "our apprehension and our measure of what happens to us as social creatures."[17]

I find Chase's description of America's literary tradition valuable because it designates the conditions of cultural division at work in the nineteenth century. But what Chase doesn't acknowledge is their continued existence in the post-McCarthy years when he was writing his book. Like its nineteenth-century counterpart, Cold War America is a culture organized around contradictions and division. One of the best ways to separate the public sphere from participation in the political life is and always has been through a pre-designation of the polis as composed of a uniform mass. All of Chase's descriptions of America's traditions tacitly sanction a separation of cultural from political life. And he legitimizes this separation by defining political dissent in terms of an opposition to group will. In his reading, political freedom consists in the power to elaborate and deploy the contradictions of everyday life. According to Chase, American literature exists for the sake of refining one's alertness to contradiction. And the power to maintain multiple attitudes toward an issue, resulting from this exercise, enables Chase to "experience" the contradictions the characters cannot.

In cultivating an experience of cultural contradiction, Chase only cultivates the separation of powers—the cultural from the political, the individual from the group, the person from his representations—at work in the greater culture. His interpretation invokes dissent or the power to disagree as its rationale but rarefies dissent into a form of ironic apprehension that only confirms his individual right to separate from any public sphere in which his attitude could make a difference. Chase's interpretive strategy works over the powers of dissent until dissent itself appears indistinguishable from the recognition of contradiction, disconnection, alienation organizing the culture. His interpretation justifies his disconnection of dissent from a public sphere and his identification of dissent with a private world. Which is another way of saying that interpretation becomes Chase's way of certifying a nonparticipative role in the life of the public sphere.

The same habit of mind is at work here as was at work in the other modern readers of nineteenth-century America. They read that culture for signs of the separation between the individual and public life that confirms their own. But throughout this discussion I have tried to point out very specific countermovements at work. And oftentimes these countermovements worked through the same forms modern Americans use to confirm their cultural contradictions. Then, allegory was an instrument in the collective life; today allegory is seen as opposed to an individual's freedom. But it can remain opposed to an individual's freedom only if that freedom is defined in terms of an infinite interiority, forever different from everyone else's.

That may be a way of understanding freedom now. But in the nineteenth century, the secession issue demanded that all Americans take account of the relationship between their individual lives and the national interest. And slavery, the issue that made secession a possibility, demanded of America's citizens a careful examination of their relation to rather than alienation from their actions. The slave made concrete the relation between what an individual wanted to do with his motives and what someone else, whether slaveowner or politician, wanted him to do. Today we can sustain the contradictions between our personal and public lives as signs of our individual freedom, but the issues leading up to the Civil War demanded that the nation come to a reckoning about the relationship between a nation's polity and its citizens' lives. And in this book I will show the part American literature played in arriving at this reckoning.

Visionary Compacts

This discussion of the modernist appropriation of nineteenth-century American literature returns us to the legitimation crisis, which was the original subject of this book. By reading nineteenth-century texts in terms of cultural separations—personal motives from political action, significance from world, the past from the present, the individual from the collective, and authority from identity—the tradition of critics of American literature rationalizes a crisis in legitimation. This crisis is not specific to American culture or to American literature but inheres in the core of modernism itself.

Modernism both affirms its historic discontinuity from a past and needs to legitimize this discontinuity by locating ancestral origins for it. Modernism refers both to an act—without a past—and to a literature about that act. Because language is intrinsically mediational, modernist literature cannot truly be that act but can only be about that act. So modernism inevitably traces a frustrating double movement. It can never coincide with the present moment, which is its subject. The literary critic Paul de Man has described this situation with all the sympathy his irony will permit:

> The continuous goal of modernity, the desire to break out of literature toward the reality of the moment, prevails and in its turn, folding back upon itself, engenders the repetition and continuation of literature. Thus modernity, which is fundamentally a falling away from literature and a repetition of history, also acts as the principle that gives literature duration and historical existence.[18]

In this reading of modernity, its behavior in relation to the past cannot be distinguished from a modern individual's in relation to a group. Both modernity and its individuals wish utterly to separate themselves from the past and the masses respectively. And both use the same terms to represent the opposition. The past against which modernity struggles turns out to be an oppressive logocentric tradition, become homogeneous out of a common predisposition: namely, to render each of its moments fully self-present. Like the tradition, the masses against which the individual must affirm his independence are rendered uniform by being reduced to a single demand: to make the individual subservient to their will. Modernism depends on both the present's opposition to the past and the individual's opposition to the mass in order to sustain its activity. For the "past" can be dissociated from the present only if it can be conceived of as undifferentiated, and the masses, in constituting the appropriate representation of the undifferentiated, permit a break from the past without regret.

These two conceptions, then, are deeply interrelated. In designating the past as a logocentric tradition, the most recent ideology of modernity, French poststructuralism, borrows a term important for a shared communal life, i.e., "tradition," in order to confirm the accompanying definition of the individual as a person inevitably cut off from a community. In defining the individual as inevitably separated from a past, modernism also disconnects the individual from any collective purposes or motives to be carried forward from a past. Commenting on this modern notion of a "present" simultaneously discontinuous from both past and future, Frank Lentricchia underscores its effect in the public sphere:

> The present properly conceived . . . is the time of praxis, but understood in its usual fashion, the "present" is inhospitable to action. Praxis

taking place in a moment really segregated from past and future, a contemporaneity isolated unto itself, wholly self-present, would in its ahistorical character possess no critical memory of our society's genealogy. It could not reach back—nor would it be able to bring to the moment, in its consciousness blanketed by a temporality utterly immediate, any sense of potentiality, of the possible, of change.[19]

Lentricchia's description points to the crucial problem modernism poses for the public sphere. In separating the past off from the present, modernism makes cultural change impossible. In order for change to be meaningful there must be something to change. But modernism, in reducing each moment into an abstract discontinuity, reproduces endless novelty in place of change. Instead of being available for either change or continuity, the past is simply discounted as the outmoded. And this endless-obsolescence procedure produces an aesthetic consciousness grounded on the legitimation crisis. What this crisis finally legitimizes, however, is a cultural identity grounded on crisis itself.

Criticism gives this culturally pervasive state of crisis density and critical mass by rationalizing it as the discovery of textual aporias. In the discovery of an aporia a critic can make the dissociation between what he knows and how he acts, the cognitive and performative dimensions of his speech and his life, seem the result of critical insight rather than cultural organization. A crisis mentality insists upon acknowledging disjunctions of all kinds. But the fundamental disjunction upon which all of this is grounded is that between mass culture and high culture. The literary critic, as a professional connoisseur of crisis, oversees the affiliation of political life with mass culture rather than with high culture. And the critic's activities are designed to perfect the separation between mass culture, where modern individuals perform the labors of their everyday lives, and high culture, where the individual experiences the separation from enabling cultural activity as the loss of a tradition. The critic simultaneously acknowledges political activity and justifies separation from it.

As Terry Eagleton has recently reminded us, criticism derives its cultural authority through its historical affiliations with political and religious dissent.[20] But recent criticism rarefies this freedom of speech into an opposition to determined significations. The verbal indeterminacy resulting from this activity declares itself as a freedom from explicit determinant political practices. Political dissent is also generalized into a pervasive adversarial or critical opposition. This generalized oppositional stance, often asserted in the name of cultural heterogeneity, is not usually associated with any specific cultural group. The term "heterogeneity" borrows its pathos from its relation to marginal cultural groups. But if these groups should express their needs in explicit terms, they would violate the critical principle of heterogeneity.

In laying claim to fundamental political freedoms—of speech, press, self-representation—yet dissociating these freedoms from any explicit cultural groups, literary commentary disconnects criticism from any cultural purpose other than generalizing its crisis attitude. And this generalized crisis sanctions the disconnection between the cultural and political dimensions organizing the modern public sphere.

A similar disconnection of the political arena from the public sphere was at work in nineteenth-century America. But instead of validating this division by turning the resultant crisis in cultural legitimation into a pervasive cultural attitude, the writers I will consider overcame the disconnection by radical renegotiations of the American social compact.

As a cultural rationale for a crisis mentality, the legitimation crisis validates the division between political authority and the authentic experiences of modern life. When consigned to an activity in mass culture from which an individual must free himself, the political becomes an autonomous dimension of modern life. Its inclusion within the low aesthetics of mass culture ensures for politics the power to operate according to its own rules. The disconnection of politics from other aspects of everyday life gives politicians their own authority. And this same disconnection produces a nonpolitical form of self-legitimation for individuals within nonpolitical dimensions of modern life. Unable to authorize their lives in terms of a political sphere they have discredited, modern individuals turn their opposition to political authority into a principle of cultural authority. Hence they can convert their "generalized opposition" to political authority into the "political authority" of everyday life in the modern world.

I have tried to show how the Cold War sanctions this division of political issues from everyday life. Its clear opposition between "our" genuine freedom and "their" totalitarianism presumes at once to define the only true political question and to decide it—as an ideal opposition. In the nineteenth century, a similar ideal opposition was at work in the organization of American life: the Revolutionary mythos also turned a generalized cultural opposition to political authority into a way of making American politics a self-determining activity.

But Hawthorne, Melville, Emerson, Whitman, and, in a different way,

Poe, wrote in order to overcome this division. When we consider this period we usually presuppose in it the relationship of a mass (or an elite) audience and an inventive artist that is at work in our times. But when these writers wrote, the public could not agree to the division of their everyday lives and the nation's political identity. Many of them were preparing to go to war in order to express their political purposes. And, as I suggested earlier, the Civil War screens our modern considerations of the period. Having been fought because of disagreements over the fundamental issues of union, slavery, and expansionism, the Civil War, like its Cold War descendant, now makes these issues seem already definitively decided—even in the historical periods before the Civil War.

I cannot do justice in this book to the many complex attitudes toward these issues that were at work in the period, but I can suggest the ways in which these issues demanded political action from all America's citizens, and the ways in which American Renaissance writers tried to overcome a division of cultural realms. For these writers, I would maintain, wrote not to impose their political decisions on others, but to establish an American public sphere in which all citizens could enter into the decision-making process.

The public sphere in nineteenth-century America was as thoroughly aestheticized then as it is now. Then politicians routinely acknowledged the relation between political and artistic activities by appointing writers and artists to political posts. Hawthorne and Melville were Custom House officers, Whitman was an effective ward leader, Emerson often shared the lyceum circuit with politicians, and even Poe was considered (briefly) for a post in Washington. Artistic work was acknowledged as implicitly political because both artists and politicians shared a common task. In antebellum America they both tried to shape the public will. In antebellum America the masses were not homogeneous. It would take the Civil War to turn different interest groups into opposed mass movements. Prior to the Civil War many politicians invoked that previous mobilization of the masses, the Revolutionary War, to urge a mass consensus. But disagreements, often within the same person, broke most consensus formations into splinter groups.

Confronted with this release of numerous, conflicting interest groups, politicians tried to consolidate them into voting blocs. They used all their oratorical power to reduce the masses into the position of spectators. But writers like Hawthorne and Melville believed in the value of shared democratic processes as opposed to spellbinding oratory. Instead of affirming the orator's power, which as we have seen was founded upon the scene of the Revolution, Hawthorne returned to the pre-Revolutionary origins of American culture. And he found there a vital reserve of unfinished cultural business. Then he devised an aesthetic strategy to make this collective life from the past the subject as well as the potential result of his tale. His friend Melville would in *Moby-Dick* simply expose the orator as a figure of self-aggrandizement. When he wrote, Melville imagined Hawthorne as an impersonation of a collective readership. Believing Hawthorne the one person in the American sphere able to recognize the falsity of political rhetoric, Melville addressed his novels to Hawthorne in order to write a more adequate public sphere into existence.

Both of these writers refused to sanction any division in the cultural realm. Instead of identifying their works as original inventions of isolated artists, both Melville and Hawthorne identified their writing with collective projects. Melville's narratives depended on an American public to whose reaction against the orator's compulsive rhetoric he gave shape. Hawthorne's, on the other hand, aspired to a communal life that existed only in his writing.

In drafting a new social compact for America, these writers wrote prefaces making explicit the relationship between their writing and that greater process of political deliberation called the public will. In the preface to *The Scarlet Letter* Hawthorne specifically situated himself in relation to an alienating public sphere. In the preface he experienced what was missing from his present political life as the return of a repressed memory. That repressed memory had to do not with an event in his personal life but with the vital collective life of the pre-Revolutionary past. In returning to the pre-Revolutionary past Hawthorne violated the terms of the Revolutionary mythos that insisted on the separation of a community's will from a politician's representations. He returned from that past, moreover, with a different moral faculty for the American people to exercise: a collective memory capable of reestablishing their relation to purposes from the past in need of present enactment.

I have called Hawthorne's renegotiation of the terms of American social life a visionary compact because in his writing he *saw* what was missing from his contemporary life. In Hawthorne's view only the acknowledgment of a collective will could make good on the principle of participatory democracy upon which the nation was founded.

Hawthorne's visionary compact did not oppose any existing ideology. Such an opposition would have personalized his project by incorporating it within the scenario of an individual's rebellion against an oppressor. Hawthorne's tales derive all their force by drawing upon an unfulfilled promise in America's founding covenant. Hawthorne's America needed to be reminded of its ongoing power to renegotiate the terms of the covenant binding Americans to one another. He intended his tales to participate in democratic processes that could be activated by the telling and the reading.

In their writing as well, such American transcendentalists as Whitman, Emerson, and Thoreau established visionary compacts, but different from Hawthorne's. Unlike him, they did not return to a collective life from the nation's past. Instead they took advantage of political fictions capitalized on by the orators and situated themselves on the still-present founding scene. Unlike the orators, however, they did not claim sole power to act upon the principles found there. Instead they asked that these principles be available to all Americans and not just the orators. "Why cannot we also enjoy an original relation with the universe?" Emerson asked at the outset of *Nature*. At a time in which the politicians compromised on founding principles for the sake of expediency, Emerson and Whitman returned to the scene of the nation's founding to recover integrity for the principles of liberty and equality and make them available as motives for the actions of all Americans. In so doing, these so-called transcendentalists did not replace political realities with transcendental ideals. They returned to the political principles founding the nation and tried to forge ways to realize them.

None of these writers disclaimed the founding principles as merely ideological. Each of them envisioned the founding principles as well as the covenant of relations as unfulfilled promises in need of the renewal that visionary compacts could effect. In fulfilling these promises, they developed new faculties, like self-reliance and the collective memory, capable of converting founding principles into motivating forces rather than past ideals. Instead of opposing the nation's principles, in an age of political compromise, these writers found those principles to be vital moral and political energies.

All of these writers share a common cultural mission. In returning the nation to its principles they literally restored it to its soul. A nation can lose its soul the same way an individual can, by compromising on its principles. But the visionary compacts they devised were by no means homogeneous. They differed as completely as did the allegiances these different writers felt toward the individual and the community. To call attention to these differences, I have organized this book around the contrasts rather than the continuities. I emphasize the differences between Hawthorne's visionary compact and those of Whitman, Poe, Emerson, and Melville. To make their differences emphatic I treat the writers as if they were themselves involved in a common process of political and cultural deliberation. The chapters call attention to an urgent cultural task common to all of these writers by calling attention to what urged each writer differently. Throughout this book I relate nineteenth-century cultural situations to modern appropriations of them for the same reason I began this chapter with a distinction between Lawrence's study of the American tradition and those of modern commentators: to call attention to what is missing in modern commentary on the period. In so doing, however, I do not avoid commentary or literary interpretation. To do so would risk turning these works into illustrations of a historical problem. But when I do interpret I bring the interpretation into relation with a greater set of cultural forces than the interpreter's will.

In returning to these visionary compacts from the past I do not wish to affirm the cultural value of these individual writers. Instead I wish to insist upon their value as a cultural reserve, a store of unrealized cultural motives, purposes, and political processes we honor but do not act upon. In a modern world, whose cultural contradictions are organized through a generalized crisis in legitimation, these visionary compacts continue to do cultural work. They can establish an enabling context for overcoming the divisions of cultural life at work in our own time.

Chapter Two

Hawthorne's Discovery of a Pre-Revolutionary Past

In truth the patriotism of a citizen of the United States is a sentiment by itself, of a peculiar nature, and requiring a life-time, or at least the custom of many years to naturalize it among the possessions of the heart.

This war, in which the country was so earnestly and enthusiastically engaged . . . put everybody into an exaggerated and unnatural state, united enthusiasms of all sorts, heightened everybody either into its own heroisms or into the peculiar madness to which one person was inclined.

—Nathaniel Hawthorne

In the preface to *The Scarlet Letter* Hawthorne comes to terms with what he finds inadequate in his culture by inventing a way to give speech to what was missing from it: any sense of shared cultural responsibility. During his years as a Custom House officer, he saw and heard persons who were aware of the duty an individual owes the public—but who were also missing from the Custom House. They were not there for good reason. They lived some two centuries before. But they nonetheless laid a more urgent claim on Hawthorne than did anything in his present surroundings. They needed him to preserve their persons in his memory, and to perpetuate their communal purposes in America's republic.

Unlike anyone else in the Custom House, these ghosts reminded Hawthorne of the ways in which persons live for the sake of sustaining and deepening the communities in which they find themselves. By removing him from a self-enclosed sphere of self-interest and returning him to a world in which even the individual's interest in himself served, through public confession, the interest of the public good, these ghosts reminded Hawthorne of a life of civic duty.[1]

But the only way Hawthorne, in an age without a past, could live such a

49

life was through the refinement of an infrequently exercised faculty. Only his reactivation of a collective memory, enabling him to remember the common purposes and motives from a shared past, and to be remembered by others in terms of those goals, could restore vitality to public life in Hawthorne's age. His fellow citizens had reduced their concern to the locus of their everyday lives, thereby refusing to put the interest of the community before their own. In contrast to them, Hawthorne found himself beholden to citizens from the Puritan past, in need of his individual interests and continued care for survival. In encountering these refugees from the nation's past, Hawthorne rediscovered the perennial basis for a human community.

An Earlier Way with the Pre-Revolution

The legendary George Washingtons who appeared in popular biographies like that of Parson Weems resigned from the military for a specific historical reason: to deactivate America's Revolutionary will. His resignation to what he called the "general weal" was an exemplary form of "republican virtue," the surrender of an individual's interests for the public interest.[2] But Nathaniel Hawthorne was compelled to resign from his Custom House post in 1850 because of a revolution in the public will. Underwritten by a spoils system that strengthened party politics, this public will derived political authority from a symbolic association with the American Revolution. And this symbolic association had earlier given Hawthorne an explicit subject for narrative reflection.

In such historical sketches as "The Hutchison Mob," "The Boston Massacre," and "The Boston Tea Party," Hawthorne worried over the ways in which thoughtless mobs had symbolically associated their actions with the great moral principles supporting the American Revolution. This symbolic association, Hawthorne believed, had made the effects of the Revolution "pernicious to general morality." In treating both Tories and patriots as resurrections of a common, tyrant-hating Puritan ancestor, the author of "The Old French War" and "The Old Tory" labored to undo those effects and establish a shared past, transcending Revolutionary loyalties.[3]

In these early tales Hawthorne devised the narrative equivalents of kinship feelings both Tories and patriots could share. As descendants of common Puritan ancestors, Tories and patriots shared feelings of reverence for the nation's past. "Ancestral feelings" could thus establish "fellow-feeling" able to make Revolutionary opposition seem morally reprehensible rather than patriotic. Or so Hawthorne believed when he wrote those early tales.

But Hawthorne's Custom House preface to *The Scarlet Letter* complicated his relation with the ancestral past. In articulating the rationale for what he calls his "ejectment" from the Custom House, Hawthorne does not trace the political debate between the Whigs and the Democrats back to a Puritan origin. Such a genealogy would have elevated their unprincipled partisan antagonism too much. Instead, Hawthorne identifies the spoils system of partisan politics to which he was indebted for his office in the Custom House as a leftover from Revolutionary times. And he finds his days within the Custom House haunted by figures from a *pre*-Revolutionary past, who ask him to get the Revolutionary mythos out of the nation's history.

At the time Hawthorne wrote *The Scarlet Letter,* such revolutions in the public will as the one that saw Hawthorne out of office were not universally discredited. In some circles they led to celebrations of Americans' mobility. For Michel Chevalier, an eighteenth-century French traveler,

> The American . . . has recourse to business for the strong emotions which he requires to make him feel life. He launches with delight in the ever-moving sea of speculation. One day . . . he enjoys in haste the moment of triumph. The next day he disappears between the crests of the billows . . . Go ahead! If movement and the quick *succession* of sensations and ideas constitute life, here one lives a hundred fold more than anywhere else; all is here circulation, motion and boiling agitation . . . An irresistible current sweeps away everything, grinds everything to powder, and deposits it again under new forms.[4]

After having become a victim of that irresistible current called progress, however, Hawthorne could not share Chevalier's celebratory mood. He recognized the cost for human community when public positions lasted no longer than the associations holding together the mobs that saw him out of office.

Reflections on the Mythos of the Revolution

When reduced to a rapid "succession of sensations," existence becomes indistinguishable from an appetite, a lust for power like that of the Whigs who grew cruel, as Hawthorne put it, "merely because they possessed the power to harm." Appetite for position reduced the attention of every Custom House functionary to a span circumscribed by the aftertastes of meals. Individually and as a group, "they spoke with far more interest and unction of their morning's breakfast, or yesterday's, today's or tomorrow's dinner, than of the shipwreck of forty or fifty year ago, and all the world's wonders which they had witnessed with their youthful eyes." [5]

In such passages as these, Whig power and Custom House opportunism emerge as related aspects of the same motive: that is, the need to consume every moment as an assertion of power over it. The cultural rationale for living as if one were participating in a quick "succession of sensations" was the same in Hawthorne's day as it is in ours: progress, the belief that every moment exists only, like the displacement of persons in the Custom House or the displacement of sensations in the psyche, to be superseded by the next. All of the figures within the Custom House would have described their public lives in terms of progress. But, as a victim of the progress from which he, as a political ally of Franklin Pierce, formerly profited, Hawthorne felt called upon to expose both progress and the mythos of the Revolution supporting it as impediments to a vital public life.

The Revolution brought into dynamic interrelation what Hawthorne construed to be the related activities of the mob and the present moment. As the decisive moment in the nation's history, the Revolution continued to give peculiar legitimacy to the "momentary associations" of participants in a mob, as well as to the "spur of the moment" opinions, prejudices, emotions organizing the everyday sensibility of Hawthorne's companions in the Custom House. When contrasted with a revolutionary moment from the past, everyday events seemed drab and ordinary. Consequently the mythos of the Revolution produced a transitory quality for events taking place in the present.

The Revolutionary mythos urged American citizens to reorganize their time as replicas of the Revolutionary moment. But the Revolution reduced time to a series of discontinuous "instants," each lasting no longer than it takes for the next to displace it—as a "has-been."

Officials in the Custom House modeled their relations on a shared fear of becoming "has-beens." This shared fear, when repeatedly engaged, turned into their common way of apprehending the everyday world. But it was not only the officials in the Custom House who were subjected to this temporal process and its attendant sensibility. Everything in Hawthorne's world could be categorized as either current, up to date with present fashions, or, like Hawthorne, outmoded. The best anyone in the present could manage was appearing revolutionary. And, as Hawthorne discovered, one managed that by making others appear obsolete.

Being revolutionary meant producing "has-beens." But an age that produced "has-beens" without a history had no way of remaining in touch with its own past. And without a sense of its past Americans could not experience their movement through time as development rather than a "quick succession of sensations." The mythos of "progress," which was really a variation of the mythos of the Revolution, enabled some commentators to read "change" as development. But with no clear sense of what anything changed *from*, no one could know what anything was developing into—except that generalized effect of progress, the new.

Progress and obsolescence became interchangeable terms—for interrelated activities. Working together they produced change. But without an accompanying sense of history, the change they produced lacked development. Development required a refined sense of the cultural past that the ideology of Revolutionary progress had taught the nation to do without.

Before his contemporaries could recover the shared task they inherited from the past, they had to be dispossessed of the Revolutionary mythos as the approved way of organizing their time. They needed a legacy from the nation's past capable of reminding them of a duty to which they could devote their present lives. Returning to a pre-Revolutionary past, Hawthorne found in the Puritans an alternative set of founding fathers. And he used the Puritan past to furnish his present not with an achieved ideal but with an unrealized vision of community, still addressing his age with a common task. Hawthorne hoped this as yet unrealized task would restore to his present age the motives it needed to make its time purposive.

To recognize the social purposes to which Hawthorne put his historical romance, we must reiterate the uses to which Hawthorne's contemporaries put the nation's history. They reduced the past to a mythos of the Revolution, thereby translating it into an abstract ideal, exempt from the need for continued development. As the nation's already realized ideal, the Revolutionary past emptied living value out of all other events in the nation's time and could not inspire later generations of citizens to new goals. It eradicated the need for any developing sense of national purpose. Defined as what had already fulfilled all that America need ever want, the mythos of the Revolution occupied two simultaneous temporal locations: the ideal past as well as the fulfilled future.

In order to make its present life meaningful, a nation needs to acknowledge the achievements and accomplishments it inherits from a past. It makes this inheritance part of the commonwealth of fulfilled goals. But before a nation can experience its present achievements as continuous with those of the commonwealth in the past, it must take up those common tasks and shared purposes that, although begun in the past, need the renewed commitment of subsequent generations for fulfillment.

In squandering all the nation's purposes and ideals in a potlatch historic event that had already taken place, the Revolution permanently impeded any renewal of national purpose. Without any inherited goals to be realized, subsequent generations had no way of realizing the historical significance of their own time.

In place of dedicating themselves to common tasks, subsequent generations reshaped present events until they reproduced the mythos of the Revolution. When designated as "Revolutionary," events could accrue mythic significance by association. In the "culture of the Revolution,"[6] every other cultural occasion aspired to become a mystic participant in the definitive national event. When acknowledged as "Revolutionary," everyday events could be described as progressive rather than (as Hawthorne experienced them in the Custom House) merely successive.

Hence the myth of progress and the mythos of the Revolution mutually sustained one another. Without the Revolution as an ideal frame of reference, progress could not have been distinguishable from mere change. Progress became an official means of appropriating every "significant" event. In Hawthorne's Custom House, events became significant only when they were called progressive. And whatever was called progressive— General Miller's move from the 1812 war to the Custom House, for example—recalled the Revolutionary event. Yet without an ongoing set of purposes, no age can experience its events as progressive, despite the official designation. In the Custom House preface Hawthorne does not subscribe to the Revolutionary mythos any more than he believes in the myth of progress. When he experiences a "revolution" in his life, it does not result from progress. He gets "ejected" as a result of a form of patronage politics to which Hawthorne owed his position in the Custom House— the spoils system. And while the spoils system may have followed the lead of every other political program of Hawthorne's time and used "progress" to rationalize its policies, Hawthorne, following the loss of his position, interpreted such "progress" as synonymous with the violent usurpation of property rights and human dignity formerly identified with the British tyrants rather than with the American Revolution.

Following his ejectment from the Custom House, Hawthorne returned to his tales of pre-Revolutionary America as both a public man and a man of letters. The public man in him, bereft of present civic relations, needed a renewed relation with official ancestors as much as the author in him needed relation to his former characters. In the Custom House Hawthorne discovered a division within his own character in need of a Puritan past for resolution. Like the Tories and patriots of his early tales, the different persons in his character shared a common motive in needing this recovered relation. Each needed to recover a vision of national purpose that post-Jacksonian American politics had not been able to realize.

This need explains why Hawthorne returned so often to historical sources for the nation's origin different from the Revolution. He did not write about the Puritans to replace the Revolutionary *mythos* of history with history proper. Such a history might have got the facts straight. But such facts would only have confirmed his contemporaries' already inflated sense of the value of their present age.[7]

Hawthorne's aim was not to write a definitive historical account of what actually happened in the past, but to recover the culturally enabling sense of what remained to be made out of a collective process begun but not concluded in the past. If the Revolutionary mythos resulted in a sense that all the nation's goals had already been formed, Hawthorne returned to a moment in the past before the Revolution had confirmed that belief.

The Repression of the Past

While in the Custom House and subject to its activities, Hawthorne could not mobilize a sufficiently reflective consciousness to return to the Puritan past. Like the other inhabitants of the Custom House, Hawthorne passed the time but without learning anything from time passing. He confronted a field of attention so undemanding of permanent record as to leave no impression or trace in the psyche for more than a passing moment. Without an adequate sense of a time past upon which to reflect, Hawthorne was unable to conceive of a transition from the Custom House to any other place.

While in the Custom House what Hawthorne very much needed was a means of coming into relationships different from mere displacement. Hawthorne met this need through a haunting encounter with his Puritan ancestors, who unlike everything else in the Custom House were not subject to the time progress keeps.

The Puritan ancestors Hawthorne encountered in the Custom House are sufficiently different from the characters in his early tales to warrant a distinction. In those tales he began with an existing division in the political character of America—that between, say, loyalist and patriot—and brought the two sides together by tracing their genealogy back to the same Puritan ancestor. This ancestor believed deeply in the fundamental principle at work in both the loyalist and the patriot, and sanctioned, after the war, their reunion in accordance with a common principle. But in the Custom House, no one believed in anything deeply enough to turn it into a divisive issue. Since they held no values in common, the Custom House officials never divided over moral or political issues. Because they were bound together only by a common fear of their displacement, their apprehensions of each other were as evanescent as the memory of total strangers.[8]

Earlier it was Hawthorne who returned to the Puritan past to resolve contemporary cultural crises, but in the Custom House tales it is the Puritans who return from the past to restore a sense of actuality to the present. Only when he is remembered by the Puritan ancestors does Hawthorne recover significance for his present existence. The ancestors appear to him when he recalls reasons for leaving his career as a writer and becoming a public official. His ancestors introduced a moral context for his decision when they asked: "What is he . . . a writer of storybooks? What kind of business in life,—what mode of glorifying God, or being serviceable to mankind in his day and generation may that be?" (12).

They implicitly demanded that Hawthorne give up his self-interested life of distracted daydreaming for public service in the Custom House. But Hawthorne's experience in the Custom House qualifies the terms of their demand. When he takes up in the Custom House a life dedicated to the common good, he finds a world filled only with distracted, self-interested men.

In experiencing himself as remembered by his Puritan ancestors, Hawthorne undergoes his first act of reflection on conditions within the Custom House. Hawthorne is not the agent but the object of this act of reflection. It takes place not in his present age but in the Puritans' past. More precisely, figures from the Puritan past reflect on Hawthorne's present circumstances because they need him to continue the cultural project they began. In reminding Hawthorne of his duty to public service, they remind him of the life he shares with their past, a life which he *ought* to continue. The optative form of their request cannot be overemphasized. The ancestors from Hawthorne's past make it clear that he has a duty to the past. They depend upon his performance of this duty for the preservation of a way of life, as if he were a cultural memory of their past but existing in the future.[9] I am going to refine this point in a moment. But now I will simply say that what remains vital from America's Puritan past depends upon Hawthorne's present age for realization.

The Puritan past recalls a set of customs, purposes, and relationships which were not completed in the past; hence they could once again become present. In fact the Puritan past is so much more demanding than are Hawthorne's present circumstances that he looks to it rather than patronage politics when he needs to justify his decision to enter public life. Since the Custom House officials knew nothing of the writer in Hawthorne, they could not ascertain what he had sacrificed in his decision to enter public life. But the Puritan ancestors' conception of public duty involves self-sacrifice as a necessary component and constitutes an implicit condemnation of a Custom House that has failed to measure up to these standards. In failing to measure up, the Custom House can be said to have failed to progress beyond the Puritans' past, to have insufficiently realized their cultural purposes. So the Puritan ancestors bequeath Hawthorne a relation to an as yet incomplete past, one in need of his present for completion.

Usually a modern man experiences the discontinuity between present and past as "the way things are." But while among the inhabitants of the Custom House, Hawthorne experiences the immediacy of present existence only as insufficiently demanding. He perceives his present world as a time without memory, and experiences the loss of cultural memory as a torpor. He lives in a world in which the present has repressed the past. And repression leads to a return of repressed material, whether within an individual's psyche or within the culture, or at least it does in the preface to *The Scarlet Letter*. For here the past overturns the authority of the present. Instead of acknowledging the power granted present time by the mythos of the Revolution, the past returns to the present age and reminds it of its strictly temporal obligations—to fulfill those aims and purposes inherited from the past. As temporal presences unfulfilled by modernity, these figures from the nation's past demand that the nation's present change its official means of keeping its time.

Separated from the past rather than related to it, each modern moment is forgetful of what it was. Hence the present becomes the locus for the oblivion to which we usually consign the past. As a victim of this amnesia, Hawthorne cannot recognize how forgettable his present has become until he can perceive what his age has forgotten. Only after he apprehends persons with no present existence within his culture can he see the pathos of his own present situation. They disclose to him what it means to be without the time necessary to realize a life. And after this disclosure Hawthorne realizes that he is as discontinuous with his present age, and as unrealized in his person, as are his ancestors. Their reappearance within his time enables him to come to terms with his difficulty with the nation's means of keeping time.

The Revolutionary mythos encouraged Hawthorne's age to conceive of the Puritan past as a self-contained unit—utterly separated from the present. But these figures from the past deepen Hawthorne's experience of the present by adding to it the memory it lacks. Although Hawthorne's age disconnects itself from the Puritan past, that past remains continuous with the present age. Hawthorne's present age occupies the place of the future the Puritans projected for themselves. And their connection and Hawthorne's disconnection make possible a peculiar temporal exchange. Without the Puritan past, Hawthorne finds his present age insufficiently real. Without Hawthorne's age as a locus in which their goals and purposes can be renewed and continued, the Puritans have no place left in time. In their time the Puritans projected an alternative present to the one Hawthorne inhabits, and they demand to know why it is not the one Hawthorne's age has realized.[10]

Upon reflecting upon his existence, these ancestors find Hawthorne himself a remnant from their past. His face perpetuates the "mould" of their features as well as their "cast of character" (12). Unlike these ancestors, however, Hawthorne cannot, while still in the Custom House, reflect upon his existence. The time kept in Hawthorne's world separates his experiencing self from any past experiences, thereby making self-reflection impossible. Instead, Hawthorne divides up his character—into a "figurative" self and an actual person. This figurative self belongs not to one of his fictions, however, but to his life in the Custom House. His "actual" person, meanwhile, belongs in an as yet unrealized present, one that began with the Puritan past. Hence he cannot reflect upon his present life unless he does so from within the realm of the Puritan past.

The Puritan past is also where his "unwritten characters" belong. They

share a significant trait Hawthorne inherited from his Puritan ancestors—
they too are in need of Hawthorne's present time for realization. When
they address Hawthorne, these unrealized creations adopt the Puritans'
voice but reverse their command: "What have you to do with us?" they
rebuke; "the little power you might once have possessed over the tribe of
unrealities is gone! You have bartered it for a pittance of the public gold.
Go, then, and earn your wages!" (30).

Like the Puritan ancestors, these unwritten characters embody a demand originating from out of Hawthorne's past. But unlike those ancestors they implicitly claim that Hawthorne performed a public service in
writing his tales. Their lives from Hawthorne's past life as a writer are as
much in need of perpetuation as are the Puritans'. But these unwritten
characters do what his ancestors would not. They acknowledge the life of
the writer as if it were as proper a calling as a Puritan vocation.

Through these hallucinated reflections, Hawthorne discovers the similarity between the duty he owes to his Puritan ancestors and his duty to
his unwritten characters. Both are in need of his present existence for
realization. The dual nature of these reflections mirrors the division in
Hawthorne's character. And that self-division reproduces the temporal division effected by the Revolutionary mythos. Hawthorne exists as a person
with a past life (of writing) but a past utterly disconnected from his present existence. Like one of his own Puritan ancestors, the author he was can
find no life for himself in Hawthorne as he now is. So Hawthorne's self-
division allows him to distinguish his figurative self, who embodies the
force of modernity's temporal displacement, from his actual self, who acknowledges responsibilities to both his unrealized characters and his Puritan ancestors.

These apparitional figures from Hawthorne's genealogical and bio-
graphical past are not resigned to their future displacement by the next figure in an endless succession. Instead they ask Hawthorne to preserve them
in his consciousness. Unlike these ghosts, the actual officials in the Custom
House resign themselves to their disappearance by passing their time with
distractions rather than common tasks.

When Hawthorne encounters his Puritan ancestors who are in need of
careful apprehension to remain in existence at all, he does not quite see
actual persons from a past. Through their presences, he literally hears and
sees what is missing from the characters in his actual field of vision. The
Custom House officials are resigned to their imminent disappearance, like

apparitions. So when Hawthorne confronts what are quite literally apparitions, he encounters what a reflective consciousness would have enabled him to realize: Without care for one another, actual persons lay no deeper claim on human existence than do evanescent apparitions.

Like characters in his early tales and out of his Puritan past, the actual persons in the Custom House must be given a life in Hawthorne's memory as well as in his present perception to be sustained in any life whatsoever. These persons, too, must be apprehended, Hawthorne soon discovers, as if they were memories of themselves, before they can possess any enduring existence.

Without the replenishment of their perceived existence with qualities from Hawthorne's memory, his fellow officials become ghostly. Supplementing perceptions with memories enables Hawthorne to intuit what he will later know: these officials bear the "mould" and "cast" of those who preceded them, and this ancestral trace lays a greater claim on Hawthorne's attention than do their actions. It is through such an accompanying memory, a much vaster memory than the personal, that a community sustains its persons, their places and things.

An Archaic Way with a Narrative

The Custom House preface makes it clear that Hawthorne was extremely sensitive to the threat modernity posed for a culture of memory. To highlight the conflict between memory and modernity, I am going to view Hawthorne's tales from the perspectives of two quite different contemporary theorists of modernity: Stephen Greenblatt's commentary provides a rationale for a world without a past; Walter Benjamin's theory of the storyteller constitutes an implicit critique of modernity.

Greenblatt suggests a relationship between the formation of a modern identity and narrative form in terms that have applicability to our discussion. According to Greenblatt, narrative self-fashioning works hand-in-glove with what he calls "improvisation." "Improvisation" means "the ability both to capitalize on the unforeseen and to transform given materials into one's own scenario. The spur-of-the-moment quality of improvisation is not as critical here as the opportunistic grasp of that which seems fixed and established."[11] The improvisational self possesses no personhood different from the role he must assume to transform another's reality into a

manipulable fiction. Even an action we can readily acknowledge as gener-
ous—the wish to sympathize with the desires and beliefs of others—serves
the interests of Greenblatt's "self-fashioning self," who empathizes with
their intimate revelations only the better to control others. Consequently,
when an improvisational self appears within cultural narratives written
and believed in by others, he does so only to interiorize their beliefs and
desires within his own improvisational belief system and then displace
them altogether.

The improvisational self grounds his power in his modernity. For the
modern individual, fixed belief indicates only an inability to change. The
improvisational or modern self capitalizes on what Greenblatt, quoting
the sociologist Daniel Lerner, calls "a mobile sensibility so adaptive to
change that rearrangement of the self-system is its distinctive mode."[12]
Whenever this improvisational self appears within a narrative, it is always
implicitly as a response to a traditional demand—to be representable in
terms familiar to the culture's narrative of itself. Since these narrative terms
can apply only momentarily, and in passing, to a self who appears within
them only long enough to display his power to turn them to his advantage,
he agrees to them only long enough to displace them. Hence this self's
improvisations provide displacement with a rationale. Through the improvisational self, the sheer force of displacement productive of each new
moment can be experienced by modern man as a liberation from the fixat-
ing constrictions of whatever came before.[13]

According to Greenblatt's implicit model of revolutionary action, the
improvisational self's forever "new" mode of situating himself within any
narrative structure becomes legitimate only when he dispossesses himself
of what is old. Thus he oppresses traditional society at the same time as he
frees himself from it. In his power to identify with both the oppressor and
the oppressed, the improvisational self exposes the cultural sham at work in
the Revolutionary mythos. The mythos promises a change in character,
but the improvisational self has no character to change. Instead he impersonates only the motion of his displacements, treating his impersonation of
change as if it were a character.

Unlike Greenblatt's improvisational self, Nathaniel Hawthorne felt oppressed only by the impromptu operations of the new. He did not, as
Greenblatt does, celebrate the "generalized displacement" resulting from
the aleatory impulses of the moment, nor did he humanize this displacement as Greenblatt does with the fiction of an improvisational self. Instead

he tried to protect inherited cultural purposes from displacement by the "new."

In this effort Hawthorne has much more in common with what Walter Benjamin calls a storyteller than with what Greenblatt calls narrative self-fashioners. In the Nazis' oppression of the Jews, Benjamin confronted dispossession by an authoritarian cultural modernism. In reflecting on ways to preserve the traditional wisdom threatened by modernism, Benjamin rediscovered the cultural value of archaic tales in an age of novels. In his analysis of modernity, Benjamin would have agreed to Greenblatt's linkage of the process of narrativity at work within a novel and the forces of displacement at work in cultural modernism. He would not, however, have celebrated the alienation resulting from such displacements as a display of freedom.

Benjamin considered the reduction of culture to passing "fashions" as akin to the reduction of the storyteller to the status of a novelist. The novelist legitimizes relations in the world conveyed by the "news." And the news media assimilate all other cultural forms, providing them with no other rationale for their existence than their status as bits of "news." Like the endless barrage of shocks modern man inherits, the "new" places a wedge between an individual and his experience of himself. When received as a "shock," experience in the modern world surges up as a sheer discontinuity, an impulse without connection to anything else within the consciousness. In organizing its "layouts" according to the principle of disconnection, the news media reprocess "shocks" into "information." Information, in its turn, divides modern individuals into public persons utterly impervious to news from the world, and private persons who live in worlds of their own.

> If it were the intention of the press to have the reader assimilate the information it supplies as part of his own experience, it would not achieve its purpose. But its intention is just the opposite, and is achieved: to isolate what happens from the realm in which it could affect the experience of the reader. The principles of journalistic information (freshness of the news, brevity, comprehensibility, and, above all, lack of connection between the individual news items) contribute as much to this as does the make-up of the pages and the paper's style.[14]

Greenblatt's theory sanctions this lack of connection by identifying it as a sign of human autonomy. His improvisational self produces disconnections capable of translating already existing cultural forms into passing "fashions," and of leaving shocking examples of manipulative control in their wake. But the improvisational self does not survive this display of power. Without any cultural form to believe in, displaced by the same power he uses to displace others, such a self can last no longer than the fashion he impersonates.

However much Greenblatt may celebrate this new man, Benjamin deplores him. And he opposes the production of the "new" by the novelist with the preservation of the "aura" by a storyteller. The novel supports a form of cultural perception confirming the desire to bring things close enough to deny their distance. The tale invests its persons and their things with an under- and after life capable of creating an intimate distance between them.

In Benjamin's telling of it, the aura seals off the discontinuity between the person and his experience. While the new demands that persons insulate themselves from its procedures, the aura preserves what cannot become present in the new. In the telling of his tales, the storyteller lets these residual forces become lively once again.

What can never eventuate on present terms appears in the tale temporally as an irretrievable pastness, perceptually as the shadows persons cast in the light, psychologically as a secret concealed within revelation, spatially as the "distant" haunting of what seems near, relationally as a strangeness no intimacy can overcome. Through the telling of tales, a culture's members enter into relation with these cultural reserves. When engaged in such relations everything persons do and say becomes permeated with what Benjamin calls an "aura."[15] The aura deepens the impressions persons, places, and things make upon one another, making them appear vivid as opposed to evanescent.

In the preface to *The Scarlet Letter* Hawthorne describes his creative process in terms consonant with Benjamin's theory of aura formation. "A child's shoe; the doll, seated in her little wicker carriage; the hobby horse:—whatever, in a word, has been used or played with, during the day, is now invested with a quality of strangeness and remoteness, though still almost as vividly present as by daylight" (31). In this description, Hawthorne experiences all of these objects as if they were permeated with a remoteness turning them into memories of themselves. And during this process, ghosts reenter from the past. "Ghosts might enter here . . . It would be too much in keeping with the scene to excite surprise, were we to look about us and discover a form, beloved, but gone hence, now sitting quietly . . . with an aspect that would make us doubt whether it had returned from afar, or had never once stirred from our fireside" (31).

Telling tales turns out to be Hawthorne's means of reestablishing touch with the past. In touch with what makes persons memorable as opposed to what makes fashions new, Hawthorne works with an unprogressive "cultural reserve" that accompanies a culture's persons but outlasts them. The cultural reserve, as what cannot be outmoded by the "new," becomes a way to recall figures back from oblivion and into enduring human forms.

Unlike Greenblatt's improvisational self, then, Hawthorne does not wish to displace or manipulate already existing cultural institutions. Nor does he wish to invent or merely imagine otherwise nonexistent characters. Instead he wishes to participate in a process capable of making persons memorable. The means of telling replaces the authorial self as the primary focus of attention in Hawthorne's twice-told tales. Hawthorne's *re*telling realigns the modernizing principle at work in Greenblatt's impromptu self as well as Hawthorne's Custom House with a cultural memory. When Hawthorne subjects the progress of modernity to the unprogressive activity of cultural reserves, the nation's past reappears as the "memory" Hawthorne's world urgently needs if it would perpetuate anything at all, including itself.[16]

Instead of meriting displacement, Hawthorne's tales bear repeating as a way of perpetuating what can never become new or enter the "news." They bear repeating in the same way as do persons who exist for Hawthorne's ancestors. His tales become a way of transmitting a cultural legacy. What his tales pass on outlasts any single person within them but accrues increased wealth by passing through a lineage of retellers of the tale. Retelling these tales turns one's private person into a site of cultural transmission where this legacy can be acknowledged and the resultant common wealth increased.[17]

The Allegory of the Person

In writing twice-told tales, Hawthorne put himself at the disposal of what we have called a collective memory, in order to provide his present culture with an appreciation of those reserves culture needs to survive. Moreover, telling his twice-told tales turned Hawthorne into an allegory of himself.

Allegory functioned not merely as a literary form but as a force in his personal psyche replete with cultural affiliations. Allegory is a culture's means of conscripting persons, places, and things into duty as reserves. It transfigures actual persons, places, and things into exemplary forms, cultural resources whose mold can be recast for future cultural use. They become cultural powers, addressing the fundamental questions constitutive of a culture.

Considered within this context, persons may be described as both themselves and allegories of exemplary figures. These presences are not what an actual person remembers; they "remember" themselves through actual persons, like Hawthorne in the Custom House, when their services become necessary for the vital preservation of personhood within a culture. Hawthorne provides, in the scene by the fireside, the best example of his experience of the self as an allegory of his own person. There he, along with the child's shoe and doll as well as the ghostly outline of the lost beloved, seems less a figure who recollects a past and more a figure recollected within a memory from the past. When he joins all these other "spiritualized" forms, Hawthorne exchanges his actual person to become like them a thing of intellect. As this fireside encounter makes clear, retelling tales from the culture's past demands that Hawthorne offer his person as a living memory—a site through which culturally valuable forces from the past can pass for renewal.

So living allegorically means doing as his ancestors commanded, that is, putting himself into the service of the commonwealth. Through allegorizing its persons, a culture can increase the reserve of symbolic characters for them to assume. After experiencing himself as an allegory of cultural memory, Hawthorne put himself on loan to the community's means of perpetuating itself. In a culture of memory, what one can be for others takes priority over what one can be for oneself. While the emphasis on the private person in Hawthorne's time caused persons to forget their status as allegories, their forgetfulness enabled Hawthorne to realize his culture's need for a collective memory.[18]

Reentering the Present

If his present circumstances separated him from his ancestral past as well as from his life as a writer, his visionary encounters led him into a special contractual relation with the past. Through this pact he became part of a past that had not yet flowed into his present. He also became a part of a world whose forms abide in a cultural reserve rather than a present existence. By a cultural reserve I mean a cultural place, existing within every cultural moment, wherein unrealized or incomplete persons and forms from the culture's past continue to exist, awaiting renewal or re-activation. Here nonsynchronous forms which began in the past but could not continue into the present remain preserved.[19] But their very status as incomplete forms enables them to lay greater claim on Hawthorne's present than do the desultory and disconnected moments in the Custom House, for they designate purposes that must be renewed if the culture is to sustain itself. In describing the cultural reserve, Geoffrey Hartman writes:

> There exists a highly structured *reserve* of forms which claims to repre-
> sent for each generation the genius of a nation, class or structure. Here
> are found the official commonplaces, the symbols and passwords that
> bind a community together, or identify its members to each other.[20]

By entering the cultural reserve, Hawthorne reversed the relationship be-tween an individual and a community that prevailed in post-Jacksonian America, where the spoils system—from which he had previously bene-fited—had repressed civic duty, putting the individual's interests before the group's. In the Custom House preface, the general interest of the United States uses Hawthorne's personal memory to return from the realm of the repressed. But when the general interest (or general will) uses Hawthorne's memory, that memory becomes a collective rather than a merely personal memory. By means of a collective memory each person remembers every other person on communal terms. He experiences the community's way of perpetuating itself, as its processes, purposes, and tasks inhabit his person. When it reflects upon Hawthorne from the past, the Puritans' collective memory exerts the equivalent of a force of will, re-minding him of a greater cultural responsibility than his self-interest.

Hawthorne begins to know the force of this memory when he enters the "second story" of the Custom House. Here a figure who is neither an actual ancestor nor an imagined character but what Hawthorne calls an "official ancestor" appears. Surveyor Pue is Hawthorne's precursor in the Custom House from pre-Revolutionary times, and he displays, before Hawthorne's distracted attention, a scarlet cloth and a little roll of explanatory manuscript. Then he delivers him to an urgent duty: "give to your predecessor's memory the credit which will be rightfully its due" (29).

No longer alive within the Custom House but the locus for the reappearance of some documents which, as pre-Revolutionary, cannot be correlated with the nation's present means of marking its time, Surveyor Pue provides Hawthorne with that sense of a past within the Custom House that will enable him to experience the recovery of his former life (of a writer) as equivalent to the recovery of a past. In demanding that he give his predecessor the credit that is his due, Surveyor Pue provides Hawthorne with the relation to a past for the Custom House that we earlier saw he needed in order to "leave it" and make it part of his past.

The importance of this encounter cannot be overemphasized. Through it, Hawthorne finds a means to perpetuate a cultural memory that would make writing indistinguishable from an ancestrally correct public duty. Moreover, when he encounters Surveyor Pue, Hawthorne finds himself within a cultural lineage—Surveyor Pue's—that the present age has merely forgotten and not subjected to its displacing force.

Unlike the present officials inhabiting the Custom House, Surveyor Pue continues to exist, but as a form who can remain alive only in memory. In locating the Surveyor in a time from the past that can no longer be replaced by the temporal operations of his present, Hawthorne envisions the Surveyor in two coexisting temporal aspects. He is a memory from the past and also a memory that cannot be replaced, through a substitute formation, in the present. In this encounter, Hawthorne enters into a visionary compact whose terms will guide his continued service in the Custom House. He receives this compact not from a functionary of the spoils system, but from a person outside the rolls of any existing party. In imagining himself recalled to public duty by Surveyor Pue, Hawthorne also envisions himself in a line of cultural succession with which partisan hirings and firings can not interfere. As a memory that cannot be made present according to the terms supervising the Revolutionary movement of temporality in his time, Hawthorne like Surveyor Pue cannot be replaced. Instead he exists as a transmission, in both his person and his action, of what continues to make persons memorable. Existing as what must be made present, the apparition of Surveyor Pue enables Hawthorne to experience himself as a figure of collective memory who must be restored to a memorable cultural life.

In finding the Custom House haunted by these figures from the past, Hawthorne feels relieved rather than terrified. In giving the Custom House a past, these ghosts restore continuity to Hawthorne's time within it. They make him feel that he has received a legacy from the past, one that he must carry forward into the future.

Personal and Collective Memory

What is crucial to acknowledge in this scene is the difference between the transmission of a collective memory and the transmission of a merely personal memory. To underscore the distinction between the two forms of remembering, Hawthorne transforms himself into a ghost, a figure through whom the public can remember its collective past. He begins this transformation with an inventory of the progress of amnesia, "prying into my mind, to discover which of its poor properties were gone" (34). After ascertaining the extent of this amnesia, he demands that he be treated as "a gentleman who writes from beyond the grave" (37). Transforming his tabulation of some lost mental properties into a request to be treated as a person who must be remembered in order to receive any human acknowledgment at all, Hawthorne completes his conversion into a "figure" of present oblivion. Then he turns his oblivion into a request to be preserved in a collective memory by invoking "the great grandchildren of the present race," who may "sometimes think" him and his tales "memorable."

This request concludes the Custom House preface and also brings to a rather startling close a transformation of Hawthorne's person into a memory. Once converted into a memory Hawthorne can take his place as a character in *The Scarlet Letter,* where a community of persons make it their duty to reflect upon and be reflected upon by each other. To indicate the results of such activities Hawthorne finds the records of a collective memory from the past among Surveyor Pue's papers.

Among Surveyor Pue's private manuscripts, Hawthorne finds papers the authorities of his own day did not, after Pue's death, deem official enough to be delivered over to the place of institutionalized memory in Halifax. In his own day, Surveyor Pue himself felt sufficiently unfulfilled by official business to become absorbed in another activity, that of collating the documents surrounding the life of Hester Prynne, who lived some eighty years before him. While sorting out these antique documents, Hawthorne discovers a worn cloth with gold embroidery and inscribing, through three bars of equal length, the letter *A*. And when he places it upon his heart he feels a sensation resulting in the exercise of what he calls "spiritual sympathy." This sympathy "begins subtly communicating itself" (28) to Hawthorne's sensibility as if it were a ghostly presence inhabiting his body.

Exercising the same license as did Hawthorne and contriving to think as if informed with a related sympathy, we might develop a context for making Hawthorne's relation to this letter understandable. An impulse that, like Hawthorne, has fallen into an age in which it cannot be fully present, the letter arises as an impression from the past but without any appropriate memory to be inscribed upon. The letter is an unrealized memory. After Hawthorne recognizes its need for a context in order to come into present existence, he ponders what coming into present existence entails.

Existing in an age without memory, Hawthorne could not wish that this impression, which is already separated from an appropriate memory, be presently recalled. His age would only forget about it. Instead of remembering it, then, in his own time, Hawthorne exercises the "figurative" prerogatives of a man "from beyond the grave" and converts his own person into a memory of himself. Transformed into a "figure" of memory he becomes the past's way to recall or retell a tale that, having originated from an "almost immemorial date" (28), has no other means of being told.

The collective memory comes to life within Hawthorne's, then, after his personal desire to be remembered by future generations coincides with a simultaneous need to be recalled by a collective past. For the charged space between these two needs—to be recalled by the past as well as by the future—is the locus for a collective memory, which transmits to the future what remains to be developed from the past.

As a figure who had never become officially past, Hester Prynne existed only within the memory of certain persons still alive in Surveyor Pue's time. They came to terms with their present circumstances by coming to terms with her memory. Hester never could have existed in a past, because she never possessed a present self, or at least she never presented herself to Pue, or Hawthorne. Never having been present, Hester always had to be made present by a work of memory. Surveyor Pue knew of her existence in the past only through the "oral testimony" of "aged persons" who never personally knew the Hester of the tale but only its afterimage, the "very old, but not decrepit woman" of "a stately and solemn aspect" (28) who continued to live among them alongside their memory of her. As a figure who must always be brought back into existence through those collective acts of recollection passed within and from generation to generation, Hester requires that the people remember her—"by heart," in order to possess any existence at all.

Memory as Civic Virtue

By recollecting a cultural context for this curiously sewn letter, Hawthorne ends the rule of displacement the spoils system wielded over the Custom House. In keeping with his pattern of daydreaming while in the Custom House, Hawthorne could have turned the letter into simply one more passing interest. Instead, Hawthorne experiences an urgent need to remember a permanent context for the letter. This need, instead of passing as had those distractions, becomes more urgent, and compels him to exercise a faculty that has lain dormant since he entered the Custom House.

The faculty he exercises is the collective memory. And, as we have seen, it positions Hawthorne outside a world of self-interested individuals, and within a world of shared interests. Earlier he perceived his reflective power as belonging not to himself but to his ancestors, his characters, and then Surveyor Pue. When he sees his power of reflection coming to him from the position of figures he had forgotten, he sees what he literally needed, that is, the ability to reflect on his own situation. Likewise, upon brooding over the inadequacy of present circumstances to preserve the scarlet letter, he envisions a world capable of "recollecting" the letter into an appropriate context, and finds it remarkably different from his own. So different, in fact, that in it the usual temporal locations of the present and past are reversed.

The past is customarily seen as utterly irrelevant to the cultural present. The starting point for what the culture is on the way to accomplishing, complete and unified in itself, the past appears divorced from the possibility for continued activity. In the Custom House, however, the cultural past appears the more present temporal formation. It is the time of the Custom House present rather than the culture's past which seems already completed. Here all the work it is necessary to do seems already to have been done—in the time it took to place the officials within the Custom House. Instead of performing further actions, the Custom House officials merely pass through a dimension of fully achieved present time. Their mere presence is all the activity the Custom House demands of its inhabitants. But this demand makes human beings seem like ghosts of an inhuman present,[21] one which goes on without the need of persons. Only the past with its supplies of incomplete actions and renewable possibilities can make those demands on a person's energies the present cannot.

The collective memory enables Hawthorne to see an entire community whose purposes are still in need of completion. When reflecting collectively, Hawthorne's memory situates him within a "recollective" community it will take *The Scarlet Letter* to realize for his present age.

The members of this community do what the members of the Custom House do not. They care for one another, precisely because their relations are grounded in a collective memory. In remembering how to use that faculty, Hawthorne did not merely see how much his age had forgotten. Though he clearly saw that, he also saw how forgettable his age had become. To recover the capacity to live in a potentially "memorable" age, Hawthorne devised a literary form he hoped would awaken the same predisposition to remember collectively he experienced in the act of writing *The Scarlet Letter.*

This hope entrusted his artistic concerns with political responsibility. Hawthorne acknowledged the political dimension of his work explicitly when he announced his intention to change his citizenship. But writing *The Scarlet Letter* rather than moving from Salem effected this change. Until he wrote *The Scarlet Letter* he had no way of correlating his artistic calling with civic duty. Writing that romance meant reflecting on questions more usually asked by a citizen out of duty to his nation than by an artist in response to his vision. What institutions, principles, and agreements should the present bring forward from the past? In what ways can persons address the responsibilities bringing them together rather than the interests keeping them apart? These were two questions Hawthorne brooded over in *The Scarlet Letter.* In exploring the differences among the characters in *The Scarlet Letter,* Hawthorne expanded his sphere of interest to include what political theorists call the general welfare.[22] Ironically, Hawthorne found it impossible to arrive at this concern while ostensibly performing his civic duty.[23]

So brooding over the characters in *The Scarlet Letter* did not detach Hawthorne from a world but included him within the decision-making activity of a truly civic community. As a figure included within the process he reflected upon, Hawthorne, at least while writing that romance, could experience his person as if it were itself produced by a community's collective memory. While remembered by that archaic community, Hawthorne re-called a set of affiliated political concerns (traditionally designated as the general welfare or the common good) forgotten by the politicians of his own age.[24]

Mob Rule and the Custom House

Without this memory to sustain him, Hawthorne would have demate-rialized back into the Custom House. To prevent this regression into a world he wanted to get behind him, Hawthorne presents an alternative account of citizen life. In dividing the Custom House preface from the ro-mance, *The Scarlet Letter* asks its readers to do what Hawthorne did, namely, reflect upon the disparity between their present lives and a memo-rable world.

As his early tales made clear, Hawthorne was apprehensive about mob rule. Hawthorne considered the mob tyrannical in its hold over the indi-viduals composing it. Formed by sudden associations of interests no more enduring for the group than is an impulse in the psyche of a person, mobs did not deny the self-interests of their members, but multiplied them.

Differences of opinion capable of distinguishing its members were gen-eralized by the mob into the unanimity of mob rule. "Mob rule" and the "tyranny of the masses" were two terms popularly used to qualify any sus-tained enthusiasm for the will of the people. Hence Hawthorne always qualified his respect for the democratic people with reservations about their potential to become a mob.

He was interested in the way the one could be converted into the other. A mob generalized an individual's impulses into a monstrous parody of what we have called the general will. But a mob could be induced to reflect on its motives. Reflection, when exercised collectively, could enable a mob to give up its immediate impulses and participate in a deliberative process.

Hawthorne used just such a reflective change in the group mind—from an impulse of judgment to a collective reconsideration—as the context for *The Scarlet Letter.* In the process of such a reconsideration the Puritans dis-cover a more enduring basis for relationship. Their shared reflection recon-stitutes a crowd of onlookers into a group. In this reconstituted group each person appears both as an isolated individual and as a participant in a more inclusive reflective process, one in which all the members of the group are perpetuated.

Collective memory is the shorthand designation we have given this process. When considered as a psychological faculty, the collective memory is indispensable for a democracy. Definable as the collective deliberative process through which a person and his community are preserved, the collective memory constituted a culturally meaningful relation between Hawthorne's present and the nation's past.[25] Whereas Hawthorne's age turned displacement into the approved way of reproducing its present, the collective memory restored a context from the past as the basis for present culture. After we identify this context, we can understand why Hawthorne's age turned it into a presupposition, and we can begin to understand its relation to collective memory. The context Hawthorne's age presupposed was the democratic process, the commitment of each citizen to the general welfare of all. But to preserve their special interests, many of Hawthorne's contemporaries acted as if the process had already been fully realized—in the past.

When consigned to the past, the democratic process shared a position akin to Surveyor Pue's. It was given "official" recognition rather than the credit it was due. Hawthorne realized he could not give his official ancestors the credit due them without restoring the democratic process necessary to grant it.

Restated in the terms guiding our discussion, he could not fulfill his visionary compact with Surveyor Pue without treating the democratic process itself as if it were a part of collective memory. It now becomes clear that no age can ignore its relation to the past and remain democratic.

The Politics of Memory

When I use such notions as collective memory and the general will, I do not wish to substitute idealizations for a description of the actual political situation in 1850. At the time he served in the Custom House, the notion of the general will—a term invented by the English Whigs during a time when neither the monarch nor the members of parliament (whose integrity was often corrupted through pension and position received from the court) represented the will of the people—had fallen into disrepute.[26] It was discredited as a result of the spoils system, the patronage system inherited from a president, Andrew Jackson, popularly considered a representative of the popular will.[27]

Moreover, the notion of the "general welfare" which formerly warranted the sacrifice of a citizen's private interests to the common good underwent a similar and more or less contemporary complication. Consequent to the arguments for a balance of self-interests, the nation's stated grounds for "social compaction" was no longer the general welfare. Instead, as Arthur Lovejoy has pointed out, most Americans believed the aims and motives of virtually all individuals and therefore of all factions were "equally irrational and 'interested' [hence] equally indifferent to the 'general good.'"[28] Without the need to oppose a monarchy or aristocracy whose interests were at odds with those of the populace, Americans had no grounds to discriminate the self-interest of individuals (who composed the populace) from the interest of the people in general.

In post-Jacksonian America, freedom was negatively defined, as a freedom from institutions of any kind. This freedom resulted from a contract freely taken up—not with one's fellow Americans but with nature. When exercised within nature, however, civic virtue could express itself only as independence from the customs and institutions of society. In the wilderness, political freedom could not be differentiated from the independence of spirit necessary for survival. Civic virtue required not the sacrifice of personal interests for the common good but only the expenditure of personal labor in the husbanding of the virgin soil. America's laborers won a reward from nature for this display of their industry—private property. Instead of requiring subordination of personal interest to the common good, such a vision of civic virtue encouraged citizens to pursue their personal interests as the best way for the nation to progress.

National progress, then, supported by expansionist policies, displaced the "general will" as the source and goal of citizenship in post-Jacksonian democracy. Even a factory worker in the crowded quarters of a city could think of himself as saving for a move westward, where nature's reward for his industry could ultimately be claimed. In this migratory commonwealth, the appeal to the broad court of the expansive landscape itself provided the solution for many political questions, or did so at least until the South, invoking the negative value of freedom guaranteed by this notion of a social constitution, insisted upon exercising its right to liberty: not from other citizens but from the Union itself.

Secession, the civic right of political independence urged by Southern states, was not contrary to the notion of political virtue secured by the Constitution. The South, the part of the nation where an agrarian economy flourished, could use as its rationale for secession the same sacred notion of "Nature's Nation" that guaranteed the rights of American political virtue. Transforming the political small print of the common pursuit of self-interest into the large print of secession from the Union, the South cast the "counterpoise of interest" theory of the federal Constitution into doubt and upset the harmony expansionism might otherwise have promised.[29]

This turn in the political argument of Hawthorne's time returned him to an older notion of civic virtue. For in following out the pursuit of self-interest rather than its sacrifice for the sake of the commonwealth, the South necessitated a reevaluation of the terms of political discourse.

Hawthorne correlated his forced displacement from office with that force of nature operating within man when he exercises self-interest. He thereby denied "nature" its ideological place as an appropriate source of political value. Instead of honoring nature, Hawthorne included it within a chain along with greed, the spoils system, and corruption, and he linked all these with everlasting oblivion. He denied the existence of a nature undefiled by time, custom, or past memory.

As we have already seen, the myth of progress was founded on the mythos of the Revolution. The Revolution achieved for American time what the frontier effected for national space, that is to say the power to be free from past inhabitants, customs, or memories. Both mythoi, that of the Revolution and that of the frontier, defined American freedom as the negation of any prior formation whatsoever.

But after having been expelled from the time and space marking his political life in America, Hawthorne experienced his own person as a political custom from which American progress had declared itself free. Occupying, along with Surveyor Pue and Hester Prynne, the place of a past for which the course of American history had no present use, he did not retreat to the private life of a writer whose solitude would turn alienation into cultural privilege,[30] nor did he exercise the right of revenge against the spoils system (an exercise that would have indicated only a residual desire for a new position). Instead he recovered his relations with other figures from an American past who conceived of the common good rather than nature as the ground for political value.

Unlike his neighbors Thoreau and Emerson, to whom he is often compared, Hawthorne did not return to nature for a fresh start. Because he could not distinguish the appetite for revenge within the Custom House from the instinct for survival supervising life within nature, he could not

choose nature as an alternative to the Custom House. Instead, he transformed the wish for a new life into an event within his narrative *The Scarlet
Letter*. There, as we shall see, the need for a new life discloses an inability to
be responsible either for one's personal or for one's cultural past.

A Citizen of Somewhere Else

Hawthorne came to terms with history's loss of his person by entering into
relations with other persons whom history had relegated to a lost past. All
the citizens of this "somewhere else" turned the need they shared, for a
common exertion of memory, into the precondition for their communal
life. Hawthorne also turned memory into the inner sensibility of a community. He himself described his creative process as one capable of lending
the full range of his faculties and sympathies to his creations; in other
words, he turned his writing into a means of letting others live through
him, even as he came into full life through them. Writing became an occasion to sacrifice his self-interest for the interest of an entire community of
persons. What resulted was what he called a republic of letters—"somewhere else."

Each citizen of this "somewhere else" was subject to the process of ongoing reflection Hawthorne associated with the moral life of a democratic
people. Like Hester Prynne and Surveyor Pue and Nathaniel Hawthorne in
the Custom House, none of these persons ever was fully present. Each appeared in the process of becoming present through an ongoing and collective reflection. In an age that had sacrificed all other associations of a
democratic people for the negative freedom of a democratic individual,
Hawthorne returned to this memory for his first exercise of civic virtue.

The Politics of Romance

Returning to such a life meant restoring the nation to an unfinished process, begun in the past, but awaiting renewed consideration by each subsequent generation. The Puritan community within *The Scarlet Letter* have
not completed their deliberations on Hester, but still need help in making
up the group's mind. In going back to the Puritans, Hawthorne interrupts
their process of decision-making. By returning to the past at a time when

the community was in the process of changing its mind about a prior decision, Hawthorne renewed his relation to this decision-making process.

But in recovering this process he did not separate it from the past. Instead he inherited the will to make his present culture eventful, but in
terms inherited from the Puritan past. Historians subscribing to the Revolutionary mythos have traditionally discredited the Puritans on the grounds
of their intolerance. They recognize that the Puritan institutions constituted the bases for our democracy and the origins of our liberties. But, in
keeping with the coherencies of the mythos of our history, these same historians have reshaped the Puritans' intolerance into a form of tyranny the
Revolution opposed.[31] But Puritan intolerance would have been an im-
provement over social relations in the Custom House. In the Custom
House, persons weren't sources of fear, but they provided opportunities
for nothing but distraction or indifference. The inhabitants of the Custom
House were tolerant not out of respect for freedom but out of indifference.
Unlike Custom House officials, each Puritan was both himself and a means
of transmitting a process of acknowledgment he shared with all others. As
an embodiment of a covenant, each Puritan was responsible for keeping its
rules.

As an inhabitant of the Custom House, Hawthorne was subjected to the
results of an opinion process, the spoils system, in whose operations he had
not participated at all. In writing *The Scarlet Letter*, he entered into relation
with a community whose rules were quite different from those of spoils-
system politics. Hawthorne returned to the Puritan world in order to find
a political process capable of reevaluating the terms of political and social
agreement. And he turned this process into a cultural inheritance by writing *The Scarlet Letter*, which continues these deliberations.

As a way of disconfirming the terms of his contemporary life, then,
Hawthorne's historical romance contrasts sharply with other versions of
history. It replaces the Revolutionary mythos of an ideal past with historical process, and supplants the sequential narrative of history proper with
an unfinished action. But Hawthorne's tale is no less different from traditional romances.[32]

To clarify the distinction between traditional romances and *The Scarlet
Letter*, I am going to turn to an essay by Fredric Jameson because it is critical of the social function of romance. The romance, according to Jameson,
organizes a realm wherein obsolescent cultural forms can enjoy an archaic
afterlife. Romance recovers a utopian realm; it is an archaic revivification of

persons and ways displaced from the modern world but contains these utopian energies by consigning them to an archaic, or already outmoded, context. For Jameson, "the archaic character of the categories of romance (magic, good and evil, otherness) suggests that this genre expresses a nostalgia for a social order in the process of being undermined and destroyed by nascent capitalism, yet still coexisting side by side with the latter."[33]

The coexistence of these categories of the archaic and the modern does not mean they enjoy equal status. The modern capitalistic world always circumscribes the locus of the romance, thereby canceling out any possibility of equivalence. "The formal problem of romance may perhaps be understood as that of slipping past the ever-wary censorship of the new bourgeois reality principle: the reader craves the mystery inherent in the form . . . But he now finds himself obliged to *justify* the henceforth scandalous and archaic activity of fantasy. So that . . . the replacements for the older magical function also serve as so many rational ways of explaining it away."[34]

In this description Jameson is both scrupulous in his logic and careful in his claims. Modern culture needs to gratify the desires it arouses, he reasons, or those desires could be mobilized into subversive political forces. To discharge these revolutionary energies, competitive cultures produce romances. Then they display a cultural power to contain, surpass, and outmode a world in which desire can be gratified—by designating it as archaic rather than "real."

But as we have seen in Hawthorne's time, a romance mythos organized the dominant self-representation of American culture. Consequently Americans did not need romances to gratify their cultural desires. The American Revolution had already gratified the only desire—for independence—any American need ever have. As a result of existing within an ideological context of an already fulfilled national desire, Americans were deprived of any vitalizing motive to realize or gratify a national desire.[35]

In place of confirming the power of an actual world to supersede a romance form, the mythos of the Revolution emptied the actual world of all historical density, supplanting everyday life with serialized discontinuities.

In writing his romances, Hawthorne did not validate the Revolutionary romance, but wrote an alternative romance. He wrote historical romances in order to restore to the present a cultural will it could realize rather than displace, or contain, or surpass. As Hawthorne writes in the preface to *The House of the Seven Gables,* the criterion for romance "lies in the attempt to connect a by-gone time with the very present that is fully away from it." [36] Unlike many of his contemporaries, Hawthorne did not believe the Revolution had realized the nation's purposes. It had only secured the nation's right to continue them.

Custom House as a Twice-Told Tale

When he was part of the cultural process called the spoils system, Hawthorne's person represented only its own imminent displacement. The spoils system used the Revolutionary mythos of separation from a past to compensate for its cultural shortcomings. The spoils system could not produce any social form more lasting than the movement of displacement. As a political process, the spoils system simply confirmed the power of majority opinion by finding public offices for those who voted with the majority and displacing those who did not.

Since the system worked independently of him, Hawthorne could find no motive for action while within it. He could recover motives for culturally significant actions only by imagining himself part of a decision-making process depending on the cooperative judgment of its members. As an incomplete social process, the action in *The Scarlet Letter* provides the collective relations missing in the Custom House. As an incomplete political action in the pre-Revolutionary past, the tale supplied Hawthorne with the motivational context missing from life in the Custom House.

Human motives depend upon a context capable of directing an intention toward a goal. But in a time organized according to a revolutionary mythos, an individual possesses no context from the past in which to formulate an enabling motive. Such a context could appear only within a pre-revolutionary world exempt from the revolutionary mythos. Hawthorne recovered both the enabling political motives and the context he needed in writing *The Scarlet Letter.*

In returning to the past, then, he was not simply remembering what happened. As we have seen, a merely personal or properly historical recollection would only confirm the power of present cultural forms to displace these images from the past. Unlike those in his present world, the persons in *The Scarlet Letter* as well as their actions were indissociable from their cultural processes. To recall these persons Hawthorne also had to reactivate their cultural process. And in reactivating those processes, Hawthorne discovered a cultural process capable of sustaining rather than displacing his person.

To acknowledge the pathos in this discovery, we must recall Hawthorne's feeling of being not simply ejected from his job but forgotten by his age. Only his reactivation of an as yet incomplete communal process enabled him to feel sufficiently remembered by his culture. As a process utterly different from present cultural practices, the Puritans' group decision could not be displaced by something akin to the spoils system. Their group decision also permitted Hawthorne's contemporaries to recognize, as he did, that political formations like the spoils system deprive culture of any means of transmitting its purposes or ideals to a future. Such processes reduce purposes and ideals to indifferent trends, no sooner stated than subject to displacement by the next. Defined as what requires continued reflection, the cultural process Hawthorne recalls renews the purposes sustaining its participants. In bringing forward this process as the legacy from a past, Hawthorne recovers relation with the will of a pre-Revolutionary American people. In bringing it forward in the form of a tale he *re*tells, Hawthorne does not claim the tale as the product of an individual artist; he takes his place within a community, to perpetuate its customs as a receiver of and believer in the collective process he transmits. His twice-told tale releases a living memory, capable of transmitting what remains vitalizing for a present age as it realizes the past. What remains most poignant about Hawthorne's transformation inheres neither in the tale he retells nor in his act of retelling. As an impulse of memory from the past, he demands a collective memory from *our* age to preserve his person.

Chapter Three

A Romance with the Public Will

When an uninstructed multitude attempts to see with its eyes, it is exceedingly apt to be deceived. When, however, it forms its judgment, as it usually does, on the intuitions of its great and warm heart, the conclusions thus attained are often so profound and unerring, as to possess the character of truths supernaturally revealed.
—*Nathaniel Hawthorne*

Throughout this discussion of Hawthorne I have tried to make explicit a connection between the literary form and social force of romance. In a world without a past, romance performed a necessary cultural task: it invested objects and persons with a cultural memory, without which persons in a culture behave the way the inhabitants of the Custom House do: they surge up before one another with all the durative qualities of ghosts.

Alexis de Tocqueville was quite attentive to the palpable absence, within American culture, of a usable past. Tocqueville also noticed how the failure by Americans to respect their common past circumscribed their locus of interests to private concerns and present circumstances. Most Americans were much more willing to gratify present needs than consider the welfare of future generations.

We have already seen how Hawthorne's use of a collective memory widened the sphere of an individual's interests, replacing self-interest with concern for the well-being of a community. But unlike a collective memory, a literary romance could also work in an opposite direction. Instead of generalizing the sphere of interest, it could gratify the reader's urge for privacy, thereby promoting a disposition Tocqueville found even more troublingly present in Americans: each wanted, he claimed "to draw apart with his family and his friends," and having "thus formed a little circle of his own, [he] willingly leave[s] society at large to itself."[1]

After being discharged from his Custom House duties, Hawthorne himself felt tempted to return to his merely private relations. Recent critics have argued that Hawthorne's romances sacrificed public for private relations, and elevated this sacrifice into a literary principle. In the alienation of the romance setting from Hawthorne's actual world, they have found signs of his chosen separation, his displacement of a world that had displaced him.[2]

The explicit subject matter of *The Scarlet Letter* seems to confirm this thesis. Hester and Arthur keep their violation of the community's customs private. But Hawthorne does not keep the private lives of Hester and Arthur apart from the lives of other members of the community; rather, he shows how Hester and Arthur put their most intimate needs into the service of the community's. In *The Scarlet Letter* their privacy becomes a resource for communal intimacy.

Rufus Choate, in an 1833 lecture in Salem entitled "The Importance of Illustrating New England History by a Series of Romances," underscored the opposition between romance and self-interest that Hawthorne capitalized on. Historical romances, Choate hoped, would correct "the cold selfishness with which we regard ourselves, our day, and our generation, as a separate and insulated portion of man and time."[3] He also emphasized the relationship between an interest in the past and what political theorists have called the "general interest." By "awakening our sympathies for those who have gone before, [romance] makes us mindful, also, of those who are to follow, and thus binds us to our fathers and to our posterity by a lengthening and golden cord."[4]

If Hawthorne felt the urge, after his experiences in the Custom House, to have done with the public world altogether, the romance he wrote enabled him to rediscover vital sympathies with that world, just as the Puritans' predisposition to judge Hester's transgression changed into sympathy for her. Just as their reconsideration of Hester deepened the private lives of the Puritan community, his romance with that Puritan community restored Hawthorne's faith in a public world.

This reciprocity between the public and private worlds is pertinent not merely to Hawthorne's relationship to romance, but to Hester's and Arthur's relationship to their community as well. To elucidate this reciprocity, I will make this interrelationship between private and public spheres an explicit topic of investigation throughout this chapter.

Judgment in the Name of the Father

In moving across the threshold separating the Custom House preface from the romance proper, Hawthorne intensifies his feeling of being forgotten in the Custom House world, then finds himself recalled to an archaic Puritan past by a remnant from it. This remnant from the past, the scarlet letter, continues to symbolize the public infamy it shares with Hawthorne; however, its infamy is the result not of a change in public opinion—as was the case in Hawthorne's dismissal—but of a community's judgment.

As he moves across the threshold of the preface into *The Scarlet Letter,* Hawthorne moves into a communal past. He gives up his status as a figure subject to public opinion and assumes a share, along with an entire Puritan community, in the process of judging Hester.

Here Hawthorne confronts the conflicting demands posed by Hester's private life and the Puritans' public world. In bearing a child outside of the family, Hester Prynne upset the balance in the relation between private and public worlds. She violated the principle of mutual trust and mutual acknowledgment upon which the Puritans based their community. Following the child's birth, the letter *A* embroidered on Hester's bosom stood in the place of a family surname and displaced the need for the community to find an earthly father for Pearl. Fatherhood is a man's avowal, before a community, of responsibility for the human consequence of an action in his private life. In the absence of any father to claim her, Pearl's father became the community's judgment, and the *A* marked the surname of this stern parent.

At the beginning of Hawthorne's romance, Hester suffered the public consequences resulting from an action in her past. Pearl was the human result of a past and private action, a result of a unique kind—one separated from any causative principle. And this separation of Pearl, a human effect, from any human cause turned the entire community into Pearl's missing father. Instead of leading us, in detective fashion, back to her father, Hawthorne's romance considers the consequences, both individual and communal, of a passion that could not be socialized in the usual way—with a marriage.

What remains remarkable about Hawthorne's romance inheres in its attention not to the antagonism between the Puritan community and Hester Prynne, but to the ways in which her private action required careful evaluation and reevaluation by an entire community, and to the means whereby her personal life became the basis for the community's restoration of its public life. The magistrates, for example, were able to reclaim their patriarchal authority following an act of adultery that severely damaged the social position of a father. Adultery, in separating the father from his familial function, was considered threatening to the legal and social authority of other father figures in the community, and thereby threatened the power of the group to reproduce itself socially.

Private Persons and Communal Selves

The existence of Pearl reminds the Puritans of the mystery in paternity. This mystery is usually domesticated by men who take a public pledge of paternity to explain to themselves the role their momentary passion played in the appearance of a child. As the mother of a child without a father to claim responsibility, Hester Prynne returns mystery to paternity, and at the same time restores great public authority to the erotic power of women. Without one man to claim paternal responsibility for Hester and her child, Hester remains a social force threatening to the status of every man in the Puritan community.

The public accommodates itself to this mystery and Hester's erotic power through its judgment. The magistrates, preachers, and military officers sitting in the balcony where they supervise her punishment recover the patriarchal authority threatened when the father of the child would not speak in his own name. The unsympathetic, utterly solemn stare of the crowd is the mediator for this patriarchal power, and it violates Hester's right to privacy in the mediation. The public character of the crowd's confirmation of the power of the patriarchate replaces the privacy of the denial of paternity by one of the men in the community. They make public what Hester would keep private. And they have to make it public, because Hester's private act of adultery has threatened the very fabric of the Puritan public world, founded on the authority of responsible fathers.

Instead of submitting to the public's exposure of her, however, Hester recovers a form of privacy even while on the scaffold, by resorting to private recollections of her life in the Old World. Hester's most poignant memory is that of her separation from her family. Her memories return her to her family in the Old World to compensate for the lack of any family (whether nuclear or extended) in the New World.

Hester's personal memories turn the Puritans' need for legitimate paternity into another demand from an oppressive Old World patriarchate—the one that required her marriage to Roger Chillingworth. Her recollections enable her to accept the Puritans' judgment against her, but do so by making it continuous with an Old World marriage arrangement, one of the customs the Puritans came to America to escape. Even in the midst of the shame which should have separated her from these onlookers, Hester's memory enables her to find familial, even sympathetic terms for the spectacle of judgment the public has made of her. But these terms of endearment only identify her with the Old World with which the Puritans have lost all sympathy.

After she encounters her estranged husband within the crowd, however, her entire relationship with the public changes. His sternness makes the Puritans' impersonal judgment feel comforting by contrast. When Hester encounters Roger she turns the rest of the crowd into a shield, its gaze a refuge capable of protecting her from his. "Dreadful as it was, she was conscious of a shelter in the presence of these thousand witnesses . . . She fled for refuge, as it were, to the public exposure and dreaded the moment when its protection should be withdrawn from her."[5] Unable to release herself from the field of Chillingworth's vision, Hester turns to the public's judgment not only for solace but as a substitute for that familial warmth she could not find in either her husband or her lover: "Out of the whole human family . . . she seemed conscious that whatever sympathy she might expect lay in the larger and warmer heart of the multitude" (50).

Before Hester can find comfort in the public exposure, however, Reverend Wilson, standing in the balcony, demands once again to know the name of the child's father. This demand leads Reverend Arthur Dimmesdale to intervene. Dimmesdale qualifies the older minister's command by addressing Hester in a way sure to solicit sympathy rather than judgment from the crowd. By interpreting her irresponsible passion as a sign of her compassion for the absent father, Dimmesdale also transforms the public image of Hester. He represents her not as an adulteress, but as a fatherless mother, like the child a victim but unlike the helpless child a victim who freely takes up the suffering of another. Thus he gives her the public opportunity to convert her social position from one of shame for her sin to one of self-sacrifice for the sin of another: "Take heed how thou deniest to him—who perchance hath not the courage to grasp it for himself—the bitter but wholesome cup that is now presented to thy lips!" (52). In these words Hester does not remain either herself or "adultery" but becomes another allegorical figure, one representing the pathos shared by all in the crowd who know what it was that was lost when the lovers in them became mothers and fathers.

In speaking to Hester but through the mediation of the public's sympathy, Dimmesdale inaugurates a double discourse that he will use throughout the romance: one with a private message encoded within a public communication. When he says, "What can thy silence do for him except it tempt him—yea, compel him, as it were, to add hypocrisy to sin?" (52), he means to say—to himself, Hester, and secretly to his parishioners—that his private judgment in keeping him out of a state of public repentance also keeps him in a state of perpetual relation to Hester.

Communal Addresses

This scene dramatizes not the disappearance of the public world, but the necessity of the public world as a precondition for continuing Hester and Arthur's romance. In it Hawthorne insists on the people as the medium necessary before Hester and Arthur can communicate with one another at all. Hawthorne does not conceive of either Hester or Arthur in opposition to the Puritan community; in representing his continued love for Hester through the sympathies he arouses in the community, Arthur simultaneously expresses his love for the community.

Arthur's adultery with Hester deepens his sense of his relation with the community. His sin enables him to experience the suffering of even the greatest of sinners among his parishioners:

> him, the man of ethereal attributes, whose voice the angels might have listened to and answered! But this very burden it was, that gave him sympathies so intimate with the sinful brotherhood of mankind; so that his heart vibrated in unison with theirs, and received their pain into itself, and sent its own throb of pain through a thousand other hearts, in gushes of sad, persuasive eloquence. Oftenest persuasive, but sometimes terrible! The people knew not the power that moved them thus. (103)

As this description makes clear, Dimmesdale does not avoid public judgment but releases sympathies capable of chastening and deepening it. Only after experiencing his fear of public condemnation can Dimmesdale speak for a parish each of whose members needs to judge communally because of a prior fear of being judged individually. Dimmesdale speaks from an enabling personal failure to distinguish his feeling of being judged from the community's. His eloquent words distribute the personal pain of judgment throughout the community, turning the process of judgment into a reciprocal and abiding activity rather than a one-time affair.

When speaking after Dimmesdale, Reverend Wilson tries to reinstate a demand for judgment free of complicating sympathies. In talking down to Hester, he returns her to the status of an adulterous woman who has already received more sympathy than she deserves. "Woman, transgress not beyond the limits of Heaven's mercy!" (53) he shouts down to Hester.

Hester responds to Wilson's words as if she were continuing Dimmesdale's sermon. She assumes a responsibility that naming her child's father would only compromise: "And would that I might endure his agony as well as mine . . . And my child must seek a Heavenly, she shall never know an earthly one!" (53). In insisting on the difference between her love, which is founded on passion, and the love maternity founds, Hester responds from that social space between private passion and familial responsibility that Dimmesdale's earlier remarks have prepared for her. In her response Hester has of course spoken to Dimmesdale. Not in a secret code, however, but through an unusual kind of sympathy embodied neither in Hester nor in Arthur but in the multitude through whom they speak.

Passion and Suffering

Occupying the social place through which lovers pass on their way to becoming husbands and fathers, wives and mothers, Hester converts the Puritans' assured judgment of her "adultery" into hesitant reflection upon what exactly is at issue when a lover lays claims upon another person's intimacy. In refusing to betray Arthur's name, Hester recovers the privacy of this relation, but she does not then treat this private recovery as an excuse for personal isolation from the community. Instead she gives up the right to privacy as the public cost of her private relation to her lover, and agrees to remain within the community not as herself but as a woman represented by the scarlet letter.

Following Dimmesdale's sermon, however, it is difficult to know exactly what it is that the scarlet letter is meant to represent about her. Occupying that place between lovers and family members that matrimony socializes out of awareness, Hester gives lively expression to the contradiction between personal needs and social reproduction. Representing both judgment and compassion, maternity and adultery, self-sacrifice and self-assertion, pride and humility, private vice and (in her sacrifice of her person to the community's needs) public virtue, Hester preserves the conflicting terms through which the entire Puritan community will continue to argue about its historical existence.

As a woman for whom maternity remains a private condition rather than a social role, Hester marks the point of intersection separating private and public persons. The patriarchs used the scaffold to turn Hester into their means of impressing on the memory of the community their judgment against adultery. But Hester, through the compassion with which she complicates judgment, turns their judgment into an opportunity for a re-evaluation of social relations. Instead of signifying a public judgment against adultery, Hester remains among the Puritans as their personal means for continuing to decide the most fundamental questions: that is, the relationships between private and social persons.

The Family and Persons

Returning the scene to the fundamental terms of social discourse, we can say Hester sinned against the family. And the Puritan public, in expressing its judgment, was recovering the priority of familial over private relations. But as soon as we recover these fundamental terms we discover doubts along with them. In a passion unavailable to domestication, Hester did not confirm the family's power over her but called attention to the contradiction involved in separating the private family from the universal human family. The private family organizes itself through exclusion. The turn to a private family is also a turn away from the public world. To remain exclusive, the family asserts its status as a haven within a world it must describe as heartless.[6] In judging against Hester in the name of the family, however, the Puritan community had to wonder whether the private family had not itself become a sanction for heartless behavior.

On the scaffold, which for the Puritans was a powerful pulpit, Hester agreed to represent the terms of an ongoing public sermon. But her very willingness made it difficult to state the precise meaning of those terms. For by willingly sacrificing her right to be a wife for the sake of love, she forced the multitude to punish self-sacrificial love in the name of the family.

While on the scaffold, Hester divides herself into a woman who loves a man outside the familial bond and a woman who remains a wife to a man for whom she feels no love at all. And this self-division calls attention to the troubling contradiction between the personal bond of love and the social bond of marriage. Can the family punish her love in the name of its exclusive monopoly on love? If it does, then it becomes clear that the family exists only to sacrifice the personal to the familial.

Moreover, in sacrificing herself to the interpretive needs of the entire community, Hester includes the community as well as her lover as appropriate recipients of her love. Hester asserts her right to keep secret her lover's name, but she also surrenders herself to the community's moral need to make of her what they will.

Marks of Distinction

For the public, Hester's significance is quite different from that ascribed to her by the magistrates. During her continued years in old Boston, Hester provided many preachers with a subject for sermons as judgmental as Reverend Wilson's. "Throughout them all, giving up her individuality, she would become the general symbol at which the preacher and moralist might point, and in which they might verify and embody their images of woman's frailty and sinful passion" (59). But while the ministers took advantage of her to represent the reality of sin, the remainder of the community regarded the scarlet letter from a different perspective. Finding in the letter on Hester's breast "a specimen of her delicate and imaginative skill, of which the dames of a court might gladly have availed themselves, to add the richer and more spiritual adornment of human ingenuity to their fabrics of silk and gold" (61), they looked to Hester's needlework to give Old World "majesty to the forms in which a new government manifested itself to a people" (62). Hester lost the right to move among the people as one of them, but, as an embodiment of the public's mark of exclusion, she turned into the means of reestablishing those social distinctions the Puritans left Europe to get behind them. In embroidering back onto their clothes those marks of distinction which their belief in equality before God denied them, Hester becomes the public's means of representing its social differentiations. The ministers may have found in her a way to confirm the law against adultery, but the people found in her a way to get around the ministers' sumptuary laws.

As time passed, Hester turned out "fashions," the most general and least permanent form of social display. This conversion of Hester into a source for passing fashions leads to a poignant comment from the narrator confessing his failure to discover a moral in this turn of events:

> By degrees, nor very slowly, her handiwork became what would now be termed the fashion. Whether from commiseration for a woman of so miserable a destiny; or from the morbid curiosity that gives a fictitious value even to common or worthless things; or by whatever other intangible circumstance was then, as now, sufficient to bestow, on some persons, what others might seek in vain; or because Hester really filled a gap which must otherwise have remained vacant; it is certain that she had ready and fairly requited employment for as many hours as she saw fit to occupy with her needle. (62)

In wearing the scarlet letter, Hester accepted the community's need to set themselves apart from her, but when she embroidered their mark of shame into it, she set herself apart from the community, and managed to do so with sufficient distinction for those unaware of her past to imagine her "a great lady in the land" (76).

Thus the excluded Hester became the producer of the socially acceptable sign of the exclusive called fashion. This reversal reestablished her in a place within the Puritan community of a very peculiar kind. For the producer of social differences for a society claiming to be without them, Hester could not be acknowledged as occupying a position within the community. Marking her as different from the community, only Hester's embroidery could mark the distinctions within it that made reciprocal communal positions possible.

In a sense, the public's way with Hester presupposed the ministers'. As the work of a figure already punished for a personal display of extravagance, the products of Hester's labor could be worn innocently by everyone else. They could be treated as signs of her social repentance rather than indications of the wearers' personal vanity. The community's identification of Hester with social mortification was complete enough to afford the community another allegory. Vanity itself, Hawthorne suggests, could feel ashamed when dressed up in Hester's handiwork: "Vanity, it may be, chose to mortify itself, by putting on, for ceremonials of pomp and state, the garments that had been wrought by her sinful hands" (62).

In thus separating Hester's work from her person, the community found a way to restate the purpose of Hester's penitence. Treating her as the appropriate scapegoat for the vanity inherent in all forms of social display, the community turned Hester into its means of social reproduction—even after her adultery had threatened it.

But Hester also had her own way of experiencing her work and her person. To Hester, the needlework was not work but a "mode of expressing . . . the passion of her life" (63). As an embodiment of her passion, the clothes she embroidered were not forms of repentance but public restatements of her private relationship with Arthur. Hence, in dressing up the community in signs of her passion, Hester cannot be said to have repented at all. Through the resources of communal intimacy she makes publicly available, Hester turns the community into her means of remaining intimate with Arthur. Her former abandon to the passion she shared with Arthur alone is converted by her self-sacrifice into socially acceptable hence publicly acknowledgeable terms.

As if to underscore the use of the public as a mediator for their otherwise silent discourse of love, Hawthorne remarks on an unsuspected result of Hester's public persona: her discovery of powers of sympathy akin to those Arthur released in the crowd in the scaffold scene. Arthur redirected the crowd's judgment against an adulteress into sympathy for the fidelity of the lover. Hester is possessed of "sympathetic knowledge of the hidden sin in other hearts" (65); she sympathizes with the sins she secretly shares with others.

Hester's reversal of the direction of sympathy affects both the public and its minister. The public alienated Hester from the community to reaffirm those public values Hester privately transgressed. But Hester turns her private transgression into a source of her own deep sympathy with the community. Through her public acknowledgment of a private transgression, Hester initiates relations with a community of private persons. Moreover her sympathy with their secret transgressions converts Arthur's parishioners into persons who could sympathize with rather than condemn Arthur and Hester's passion.

Lovers and Mothers

Despite Hester's power to convert into public terms the passion she formerly kept utterly private, she nevertheless publicly recognizes the limits of passion. She must acknowledge these limits, moreover, because of the child who turned her momentary passion into a more enduring form.

Hester might have claimed a social debt from the community, for by producing social distinctions she supplied a resource missing from many Puritan societies. But Pearl changes the nature of her debt to the community, and introduces her to a social relation other than her private one with Arthur Dimmesdale.

When Hester looks after Pearl, she maintains the only relation she can openly maintain with her lover. But the child addresses the mother in the lover. And her address evokes in Hester a response at least as intense as the one evoked by Arthur. And this child, in her need of a father, provokes the guilt in Hester that none of the townspeople could. Earlier we suggested that Hester divided the lover in her character from the mother in it. But Pearl brought the "object of her affection" together with the "emblem of her guilt." By conflating realms that Hester needed to keep separate, Pearl also brought Hester into a truly sympathetic relation with other figures in the community. Without Pearl as a consideration, Hester could freely transform every townsperson into a medium through whom she could make Arthur feel her continued love. But Pearl demanded love for herself alone, and to meet this demand Hester could not limit her sphere of relations to Arthur, nor could she direct all of her actions toward him. With Pearl as part of her private sphere, Hester could no longer use her status as a figure of Christian self-sacrifice to send a message of passionate affection to Arthur.

Without a father to close the circle of her family affections, Hester had to enlarge the sphere of maternal affection. Treating every needy member of the community with the same devotion she directed toward Pearl, Hester turned into "a well-spring of human tenderness, unfailing to every real demand, and inexhaustible by the largest. Her breast, with the badge of shame, was but the softer pillow for the head that needed one" (117).

On the scaffold, Hester could prove her continued love for Arthur through her refusal to give Pearl a father. Her silence asserted the priority of Hester's passion over her maternity. In the seven years following, however, Hester discovers the social expense for Pearl of being fatherless. Pearl also makes a different relation with passion necessary. On the scaffold Hester held onto Pearl as the only immediate relation to the cause for her passion. In embracing the screaming, convulsive infant, she reaffirmed her passion. But when Pearl grew into a girl of passionate impulsiveness, Hester had to reconsider her earlier reaction. "In giving her existence, a great law had been broken, and the result was a being . . . all in disorder

. . . Throughout all, however, there was a trait of passion . . . Her nature appeared to possess depth . . . but . . . it lacked reference and adaptation to the world into which it was born" (67).

When in relation to Arthur alone, Hester could deny the public's need for the name of the father. But when confronted with a child who needed the name of a father to give it appropriate reference in a world, Hester had to consider her passion culpable rather than laudable. Without a father's surname to confer upon Pearl, Hester had to acknowledge Pearl's origins in terms of her now unwanted passion. "Hester could only account for the child's character . . . by recalling what she herself had been, during that momentous period while Pearl was imbibing her soul from the spiritual world, and her bodily frame from its material earth. The mother's impassioned state had been the medium through which were transmitted to the unborn infant the rays of its moral life" (67). In her unfathered state, Pearl separates Hester's passion from its reference to Arthur. Without Arthur to claim her passion, Hester considers the implications for Pearl's existence of a life founded on nothing more stable than the impulses of passion.

When she considers Pearl in terms of a passion unprotected by the cultural institution of paternity, Hester cannot remain proud of her refusal to give the child a father. Hester fears that she has lost relation with herself in losing relationship with the cultural institution of paternity. When she prays, "O Father in Heaven—if Thou art still my Father—what is this being which I have brought into the world" (71), the separation between the father she addresses and the unfathered being she alone is responsible for bringing into the world reminds Hester of her need for some principle of paternity.

Hester does not stand alone in her need to father Pearl. The rest of the community shares this need. Pearl exists as an impulse humanized by a physical form but estranged from any social institution capable of assuming responsibility for that form's perpetuation. As an illegitimate child, she disrupts the culture's customary ways of naturalizing its institutions. As a force who appeared "naturally," that is, without the intervention of a cultural convention, Pearl's very existence threatens every other cultural convention as well.

Members of a culture customarily convince themselves of the "givenness," the social necessity of their institutions by explaining them to their children. Through these explanations, the institutions lose their merely conventional status and become "how things are." A culture's conventions come to seem "natural" and are able to recede into the background. But since Pearl remains a force unassimilable to the conventions everyone else assumes to be "natural," she cannot be persuaded of the truth of these explanations. Instead of accepting conventions as the facts of life, she asks questions bound to unsettle the institutions from their background status, and expose their contingent rather than given status.

When confronted by this threat from Pearl, the Puritan community brings Hester once again before a tribunal of the law, where they attempt to give the child an adoptive cultural father. To recover some of the cultural authority Pearl threatens, the magistrates of old Boston summon Hester and Pearl to the Governor's mansion, where Hester is asked to give cause why the child should not be handed over to the state. In response, Hester makes Arthur claim public responsibility for the child he fathered in private. Moreover, she gives Arthur public notice of her decision to be mother of her child rather than his lover. Her appeal to the young minister, which comes only after all of her other legal representations have failed, mixes veiled threats to expose Arthur with demands for his sympathy. This time, however, it is the mother in the lover who commands all of Arthur's sympathies. And that mother commands him to assume the responsibility of a father:

> "Speak thou for me . . . Thou wast my pastor, and hadst charge of my soul, and knowest me better than these men can. I will not lose the child! Speak for me! thou knowest,—for thou hast sympathies which these men lack!—thou knowest what is in my heart, and what are a mother's rights, and how much the stronger they are, when that mother has but her child and the scarlet letter! Look thou to it! I will not lose the child! Look to it!" (83)

Arthur of course gives the child the representation it needs to satisfy the law. As a gift from the hand of God, Dimmesdale reflects, the child exists under the tutelage of a higher Father who sent it to convert Hester's passion into unselfish care. In this response, however, Arthur does not answer either the law's or Hester's implicit threat of public exposure. When he articulates that complex mixture of joy and grief Hester experiences in her life with Pearl, Arthur expresses his sympathy not for the lover but for the mother in Hester. His words comfort her through his genuine sympathy and his newfound understanding of her plight. Through his sermon on Pearl, Arthur separates the passion he formerly felt for Hester from the paternal responsibility he presently feels. As a result of his words, Dimmesdale discovers the meaning of care—his care for the child and mother. His words convert his private intimacy with Hester into secret familial affection: "This child of its father's guilt and its mother's shame hath come from the hand of God . . . And may she feel . . . that this boon was meant, above all things else, to keep the mother's soul alive . . . Therefore it is good for this poor, sinful woman that she hath an infant immortality, a being capable of eternal joy or sorrow, confided to her care" (84).

In speaking for Hester before the law, Arthur also manages to speak to Hester through the law. In appealing to her impulse to elevate the passionate impulses at work in the child into a form of eternal joy, he simultaneously expresses his continued care for what he calls the "eternal" as opposed to momentary nature of their relationship.

The Human Family

Crucial to any understanding of Hester are her effects upon the family. In giving birth to Pearl outside of the protection of the family, Hester refused to socialize passion into home feelings. As if in response to Hester's refusal, Pearl addresses Hester with a sense of all the social consequences accompanying the force of a passion unprotected by the social form of the family.

When Pearl was still an infant, Hester could treat her own cultural exclusion as a sign of independence. But when she saw how illegitimacy "unreferenced" Pearl, Hester reevaluated her own relation to the rest of the community. With Arthur she felt proud in her passion; through Pearl she experienced guilt—not for her passion with Arthur but for the suffering of a child whose communal welfare was betrayed by that passion. Only guilt in relation to Pearl could connect Pearl with a stable past.

Hester's guilt changed her relation to the passion itself. Instead of wishing for a renewal of the passion, Hester asks for "endless retribution" (60). An acknowledgment of mutual guilt shared with the rest of the community, Hester's repentance for her guilt recovers relations to the world her private passion had broken.

Earlier we pointed up the ways in which Hester's exclusion from the community turned her into a principle of communal intimacy. Her repentance has an even more startling effect. In repenting for the fatherless Pearl,

Hester became the representative familial principle for the entire community. And her display of maternal care for whoever needed it had the effect Hester desired: "every good Christian man hath a title to show a father's kindness towards the poor, deserted babe" (85). In being maternal for others in need of help, without asking for "the humblest title to share in the world's privileges" (116), Hester exercised familial duties but without claiming any familial rights or privileges. She becomes the community's way of extending the bonds of mutual sympathy beyond the sphere of the immediate family. Having been deprived of traditional family ties, Hester "was quick to acknowledge her sisterhood with the race of man" (116).

In giving her sympathy to all, Hester ceased to be a private person the family needed to exclude in order to maintain its power. Her "power to sympathize" (117) expanded the terms of familial inclusion to the point where the community acted like a universal human family in regard to her. "In private life" individuals "had quite forgiven Hester," not for sin of adultery but "for her frailty" (118). Instead of pointing her out to strangers for her transgression of the community's boundaries, the townspeople claimed the maternal Hester as a source of communal charity. "It is our Hester—the town's own Hester—who is so kind to the poor, so helpful to the sick, so comfortable to the afflicted" (118). She turns into the figure through whom the community knows its heart to be communal as opposed to personal.

Narration as Repentance

In repenting for Pearl's "unreferenced" life, Hester introduces a new relation into the Puritan community. Before, as we have seen, she used the people as a transparent medium through whom she could address her lover. Her repentance transforms the public into a figure she can directly address. When Hester spoke to Arthur through the community, she acknowledged the group only long enough to speak through it. But through Pearl Hester discovered, on quite personal terms, the consequences for human identity of a life grounded in passion alone. So Hester gives up her attachment to the passion she experienced as a lover and initiates Pearl into a wider human family. In sacrificing her private person for this "universal human family," Hester also disrupts the family's usual prerogatives. In sacrificing the lover in herself to the mother who lives for the community,

Hester does not move from one private sphere, the relation between lovers, to another private sphere, the bonds of affection within a family. By assuming responsibility for the motherly care of all in need, Hester surrenders her right to a private family for the good of the entire public.

Put differently, Hester's penitence changes the terms through which a community makes certain relations eventful. Her penitence, in refusing to call attention to her person at all, widens the sphere of her personal relations. Hester's gift of her deeds to the community creates quite an unusual social situation. Judgment and the rules of law underwriting it presuppose that the punishment should fit the crime. Giving more to the community than the terms of her repentance demanded, Hester turned self-sacrifice into a gift rather than a legal compensation. And in receiving the disinterested gift of her deeds, the Puritans returned a disinterested impulse of generosity—the response of a benevolent despot rather than a righteous magistrate. "Interpreting Hester Prynne's deportment as an appeal [to its generosity], society was inclined to show its former victim a more benign countenance than she cared to be favored with, or perchance, than she deserved" (117).

This change can be stated more clearly in nonjudicial terms. In providing the Puritans with "another view" of her character, Hester Prynne changed the tale the community told about her.

In *The Scarlet Letter,* none of the characters are independent of the positions they occupy in the communal narratives. When we conceive of Hester only as a private self in opposition to the community, we lose the sense of the part the community, in its retelling of her tale, plays in her personal life. Thus far we have discussed Hester's power to constitute what we might call the private life of the people. But the relationship between the community and Hester is much more reciprocal than this description might suggest: Hester is no less constituted by the community's narratives about her.

As the community's means of actively reflecting upon its members, tales carry forward both persons and the relations capable of preserving them. Throughout his "re-telling" of her tale, Hawthorne brings his account into relation with other accounts of Hester's life. After her successful visit to Governor Bellingham's mansion, for example, Hester occupies two narrative places at once, as Hawthorne qualifies his account with other testimony. "It is averred," in this version of Hester's life, that upon departing from the mansion Hester successfully withstands the witch Mistress

Hibbins' temptation to promise herself to Satan in the forest. This other version of Hester's life reclaims a context from the Past: the Puritan belief in witches. "Had they taken her from me," Hester proclaims in this alternative narrative, "I would willingly have gone with thee into the forest, and signed my name in the Black Man's book too, and that with mine own blood" (86).

Hawthorne's tale does not deny this account its place within the Puritans' narrative community. But he relegates it to the status of a background legend, an alternative narrative Dimmesdale's account makes unnecessary. The witch narrative could lay claim on Hester, in Hawthorne's telling, only if the other narratives lost her to it. To insist on his story's power to possess her more securely than could the witch account, Hawthorne writes, "But here—if we suppose this interview between Mistress Hibbins and Hester Prynne to be authentic, and not a parable—was already an illustration of the young minister's argument against sundering the relation of a fallen mother to the offspring of her frailty. Even thus early had the child saved her from Satan's snare" (86).

In reinstating Hester within Dimmesdale's moral argument for her right to the child's custody, Hawthorne reclaims his place "as a citizen of somewhere else." But he also reclaims her from the custody of his ancestors, who would have been the more ready to include her in the witch narrative.

In telling Hester's tale, he is no less told by the community constituted by the tale telling. His choice of tale consigns him to his own position within the Puritan community. Like the others who attend to Dimmesdale's words, Hawthorne comes to understand Hester through his meditation upon Dimmesdale's representations. In acknowledging Dimmesdale's account, Hawthorne does not dismiss these other narratives. His struggles to bring his narrator's account into lively relation with these others mark his efforts to discover his place within the community. Through his impersonation of the need to believe in the communal covenants, Hawthorne discovers his place in a community no one has preserved in a living narrative.

In negotiating Hester's and Arthur's places within his narrative, then, Hawthorne does not merely adjudicate among conflicting accounts. He includes conflicting versions to articulate his own doubts about the Puritans' compacts. He does not, however, overemphasize his doubts.[7] His narrated doubts do not dismiss but invite other accounts as opportunities to enter into reflective relations with other segments of the Puritan community.

None of the characters or events in these tales exist for their own sake;

they all turn into the communal relations necessary to come to terms with them. Through his narration, Hawthorne discovers the position he may have occupied in the Puritan community, thereby gaining the ability to hear what he would have sounded like were he alive then. More often than not, the present-day man of words discovers his present self impersonated by a man of the Word. In the many moral asides throughout the tale, Hawthorne does not assert a definitive moral to be derived from a situation, nor does he establish an implicit ironic context designed to expose the inadequacy of any moral.[8] But he does discover through a genial moral attitude an appropriate way to be recalled by those past events.

In writing about the past, Hawthorne never wished to reassert the superiority of the "enlightened view" of his present age. Nor did he wish merely to be reassimilated to the Puritan past on its own terms.[9] Both of these alternatives would only have corroborated the state of displacement he experienced in the Custom House. But Hawthorne did wish for relations with others capable of providing an enduring sense of existence. In telling a tale in which the narrator must be held accountable for his terms, Hawthorne rediscovers in his narrating voice that state of mutual interindebtedness at the heart of any vital community.

Like Hester, the narrator repents for his unpardonable sin of independence from the community.[10] In exchanging the alienation inherent in any single account of the action for a recounting or twice-telling of his tale in relation to other, equally acknowledgeable accounts, Hawthorne's narrator embodies the narrative equivalent of Hester's penitence. Hawthorne calls explicit attention to the relation between narrating and coming to penitential terms with exclusion when he writes, "The reader may choose among these theories. We have thrown all the light we could acquire upon the portent, and would gladly, now that it has done its office, erase its deep print out of our own brain!" (182).[11] Here Hawthorne discloses the scarlet letter imprinted within his brain, not as what ensures him a distanced, objective view but as what enables him to engage with the rest of the community in heartfelt consideration of the issue of Arthur's guilt.

Privacy as a Temptation

As Hawthorne tells it, Hester Prynne feels most in need of a private life after she has, in the public view, atoned for her adultery. When "enough" members of the Puritan community stopped interpreting the scarlet letter by its original signification, they implicitly released Hester from her public duty, the repentance demanded by the scarlet letter. However, Hester had no private life to which she could return. As we have seen, she generated, through her repentance, bonds of affection for the public sufficient to transform it into her private world. Through its relationship to Hester, the community socialized privacy into a form of communal bonding. Changing its single-minded judgment of the adulterer into generosity toward a "sister of mercy," the community discovered a surplus of new relations for her. Hester became the community's means of discovering what we might call its private reservations about its public judgment.

In the exchange of tales about Hester, the community discovered how its persons incarnate a communal unconscious. Persons within communities are themselves as well as the judgments, affections, aspirations, condemnations, reservations, anticipations the community has invested in them. The tales, gossip, legends accompanying persons in their transit through society keep these communal affections in circulation. Tales turn these affectional investments into the community's storehouse of bonding powers.

In the conflicting tales she provokes, Hester deepens the collective memory of old Boston into the communal equivalent of contemplative care. Hester in her turn finds sufficient justice and intimacy in the public world to make a return to private life redundant.

Usually privacy recovers, through the intimacies exchanged in the familial circle, a liberation from the control over the emotions at work in a public world.[12] Privacy protects people from taxing social obligations. In our own time, the discipline of psychoanalysis provides the private individual with a silent support system. Through analysis, an individual can reexperience an in-depth "primary process" world as private compensation for the frustrations, repressions, and compelling demands of public life. The primary process promises a more rewarding life world within the self rather than out in the world.[13] But Hawthorne discovers in the everyday objects of his public world an "other" life invested with communal reflections. In writing about these objects, he comes in touch with a transpersonal memory capable of releasing these "reserved" reflections. This transpersonal memory has more psychic power than any personal unconscious. When remembering in cultural as opposed to personal terms, an individual can discover a "secret life" inhabiting the familiar objects of his world and reestablish his allegorical relations to them.

For any theorist who identifies freedom with the "right to privacy," an allegory exists as a communal judgment from which an individual should assert independence. Consequently, when modern commentators consider the allegorical component in Hawthorne's work, they celebrate the multiple meanings attending every scene as a defeat of allegory by the free individual. In providing more meanings than any one interpretation can command, these commentators argue, Hawthorne recovers a freedom from the social constraints an allegorical meaning demands.[14] But in Hawthorne's work, the multiple allegorical meanings associated with any single individual are assigned by other individuals in the community. Hawthorne's allegories turn persons toward one another's understanding. Living an allegory of oneself acknowledges the duty to exist for others as well as among them.

Members of a community do not demand that each member remain one allegorical signification. Through the exchange and transformation of allegories, individuals produce new possibilities and add them to the communal store. The change in significations demanded through conflicting understandings of one another's allegories deepens the relations among members of a community.

In a culture like Hawthorne's with a past, allegories confer a depth of potential significance, capable of instilling a sense of antiquity, a quality of "time immemorial," in the social bond. Through one another's allegories we discover the ways in which we ourselves perpetuate a cultural lineage. The renewed relations with one another demanded by the living allegories of ourselves generate a surplus for cultural existence, eventuating along with our persons but much older (in the sense that it can never be made utterly present in the present) than any person can ever be.

To distinguish an individual allegory from communal allegories, Hawthorne separates Hester's existence within the community from Roger Chillingworth's. Roger is the only member of the Puritan community who has not changed his relation to the scarlet letter. Revenge puts all the human "sympathy" at his command into the private service of discovering Hester's lover. After he sneaks his way into Arthur's heart, Roger enjoys a vision of Arthur to which no one else in the community is privy.

In a sense Roger replicates Arthur's sin of adultery, for in taking possession of Arthur's most intimate self-revelation, he denies it to those other parishioners to whom Arthur feels wedded. But Roger's "private" relation exceeds the bounds of vengeance. Roger turns his own inability ever to be on intimate terms with Hester into a terrible form of intimacy as he privately enjoys the guilt and remorse through which Arthur maintains his tie with Hester.

In the interview with Roger in prison, Hester turned their marriage vows into a bond of secrecy: she would remain in relation to Roger only by not acknowledging their relationship. This vow of secrecy had a pleasing ironic result. It turned their relationship into a mutually agreed upon contract, rather than the intolerable truth of their lack of intimacy.

Secrecy made Roger's privacy inviolable. Independent of any obligation to the public world, unresponsive to any private relation other than those exacted on his terms, Roger Chillingworth turned himself into an allegory whose only signification was privacy. Unlike the rest of the community, Roger Chillingworth used allegory to confirm his independence of anyone else's understanding. Listen as Chillingworth takes personal possession of all the meaning his allegory can have: "By thy first step away, thou didst plant the germ of evil; but since that moment it has all been a dark necessity. Ye that have wronged me are not sinful save in a kind of typical illusion; neither am I fiend-like, who have snatched a fiend's office from his hands. It is our fate" (126). Chillingworth here asks Hester to read his character as an allegory of nothing but his private will made absolute as fate.

The Return of Privacy

After Roger lays absolute claim on Arthur's private person, however, Hester breaks the vow of secrecy. To recover her own privacy—she renews her relations with Arthur Dimmesdale. Given the public's role as a go-between in that relation, Hester must first discredit the public's claim to their relationship.

We already saw how the guilt he shares with Hester enables Arthur to speak to his congregation with all the eloquent pathos released by common suffering. Their guilt instills him with a bond of communal intimacy intense enough to make him seem the personal lover of every member of his congregation. Guilt "gave him sympathies so intimate with the sinful brotherhood of mankind; so that his heart vibrated in unison with theirs, and received their pain into itself, and sent its own throb of pain through a thousand other hearts, in gushes of sad, persuasive eloquence" (103).

Consequently, to recover an exclusive relationship with Arthur, Hester must separate him from his congregation. But here Hester encounters a great difficulty. Her relation to Arthur is founded on the same guilt Dimmesdale shares with the rest of his congregation. Before she can recover *her* Arthur, she must displace one lovers' triangle (the public one composed of Hester, Arthur, and the community) with another one (the private triangle comprising Roger, Arthur, and Hester). She must turn his guilt before his congregation into the guilt owed to Roger alone. And since Arthur turned communal repentance into pathos—the principle of rhetorical persuasion with which he addresses his congregation—Hester can fulfill her purpose only by interrupting him at the moment he would speak most persuasively.

Throughout this romance, every reader has privately hoped Arthur and Hester would come back together. Hawthorne indulges this wish by concentrating on what keeps them apart: the needs of a congregation and the revenge of Roger Chillingworth. Arthur unknowingly brings these two factions together when in their second forest tryst he addresses Hester not as her lover but as her pastor: "Had I one friend—or were it my worst enemy!—to whom, when sickened with the praises of all other men, I could daily betake myself, and be known as the vilest of sinners, methinks my soul would keep itself alive thereby" (138). But when Hester replies, "Thou hast long had such an enemy, and dwellest with him under the same roof" (138), she changes the terms of Dimmesdale's address. By invoking an abstract allegorical enemy, Dimmesdale treated Hester as a parishioner. Hester's response turns the abstract allegorical figure in her pastor's speech into an actual person, the husband he betrayed.

As Hester's husband, Roger Chillingworth turns Arthur into Hester's lover. Without his public persona as her minister, Arthur can acknowledge only his personal relationship with her. Throughout this scene Arthur discovers his identity as Hester's lover, but at the expense of the pathos he felt as her minister. He reacts to her revelation that Roger is her husband first by personally refusing Hester the forgiveness he demanded his congregation show her in the opening scene. Then he grants her forgiveness, but only after asserting his personal difference from Roger Chillingworth, whose "revenge has been blacker than my sin" (140).

In this scene Hester regains a lover; but Dimmesdale experiences her gain as a loss of his character. Without his guilt before his congregation to protect him from Hester's private demand, the pastor becomes her parishioner. Hester's ministry is personal love. When instructing him of their mutual indebtedness to love, Hester begins with a lesson Arthur can learn readily, for he taught it to her: "Let God punish! Thou shalt forgive!" (140).

Theirs, as Hawthorne reminds us, had been a "sin of passion, not of principle, nor even purpose" (143). Without the principle of guilt, into which Dimmesdale had earlier converted his passion, Dimmesdale feels abandoned by all but Hester. She responds by redirecting his despair toward hope for "a new life" (144).

This wish for a new life, as we have seen, is part of everything that Hawthorne found wrong with America. He associated the wish for the new with the loss of care-full relationships. When Hester removes the scarlet letter from her breast, she separates herself from the communal ties of collective intimacy, mutual respect, and care she and Arthur together effected for the Puritan community. In so doing, Hester does not affirm her hope but only renews what Hawthorne believes to be her relation to despair.

When Pearl sees her mother without the letter, she reacts with despair. In Pearl's mind they have recovered their passion at her expense. In a remarkable moment, Hawthorne describes Pearl's estrangement from her parents in terms of a "boundary between two worlds" (149). In refusing to cross the brook and join her parents, Pearl makes the connection between a new life and the loss of relation clear. As a new life their passion made visible, Pearl beckons to them with all the force of their presently denied responsibility to the past. Pearl asks that her parents become old enough to assume the responsibility necessary to remember her back into their lives.

Whereas their earlier passion brought Pearl across the absolute boundary separating the unborn from human forms, Hester's resumption of the scarlet letter, her acknowledgment of the mutual indebtedness human relations entail, draws Pearl across the boundary between worlds—a second time. She restores human care as an unpayable debt human relations always renew.

The Revelation of the Scarlet Letter

But Pearl was not the only figure excluded by the wish for a new life. What Pearl was to Hester, the entire Puritan community was to Arthur. Whereas Hester demanded that he surrender public responsibility for his other parishioners in exchange for his personal passion for her, Arthur, on his way back to the rectory, changes the terms of that exchange.

His change of terms mirrors the difference between his understanding of their new relation and Hester's. Whereas Hester's love transcended her wish for any other relationship, Arthur loved the rest of his congregation as much as he loved Hester. In becoming intimate with Hester, he violated the privacy of one of his congregation. His sermons converted this personal violation into a synecdoche for a communal violation, making him indebted to the rest of his congregation as well.

In the forest Hester claimed a debt he owed her alone. But on his way back home Dimmesdale made good the claims of all the rest of his parishioners. Finding himself tempted to violate the privacy of every one of his congregation he encounters, he is surprised by the universality of his private love. In discovering his universal love, he does not merely reactivate the lust he felt for Hester (though he is tempted by a young woman whose purity depends upon reverencing his sanctity). Lust would only have sealed his captivation by Hester alone. The other temptations—to blaspheme the Eucharist so revered by an old deacon, to deny the immortality of the soul to an old woman, to teach children to curse—all of these inclinations point in another direction.

We could, as do many commentators, attribute these temptations to the liberation of Arthur's passions from repression. We could, that is, were it not for Hawthorne's thoughtful qualification: "At every step, he was incited to do some strange, wild, wicked thing or other, with a sense that it would be at once involuntary and intentional, in spite of himself, yet growing out of a profounder self than that which opposed the impulse" (155).[15] In characterizing Arthur's impulse to violate the private lives of all of his parishioners as coming from a profounder self, Hawthorne dissociates it from passion, which he associates with the superficial self. Arthur's "profounder self" demands that his passion direct itself indiscriminately to all of his parishioners, rather than to Hester alone. Only after being tempted to violate the privacy of all of his parishioners can Arthur recover his communal relations, but at the expense of his new life with Hester.

After having been tempted to an exclusive intimacy with all of his parishioners, Arthur recovers the right to speak for all of them. On his way back from an exclusively private relation he communalizes his guilt, then turns this communal guilt into many scarlet letters, the fiery script with which he writes his election sermon.

In the election sermon he delivers the next day, Dimmesdale turns his private wish for a new life into the hope to redeem the past. This sermon fills all of his congregation with a sense of the passion he feels for them. After delivering it, Dimmesdale heads for the scaffold Hester alone occupied at the beginning of the tale. And here he discharges himself of his private debt to her.

In revealing the scarlet letter on his breast, Arthur reveals to the community its own principle of communal relations. Unlike other members of the community, Hester listened to his election sermon for signs of its pathos. As an emotional separation from the right-mindedness of his sermon, pathos, she believed, indicated the love he shared with her alone. But on this last day, Arthur did not speak through the people to her, nor did he speak through her to the people; he spoke with the same intimacy to all.

His death after the revelation of the scarlet letter on his breast secures an unforgettable quality to the scene. In effect this final scene commemorates the first scene, and the entire tale structures itself around this commemoration. The romance began with a scaffold scene in which Hester was to burn an impression into the memory of the community. But the minister's words qualified this impression, accompanying the judgment with sympathy for Hester. The second scaffold scene, in which Arthur revealed himself in the night, disclosed what the community knew unconsciously in the first scene. In the first scene Arthur spoke for Hester; at night he disclosed why he had spoken for Hester. The pathos in his words revealed to the community why he had spoken with such sympathy. And in changing their judgment of Hester into mercy, the community had already implicitly exonerated their minister as well, by acting upon the unconscious or secret demand in his sermon.[16] The final scaffold scene removes any merely private basis for this sympathy. In revealing the scarlet letter to the community rather than Hester alone, their minister discloses the letter as what founds the community's relations.

In dying, Arthur demands that a memory of this sign accompany each transaction within the community. So translated, the scarlet letter will be not a memory of his private self, but a memory of the communal relation he spent himself to secure. But when renewed as a communal relation, Dimmesdale does not return alone. In the forest scene Hester tried to cure Arthur of his despair by hoping for a new life. In his election sermon Arthur generalized this private hope into a hope for all of New England. In generalizing her private hope into the universal hope for a New World to be reactivated by the generations following in the lineage of the scarlet letter, Dimmesdale asked that every new citizen bring Hester back into renewed relation with him. Hawthorne met the demand when he wrote *The Scarlet Letter* over two centuries later. As a consequence he discovered what it could mean to be a citizen of somewhere else, a new world that still demands to be realized.

Chapter Four

Walt Whitman and the Vox Populi of the American Masses

There shall . . . be a new friendship . . .
It shall circulate through the states, indifferent of places,
It shall twist and intertwist them through and through each other—
   Compact shall they be, showing new signs,
Affection shall solve every one of the problems of freedom . . .
                                                            —*Walt Whitman*

Walt Whitman has been called the great poet of the democratic masses, with good reason.[1] He believed the masses to be the foundation and proof of the political experiment called American democracy. And his belief in the masses differs so dramatically from Hawthorne's constitutional distrust of them that a contrast between their views seems necessary.

Hawthorne had historical as well as personal reasons for distrusting the masses. A mass action resulted in his firing from the Custom House; the masses did not read his romances; and, in his view, the masses believed in their passions much more than in democratic principles.[2] After being fired from his Custom House post, Hawthorne suppressed his personal resentment against the American masses with a simple wish to become a citizen of "somewhere else." This wish contained an implicit political program. In his new locale he hoped to find the qualities of endurance and affection missing from the relationships struck up by the common men of post-Jacksonian America. Unlike these mass men, Hawthorne looked for this new locale not in America's West but in her past, one in need of renewal rather than worship or disregard. This search returned him to the Puritan era, for that was the period when the conflicting demands of the individual and the community received the most careful scrutiny.[3]

The Puritans acknowledged the sanctity of each individual's relation to God as well as the cultural errand of the community as a whole. Part of that cultural errand was the duty to be as concerned for the salvation of one's neighbor as for the salvation of oneself. In coming to personal terms with

God, each Puritan simultaneously "confessed" those terms to the other members of the community. Such revelations prevented individual members of the community from preferring their personal sanctity over the community's. Through Arthur Dimmesdale, Hawthorne contemplated the result of such public revelations. Once made public, Dimmesdale's personal struggle for repentance before God became a resource for deepened relationships among the rest of the community.[4]

Michael Zuckerman has described this reciprocal relationship between the individual and the Puritan community.

> Once admitted to a congregation of visible saints, he [the individual] had in his turn to hear the confession of other candidates. He had to know himself precisely in order to obtain a "standard of sanctity" by which to judge the experience of others and carry on relations with his spiritual kinsmen. He had to display a daily "zeal for the morality of others" in order to uphold the social covenant on which he predicated the temporal prosperity of the community and in order to be confident of the covenant of grace on which his own eternal destiny depended.[5]

The Puritans provided Hawthorne with a version of the ideals of Hawthorne's own contemporaries. Like the urban masses, the Puritans migrated to a new world, but their separation from Old World customs did not result in a magnification of the individual's rights over the group's. Each Puritan had a moral duty to establish relations in the New World capable of justifying the break from the Old World's ways. The moral perfection of the individual depended upon his capacity to offer his inner life as a resource to the rest of the community. Consequently, the Puritan individual did not define personal freedom as a release from relations with others. Each Puritan rose to freedom through and with his community.[6] Unlike the squatters in the West, the Puritans believed in the equal but interdependent powers of the individual and the group.

In his recollection of the Puritan past, Hawthorne reaffirmed his faith in communal values. But he also justified his condemnation of mob rule. When he attributes a "deep heart" to the people, he explicitly distinguishes a people with heart from a heartless mob. In *The Scarlet Letter,* the mob becomes a people only after they surrender their impetuous impulses and initiate sustained reconsideration of Hester's sin.[7]

Unlike Hawthorne, Walt Whitman celebrated the masses in and for themselves, a composite formation he called the "man-en-masse." Instead of demanding that an individual give up his impulsive life for the reflective

life of a community, Whitman believed the impulsive life should be inten-
sified. Whitman located a private reserve of other selves in the heterogeneous impulses within each separate individual. For Whitman, this potentially multiple individuality provided the basis for the equality, liberty, and
happiness essential to the American democracy.

Troubled over the social inadequacy of merely personal impulses, Hawthorne demanded they be exchanged for the shared affections of a greater
community. But Whitman celebrated the multiple demands urged by inner
impulses as the "en-masse" or collective aspect of what he called the individual's "body electric."[8] This "body electric" was for Whitman the democratic equivalent of what Renaissance theorists referred to as the king's second body. The second body of the king, by incorporating the virtues of
permanence, immutability, and transferability, provided the physical rationale for the institution of kingship. Whitman's "body electric," the in-
cipient crowd formation at work in everybody, constituted a physical basis
for the spontaneous and momentary associations of urban life. In the doctrine of the "body electric," Whitman develops a correspondence between
an individual's inner impulses and the democratic masses. Like the multiple
impulses surging up in a person, urban crowds are transitory sources of
energy. For Whitman, crowds extinguish differences among persons: in the
electric suddenness of movement in and among crowds persons encounter
equality as an everyday experience. As the means of making visible the
democratic virtues of equality and fraternity, these masses constitute the
very life of a democratic people. As Whitman wrote in 1871, it was out of
his intercourse with these crowds that he discovered his vocation:

> When I pass to and fro, different latitudes, different seasons, beholding
> the crowds of the great cities, New York, Boston, Philadelphia, Cincin-
> nati, Chicago, St. Louis, San Francisco, New Orleans, Baltimore—
> when I mix with these interminable swarms of alert, turbulent, good-
> natured, independent citizens, merchants, clerks, young persons—at the
> idea of this mass of men, so fresh and free, so loving and so proud, a
> singular awe falls upon me. I feel, with dejection and amazement, that
> among our geniuses and talented writers or speakers, few or none have
> yet really spoken to this people, created a single, image-making work for
> them, or absorbed the central spirit and the idiosyncracies which are
> theirs—and which, thus, in highest far remain entirely uncelebrated,
> unexpress'd.[9]

Whitman did not value communal life at the expense of men-en-masse.
He believed sectarian groups, however well-intentioned, only gave seces-

sionist politics an ideal rationale. At the time Whitman began writing *Leaves of Grass,* the political descendants of such sectarian groups threatened the very fabric of the nation. What Whitman wanted instead was a "fusing relation" capable of transcending sectarian impulses rather than sublimating them. Hawthorne's romances, like his politics, were built upon a patriotism that did not extend beyond the region of New England's founding fathers. Hawthorne's American "somewhere else" would have excluded not only the urban masses but the western territories they were destined to populate.[10] Whitman grounded his inclusive democratic nation in a sense of "adhesiveness" prior to dissent, or even argument. Each citizen of Whitman's inclusive democracy could presuppose that "what I assume you shall assume." The figures within *The Scarlet Letter* came together by using dissent the way Dimmesdale did: to reestablish the basis of the community. But as is clear in their attitudes toward Quakers, Indians, and strangers, the old Boston Puritans of *The Scarlet Letter* did not abandon their sectarian predisposition. Like Hawthorne, the Puritans would have been as "tolerant" of secession as they were proud of old Boston.

Unlike Hawthorne, Whitman could not tolerate the notion of the South as a separate nation.[11] A Democrat bred on the faith in the common people brought to fruition by Andrew Jackson, whom he deeply admired, Whitman conceived it his duty as a national poet to reconcile two principles constitutive of an American democracy—the people and the Union.[12] Before we can understand how Whitman healed the rift between these two great Democratic principles, we must understand the forces drawing them apart. The election of 1800 made clear the division between the federal government and the populace, but the split between the Union and the people first became apparent during Jackson's rise to prominence.[13] Harnessing his political policy to two impulses common to the urban masses—the urge to be free from the constraints of the past and the wish for land—Jackson turned the common people into a political faction.[14] Jackson capitalized on the resentment of all those who experienced the crowded conditions of urban life. He called attention to the differences between the rich and the poor, established families and immigrants, eastern states and western territories, business entrepreneurs and laborers. Under other presidents, and in other circumstances, such resentment could have resulted in urban riots and mob rule, but Jackson turned the face of social resentment to the West, and its definitive result was a run for the western territory.[15]

Thus Jackson divided the nation into an old America, comprising New

England and established eastern families, and a new one. These citizens of somewhere else in the West were held together not by Puritan covenants but by associations lasting no longer than the threats from Indians, conditions, or the outlaws among them.[16] Unlike the Puritan exodus commonly invoked as a precedent, the western movement depended upon breaks with social bonds of all kinds—no matter whether with past generations, prior policy, one's neighbors, or one's own person. Conflicts of interests were bound to arise among a people who cherished no common belief other than their independence from all restraints.[17] And as the party founded on the absence of distinctions among the people, the Jacksonian Democrats lacked any means of resolving these conflicts.[18] And the fundamental conflict was with the authority of the national compact.

By enhancing the power of undifferentiated masses, Jackson's policies diminished the value of two of the nation's fundamental principles, union and liberty. Empowered to be free through the accumulated will of the masses, no democratic individual could claim freedom as a personal right.[19] When treated as the appropriate arbiter for deciding whether western territories should become slave states, "freedom" itself turned into an issue for a majority vote.

The Jacksonian Democrat equated freedom with the impulse to break free of any social form whatsoever, and reduced union to the brief association necessary to form the majority opinion at a polling station. Hawthorne's disgust for the mob rule presiding over Election Day led him to write about the Puritans' day of election. Unlike the majority, the Puritans did not discharge their communal responsibility with a vote. They used the day of election to reevaluate the terms through which they could justify feeling chosen by God for some earthly errand.[20] But Walt Whitman remained devoted to the masses out of which he arose. And he believed in the gatherings through which the democratic masses celebrated their inner life.

National Holidays and Majority Opinion

Today a certain cynicism surrounds the ritual expressions of America's civil religion. Our holidays are occasions for speeches without ceremonial significance, and we seem unwilling to take national celebrations seriously as expressions of our common life. But for Whitman such celebrations were occasions through which the democratic masses could take psychological possession of the republic. Through these ritual celebrations men and women recognized the commitments, beliefs, and motives they shared in common.

Often Whitman's poetry seems to take place against the backdrop of a national celebration. For Whitman a national celebration performed a cultural task. It dissolved the conflicts of interest the people voted up or down with the candidates on Election Day. On a national holiday, citizens put aside partisan debates to take part in a mass demonstration of belief in common ideals. In Whitman's view, these celebrations produced an internal life, a cultural unconscious for the masses more enduring than the opinions politicians mobilized into majority votes.[21] These national spectacles, ritually reenacted, constituted for urban crowds that "central spirit," that "image-making work" that Whitman's poetry aspired to be. On these occasions of national as opposed to partisan demonstration, the masses gather to participate in a collective relation fashioned not so much by consciously held purposes as by unconsciously held values, the living spirit of a revered past.[22] They display the continued power of the truths the founding fathers declared to be self-evident.

As self-evident values, these principles should be by definition beyond dispute.[23] Belonging to a realm more appropriate to presuppositions, they can remain unstated precisely because they form the context rather than the texts for any partisan dispute. Only in such celebrations as the one taking place annually on the Fourth of July need these invisible because self-evident truths become manifest at all. On these occasions they express themselves as the indisputable power to organize the masses into the American people.

In organizing the masses into the people, these holidays produce a shared "cultural unconscious."[24] Participants in these mass demonstrations lend their personal unconscious to the occasion. They literally permit the truths celebrated on these occasions to replace private psychic content, as having prior claim on the unconscious. At the time Whitman wrote, however, the principles that should have remained unconscious were themselves the subject of dispute. And their right to remain unconscious became the subject of a partisan debate destined to eventuate in the mass demonstration we commemorate as the Civil War.

For Whitman the seeds of war were sown in fields of political divisiveness. Post-Jacksonian politics enabled the Democratic masses to experience their dissociation from the cultural past as the manifest destiny of the nation.[25] The western territories enabled recent emigrés from eastern cities to reinterpret the estrangement they knew in their urban life as a peculiar kind of freedom, the "perfect freedom of strangers."[26] They did so, however, at obvious expense to the life of the nation. They expressed nationalist instincts only as a demand for territorial independence, and their demand to be "a nation of strangers,"[27] when associated with the Southern states' demand to secede, posed an obvious threat to the nation.

Urban Life and Jacksonian Politics

As a longtime resident of Brooklyn, Whitman knew firsthand the dilemmas posed by post-Jacksonian democracy. He was a frequent participant in debates over states' rights and western expansionism. As a Free Soil Democrat sympathetic to the interests of the workingmen and women of New York, Whitman found himself entangled in an even more troubling political contradiction. Professing belief in the freedom of their labor, Whitman, for a time, held slavery to be a just institution. After mulling over the pre-Marxist interpretation of the relation between capital and alienated labor proposed by John Calhoun and Orestes Brownson, Whitman was persuaded for a short time that abolitionism, in its opposition to Negro slavery *alone,* only justified the wage slavery of Northern laborers.[28] Opposed to slavery of all kinds, he could not oppose Negro slavery and condone wage slavery. Even after Whitman changed his mind about slavery, he believed the principle of liberty had been compromised by partisan politics.

On Election Day April 12, 1842, Whitman witnessed a further consequence of the exclusive definition of liberty he shared with the Free Soil party. In New York the resentment he "whipped up" in his *Aurora* editorials against Irish Catholics led to open combat, as a no-popery mob attacked St. Patrick's Cathedral and stoned the bishop's residence. The results of this demonstration of mob rule led Whitman to qualify his earlier position: "We go for the largest liberty—the widest extension of the immunities of the people, as well as the blessings of our government," he wrote in the next day's editorial.[29] In such editorials, Whitman considered the consequences for the nation when its founding principles become the exclusive property of factions. When used to justify demonstrations like the Election Day riots, liberty and union lost their status in the cultural unconscious and became electioneering slogans.

Whitman believed national dissension originated when the founding principles lost self-evidence. The dimensions of this loss became clearest in the changed relation between the individual and the democratic masses. Instead of sharing liberty as a common value, the democratic individual had to choose from among a variety of political contexts for liberty. Southern slaveowners, abolitionists, secessionists, proponents of expansionism all claimed liberty as their rationale. And each defined liberty in terms of an opposition. For the abolitionists the slaveowners posed the greatest threat to liberty, for the expansionists the Whigs impeded freedom, while for the secessionists it was the Union. Through a shuffling of terms, these otherwise unrelated opponents could be brought into alliances—with startling results. Southern politicians could borrow the rhetoric of righteous indignation from the abolitionists, and treat the loss of states' rights as a form of slavery more unjust than that of the Negro.[30] The individual would have to decide on which was worse—the enslavement of "sovereign" states or Negro slavery. Through its use as a common means of formulating political disagreements, liberty lost its value as an inalienable, self-evident truth.

The Common Man and the Common Self

Among other, unrelated motives, it was the need to restore "liberty" and the other founding principles to their former status that led Walt Whitman to give up on his careers as a journalist and ward politicians, and to renew his wish to create a "single, image-making work" for the democratic masses.[31] Journalists and politicians had helped forge the contexts that compromised these principles. Whitman aspired to develop a "language experiment" whereby these principles could recover their place within the inner life of all the people. After 1855, Whitman no longer wanted to persuade the nation of the truth of a partisan political program. After he decided to become the nation's poet, Whitman tried to recover for the American masses what Jean-Jacques Rousseau called the "common self."

A person develops a common self when he undergoes experiences and reveres things held in esteem by all the people. A common self is produced by social relations but it also sustains them. As James Miller explains in his study of Rousseau, the common self designates that part of our experience as individuals which moves each of us, in certain contexts, to say "we and to act in accordance with that identification . . . thinking and acting in terms of this common self raises to the level of an explicit joint purpose what, in any vital community, already exists as a disposition tacitly held in common."[32]

We develop this common self in shared experiences, like national celebrations, where "we" celebrate the power of our founding principles to continue motivating us. These celebrations make explicit what is otherwise "tacitly held in common"—the motives all of us share. Every participant can begin such celebrations with Whitman's famous opening lines to "Song of Myself." Everyone can say, "I celebrate myself and sing myself," and mean the same self because a national celebration enables everyone to know that "what I assume you shall assume."

But in the epoch of the common man, no American could make such assumptions. That part of our experience as individuals which moves each of us to say "We" had itself been sundered from us, and attached to divisive political issues.

Unlike the common self, the common man lacked any enduring joint purpose. Politicians like Andrew Jackson exploited their origins in the "life of the common man" to rationalize their self-interests. As a political fiction, the "common man" justified the inability of most Americans to participate in government. The "common man" was encouraged to believe himself an interchangeable part in a vast political machine. Since governing required no special expertise, party leaders argued, any one part could do the work of any other. The only work they needed to do together ended with the vote.[33]

Unlike the common man, the "common self" embodied motives for action equally available to the individual and the masses. As the locus for an internal life belonging to America en masse, the common self did not represent any individual's will. Within the common self were principles and purposes so deeply held that they lay beyond the control of political factions and self-interest. Possessing the force of unquestioned assumptions, the common self could articulate the general interest, what Whitman called the "central spirit" of *all* the democratic masses.

When speaking from the platform of the common self, an individual could speak with a voice of conviction, resulting from shared presuppositions anterior to the appearance of individuals or their factions. Whitman impersonates this voice throughout his poetry; it enables him to insist, in the preface to the 1855 edition of *Leaves of Grass,* that each individual must feel a "fusing relation" with the nation en masse. Throughout his career,

Whitman would derive his power as the nation's bard by presuming to speak as this voice of conviction.

Liberty and Compromise

Notions like the "common self" and the "voice of conviction" sound suspiciously like cultural superstitions, products of an alien ideology our more enlightened thinking has surpassed. Locating this voice of conviction within a "cultural unconscious," thus making it unavailable for open discussion of its merits, probably confirms these suspicions, for a notion unavailable for discussion we identify as ideological. When used in this way, "ideology" refers to a set of terms or practices that conceal presuppositions or mystify them in order to mask the contradiction between how we live and what we want to believe about how we live. While it remains masked, the contradiction remains in the unconscious.

When put into explicit ideological terms, the "common self" could be (and has been) said to mask the class distinction between factory owners and factory laborers. But at the time Whitman wrote, this class distinction—along with the conflicting claims of states and the Union, merchant capital and commodity capital, slaves and masters—was not masked but available for free and open debate.[34] Through notions like the "man-en-masse" or the "body electric," Whitman wanted not to conceal these distinctions but to rediscover a set of shared assumptions indicating what should be done about them.

When I used the term "cultural unconscious," I intended the opposite of an ideological meaning. Whitman wanted not a secret haven for the contradictions his culture suppressed but a locus for what everyone in the culture could agree was self-evident. To be self-evident is to need no justification, no proof, hence no discussion.[35] In the nineteenth-century debates over liberty and union, when Americans subjected these self-evident truths to discussion, they broke the terms of agreement upon which the culture was founded. They reentered the scene of the nation's founding and implicitly said, "We no longer hold these truths to be self-evident."

In choosing to describe liberty as a self-evident truth, the founding fathers identified it as a natural right protected by natural law.[36] By natural law, they meant a system of law binding on men by virtue of their nature, independent of any convention or positive law. We need nothing but "natural" reason in order to recognize this law, so its proponents would claim, and it is because we recognize it that it is binding.

In the national debate over slavery, politicians redefined liberty as a positive law, subject to the enactments of legislature. The Fugitive Slave Law distinguished the natural right of liberty from a state's right to self-rule. Liberty was toppled from the realm of nature, where it was protected by nature's law, and into the realm of political expediency, where it could not be the principle for deciding the debates on slavery. Politicians distinguished liberty as a natural right from liberty as a political convention by turning natural liberty into an ideal principle, quite separable from the realm of legal practices. Once set apart from the practical realm, natural liberty could be honored in principle while ignored in practice. In voting the Fugitive Slave Bill into law, for example, Daniel Webster would agree "in principle" that all men should be free. Having expressed his piety for this principle, however, Webster turned to union for a higher law to guide his actions. In turning to union for guidance Webster did not honor the principle of liberty. He honored the arena of political practices where politicians could renegotiate the nation's compact in whatever terms seemed practical.[37]

Throughout his years as an editor and ward politician, Whitman experienced firsthand the contradiction between national principles and political practices. Throughout these years he refused to compromise principle for expediency. His denunciation of slavery and opposition to the Fugitive Slave Law lost him the job as editor of the *Brooklyn Eagle*.[38] A speech he delivered at Tammany Hall made Whitman's priorities quite clear:

> I beseech you to entertain a noble and more elevated idea of our aim and struggle as a party than to suppose that we are striving to elevate this man or that man to power. We are battling for great principles—for mighty and glorious truths. I would scorn to exert even my humble efforts for the best Democratic candidate that ever was nominated in himself alone. It is our creed—our doctrine, not a man or set of men, that we seek to build up . . . The guardian spirit, the good genius who has attended us since the days of Jefferson, has not now forsaken us.[39]

Despite these expressions of loyalty to the party of Jefferson and Jackson, Whitman would soon abandon the party and take up his vocation as the nation's bard. As the issue of slavery became the subject of compromise,

Whitman discovered that he could not serve his party and follow his principles. But he also discovered that he could no longer address these principles as tutelary spirits or guardian angels. This rhetoric had already been adopted by the parties of compromise to secure liberty in an ideal realm, quite apart from the world of politics.

Whitman intended his poetry to perform an explicit political duty. In turning from politics to poetry, Whitman reversed the politicians' maneuver. They elevated liberty into an ideal principle, more worthy of worship than practice. Whitman's poetry generalized liberty into the motive common to all actions, as cheap and available as vitality itself. Then he treated everything in America—whether in man or in nature, in the psyche or in the body, in the slave or in the slavemaster—as a realization of liberty.[40] By returning liberty to a context where argument over its nature was clearly inappropriate, Whitman removed it from the platform of contending parties.

Now, when I say that Whitman treated everything in America as if it were the realization of the natural right of liberty, I make Whitman's poetry sound as if it performs the classic function of an ideology. In his *Dictionary of Political Thought,* Roger Scruton writes that the classic "function of ideology is to naturalize the *status quo,* and to represent as immutable features of human nature the particular social conditions which currently persist."[41] When used ideologically, the word "natural" masks whatever conventions and practices those in power wish to be the ruling illusions of the day. A good rule for a student of ideology to follow might be that whatever an ideology defines as natural is not. The need to designate something as natural should give fair warning to the wary.

But Whitman used natural law as a weapon against the ruling ideology of his day, a way to mark the difference between national polity and the laws of nature. If we could imagine natural law as a legal system with precedents like those of positive law, we could say that Whitman had a legal precedent for his poetry. The nation's founders put natural law to a similar use when they distinguished America's liberty from Britain's tyranny. Whether any of the founding fathers believed natural law to be anything other than a legal fiction necessary to justify the Revolution is a much debated point.[42] That they founded the country on the basis of natural law cannot be debated. Whitman wrote *Leaves of Grass* not to enter another debate but to return America to her basis in nature. For Whitman that meant making natural law available as an experience, a resource for real rather than symbolic actions.

The Nature of Slavery

For Whitman, the self-evident was not one more experience to be undergone in nature; it was the experience of nature, both our experience of nature and nature's experience of itself. Unlike any other experience an American would undergo, this one, Whitman believed, gave entry to the will of nature, enabling one to act with nature's energies and purposes.

To say that Whitman made nature's law available as an experience presupposes what most Americans no longer believe to be self-evident—that nature possesses an inner life, complete with will, sensations, reason, and emotions. This belief was to become the credo of many late-nineteenth-century naturalists, but also corroborated the authority of natural law. The inner life of nature was, our founders believed, the creative activity of the creator himself at work. Daniel Boorstin points to this belief about nature's workings as widespread enough to answer anyone's doubts about natural law. While there may have been "wide disagreement . . . as to the possibility of revelation," he observes, "all appear to have believed that the creation itself was the primary source of knowledge about God."[43]

Belief in the inner life of nature provided the patriots with the rationale for their "Declaration on the Reasons for Taking Up Arms." Ethan Allen gave the clearest explanation of the grounds for Americans to turn God, nature, the law of nature, and nature's God into interchangeable terms in the evolving American structure of consciousness. In *Reason The Only Oracle* (1784), Allen writes:

> The whole, which we denominate by the term *nature,* which is the same as creation perfectly regulated, was eternally connected by the creator to answer the same all-glorious purpose, *to wit,* the display of the divine nature, the consequences of which are existence and happiness to being in general, so that the creation with all its productions, operates according to the laws of nature, and is sustained by the self-existent cause in perfect order and decorum, agreeable to the eternal wisdom, unalterable rectitude, impartial justice and immense goodness of the divine nature, which is a summary of God's providence. It is from the

established ordinances of nature that summer and winter, rainy and fair seasons, monsoons, refreshing breezes, seed time and harvest, day and night interchangeably succeed each other, and diffuse their extensive blessings to man.[44]

In this quotation and throughout the Revolutionary period, nature's law would be invoked not to "naturalize" the status quo, but to demand a correspondence between the rule of government and the workings of nature. Nature was the general rule of government on earth, so our founders argued. When man acted according to nature's dictates, he followed nature ruling from within himself. The law of nature became Revolutionary man's rationale for overruling the arbitrary will of tyrants.

From the beginning, then, natural law was invoked as the only true government. By Whitman's time, however, slaveholders and their advocates in Washington were invoking the right to property guaranteed by natural law as the basis for their "natural right" to hold slaves.[45] They invoked natural law as a defense of an "unnatural" institution.

In the slaveholders' defense, it must be said that the right to property, as what guarantees the inalienability of all the other liberties, had become their natural ruler. There were specific and complex historical reasons for this development. The conjunction of the quite separate political issues of slavery and western expansionism can be numbered among them. The "land grab" movement, as the western migration was sometimes called, turned nature into land. If the inner life attributed to nature could be owned as property, why not the inner character of a man?[46]

In deciding who rightfully owned the western lands, post-Jacksonian Americans considered the claims of the squatters who worked the land, the bankers who lent them the money, and the speculators who bought it for its resale value. No one, of course, considered the natural rights of the land itself. Yet according to the theory of natural law, nature itself, like man in nature, was created with certain inalienable liberties. Its pure and simple display of those liberties was the precedent for man's claim to his natural liberties. While these liberties may have been obscured in man, they appeared self-evident in nature.[47]

In describing their rule over nature as a "natural right," nineteenth-century Americans reduplicated the Revolutionary model, without realizing that they were playing the role of tyrant rather than rebels. Similarly, in the peculiar institution of slavery, the slaves were to their masters as the Americans had been to the British; so the abolitionists claimed in their rhetoric of opposition. And many of the advocates of slavery agreed, for different reasons. Some of these reasons, as Richard Slotkin has argued, were psychological.[48] By behaving toward slaves (and Indians, and immigrants, and Jews) as had the British aristocrats toward them, they could dignify their newly won freedom by giving it an aristocratic bearing. This role reversal also performed a more specifically social function. It accommodated the patriots to their former enemies by establishing a role they shared in common.

Slavery performed economic labors as well. By turning freedom itself into a property, it smoothed the way for "laissez-faire" economists to equate human freedom with the activities of a free man in a free market.

In the debates over slavery, many abolitionists did not distinguish freedom from property, but implicitly agreed with their opponents. Their disagreement was over who should own the property, a master or a man. Nor did they see any connection between nature in the West and slavery, except insofar as the free or slave status of the western territories was concerned. This issue, whether a territory should become a free state or a slave one, led to an even greater question: whether the nation should remain united or separate. Thus the right to property was made to function as a natural arbiter of the legitimacy of the Union.

The right to property replaced natural liberty as the "principle" of compromise. Property was a right that seemed to satisfy the interests of all the discussants. It permitted the slaveowners to exercise their natural right to own slaves and the Union its proprietory power over the states. This compromise only continued a long series of redefinitions of natural law that began with the American Revolution. In continuing the series, the Great Compromise only proved the argument of ideology. Throughout these redefinitions natural law did indeed become synonymous with whatever institution a legislator wanted to seem natural.[49]

But when the theory of natural law was invoked to legalize the right of one man to hold another man as property, Walt Whitman refused to accept the law as nature's. He did not lose faith in the laws of nature. But he did refuse to acknowledge the right to property as a higher principle in nature than liberty. And when he gave up politics and turned to poetry, he did what politicians would not do: make it self-evident that liberty was the ruling principle in nature's law and over "Nature's Nation."

Natural Law and Whitman's Vision

In early America, the historic liberation from feudal institutions like slavery could be experienced as liberating only by preserving those institutions. And the preservation of the institution of slavery made it possible for Americans to interpret natural liberty as a cultural possession.

For Whitman this confusion clarified the error in the Revolutionary model. He saw how the model perpetuated Old World conditions, how the opposition to an old world was itself an institution inherited from the Old World. He also saw that the consequences this model had for the Old World were about to be replicated in the New World. As long as the Revolutionary model ruled, the nation itself was destined to replicate the Civil War conditions preserved in the model.

Whitman had had a foretaste of the Civil War in the Brooklyn no-popery riot. In the next day's editorial he explained that he had lifted his voice against the immigrants from the Old World to inspire confidence in the new republic. Now he would: "see no man disenfranchised, because he happened to be born three thousand miles off. We go for the largest liberty."[50]

It was not, however, until he became the nation's bard that Whitman found the polity necessary to make this "largest liberty" a natural resource. In the preface to the 1855 edition of *Leaves of Grass,* Whitman did not shape the relationship between Old and New Worlds into an oppositional model. He removed the opposition from the model by representing the relationship between the Old World and America as a natural development rather than a historic action: "America does not repel the past or what it has produced under its forms or amid other politics of the idea of castes or the old religions."[51] Whitman begins as if to disarm, from the outset, the need to define the nation too impetuously. America had already outgrown the need for petulant antagonisms, and could acknowledge Old World cultural achievements "with calmness."[52] As Americans develop their own ideas to meet their own conditions, those they inherited from Europe will literally drop away, Whitman suggests, as will unnecessary limbs in the evolution of a species. No explicit antagonism is necessary to hurry this development along, because the power of liberty itself, acting from within Nature, has already realized this development.

In Whitman's revision of its origins, America did not result from a revolution. That war preserved a model of freedom based on masters and

slaves. America need no longer found her freedom on the basis of continued oppression, because America had freed the oppressor from the need
to oppress. In Whitman's preface, America is not opposed to Europe, but
portrayed as the regenerative power enabling Europe to outgrow itself. As
this power, America was already present in the Old World. It existed in
every European's aspirations for a better world. But once it fulfilled those
aspirations, America enabled Europeans to separate the Americans in
themselves from the Europeans in themselves.

As the fulfillment of European ideals, America was also free from European history. And what is free from history returns to nature. Unlike the
nature invoked by Hobbes and Locke, however, this second nature was not
prepolitical.[53] According to Whitman, nature was what mankind could reenter only after passing through history.

Unlike the history men pass through, however, this second nature
existed without reference to a previous world. As the fulfillment of the Old
World, America no longer had any precedents in that world. So in his radical redefinition of the nature of America, Whitman takes the founders at
their word. And because his contemporaries were redefining America in
terms more congenial to Europe's history, he described America as a nation working in accordance with the laws of nature.[54]

What Whitman meant by nature's law was what Ethan Allen meant by
the law of nature, not what Hobbes meant by natural law. As a nation
founded on nature's laws, America could not be made to follow Europe's
customs. What appears according to nature's laws does not follow men's
precedents. Existing without precedent, everything in nature is quite literally "self-evident."

Natural law did not work according to men's designs, but was, by its
nature, that which revealed its designs through mankind as well as his environment. By defining natural liberty as a regenerative power, Whitman
means it to be a force capable of reforming the nation's legislators who
founded their compromises upon it.

Let me suggest a context—what Whitman called a "democratic vista"—
for Whitman's natural liberty. He was arguing the case against slavery by
the laws of nature rather than by the rules and conventions of the nation's
legislators. The legislators, in forging their compromise, had turned to the
founding fathers' words as precedents. When they returned to the founding documents, they turned liberty into a property right, and the slaves
owned by Jefferson and Washington into proofs for this interpretation.

Their legal interpretation turned liberty into an instrument of political opportunism. And the uses to which they put it had already compromised its nature as a self-evident truth.

To restore liberty to self-evidence, Whitman returned to the founding scene to do for the founders what they could not as yet do for themselves. Unlike other principles in human history, our founding ones were themselves without precedent. The founders used words, like "natural liberty" and "equality," which as yet had no referent. Unlike other words, which had a history, these words could receive their meaning only after their first usage—in the people, institutions, and forms of life they made possible.[55] That is why Whitman called these words productive of an "ever-apparent" life; they were words that called forth forms and forces able to realize them into life.

Like other men in the eighteenth century, the founders did not know the meaning of their own words. Many of them acknowledged their ignorance by claiming the future of America as the place to clarify the significance of the founding covenant. The future, in an odd reversal of temporal categories, was to take precedence over the past, as the place where these otherwise unreferenced words could find appropriate referents.[56]

Whitman based his case against slavery on this reversal of temporal categories. Whitman had experienced, in his life among the democratic masses, the self-evident truth of liberty, and he returned to the scene of the founding to make this truth self-evident to the founders: liberty made slavery impossible in America.

To give this return the emphasis Whitman intended, we must consider the nature of the medium enabling him to return. In restoring the spirit of liberty to the letter of America's law, Whitman does not oppose the founder's words. Nor does he condemn their lives as failures to live by their word. In place of opposition, Whitman puts regeneration to work. He describes the movement from Europe to America as the "natural" development from what no longer adapts man to his surroundings to what does. He does not use nature to "lord it over" an Old World remnant in America. That would only duplicate the usage to which the legislators had put natural law. Instead he democratically associates himself with the regenerative process of nature, certain of its success.

I call his relation with nature's law a democratic association for a reason. The association is not one founded on force or opposition. Neither is it the exercise of a greater power demanding obedience from a dependent. The relation is a free one in the most fundamental sense, in that it releases the adherents not *from* a despotism but *to* a renewal of all that is best in themselves. Those held together by this law are not subjects ruled by a monarch. The law of regeneration lacks any ruling principle. It does not rule over a field but releases whatever is most vital in whatever already exists. As the power of renewal at work within, the law of regeneration cannot be distinguished from the mass of different shapes this renewal assumes.

In regeneration Whitman discovered the democratic principle at work in both nature and the nation's founding. Like the self-evident truths of the founders, the law of regeneration has no referent other than the phenomena revealing it. It makes visible what can be. Like a democratic people, none of the phenomena held together by this law are compelled to follow its principles. Its law cannot be distinguished from an inner motivation to become better. And the results of this motive are a continual surprise.

When experienced from within the individual, this law expresses itself in the wish to be all one can be. And this motive connects the individual with all that can be made of this motive—in other words, with everything else in existence. It puts the individual in relation to what we could call a "mass logic." A mass of particulars make explicit what is implicit in this motive by channeling it through their appearances. What results is an action on a mass scale: "Here is action untied from strings necessarily blind to particulars and details moving in vast masses."[57] Overseeing this mass action is a single recognition: everything that works according to the law of regeneration is both itself and everything else it can possibly be. The individual is not opposed to the masses, as he is in any theory grounding liberty in a single individual. The masses free or "untie" the individual from bondage to his own person, releasing him to all the possible embodiments he might have assumed equally well. In assuming all the possible forms he might, the individual both completes himself, hence knows perfect liberty, and experiences himself completed by everything else, hence knows democratic equality. The regenerated "understand the law of perfection in masses . . . That its finish is to each for himself and onward from itself . . . that it is profuse and impartial . . . one part does not need to be thrust above the other."[58]

Regeneration transmutes the single individual into a democratic relation, the man-en-masse. Because every individual exists as the possibility of becoming everything else, nothing can be defined as inferior or superior, dominant or dominated. Everything is a possible expression of all one can be. And since, according to the law of regeneration, the individual cannot be happy until he is all he can be, Whitman defines democracy as what makes him happy by making his relationship democratic.

The democratizing power of the law of regeneration cannot be emphasized too much. Unlike any other principle or law or any conception of their workings, this law cannot subordinate its subjects. It does not sanction the relations between a tyrant and his rebels any more than it condones slavery. Nor can it justify the compromise formations sustaining the institution of slavery. But it can "regenerate" these political institutions as well as the compromises sanctioning them.

By identifying life, liberty, and the pursuit of happiness as the work of nature's law of regeneration, Whitman retires compromise from its duties in a democracy. Compromise puts particular interests above those of all the people. Regeneration defines all the people as the individual's means of being all each can be. Here is the essence of its political service. By defining all interests as equal expressions of all the individual could want, the law of regeneration binds the interests of one to the interests of all others. Put differently, the law of regeneration redefines the external world as the revelation of an individual's inner life. It is all he can be.

In order for such a definition to work, the individual has to agree to the relation between his desires and his world. That is where the nation's bard comes in. It is the poet's function, Whitman claims, to make apparent this democratic relation. At a time when confusion and compromise have obscured this relation, the poet's task in terms of Whitman's desire to give form and shape to what he called the "spirit" or "genius" of the masses. To give shape to the genius of the masses Whitman had to reshape his person into a crowd identity.

A crowd is quite similar to what we earlier called a common self because it too enables an individual to say "We" out of a recognition of a shared or group experience. But unlike a common self, a crowd identity has physical properties—the size and shape of the crowd incarnating it—as well as an affectional and intellectual life all of its own. When embodied in any single person, this "crowd identity" does not belong to that person. It is what enables a single person to belong to the group.

For Whitman the poet was the crowd identity of all the people. He set for his poetry the greatest of democratic tasks. He wanted the individuals in America to use his poetry as the way of forming a democratic ensemble:

> Their Presidents shall not be their common referee so much as their poets shall. Of all mankind the great poet is the equable man. Not in

him but off from him things are grotesque or fail of their sanity. Nothing out of its place is good and nothing in its place is bad. He bestows on every object or quality its fit proportions neither more nor less. He is the arbiter of the diverse and he is the key. He is the equalizer of his age and land.[59]

The key to the poet's arbitration is carried by the final line. The poet makes the individual equal to his age and land by revealing the age and the land as the equivalent of the deepest wish within the individual. The age and the land are the revelation of all an individual can be. So for Whitman all the present world is the revelation of all that an individual could ever want. The poet sees that the inner desires of a single individual are utterly correspondent with the external world, that the external world makes these internal wishes manifest. And he writes his poetry to let the nation's individuals see this as well. In seeing the world as the acknowledgment of all of his inner life, the individual can see all the world as the outer form of his inner life.

Whitman used the word "acknowledgment" to distinguish democratic relations from the relations produced by disciplines of knowledge. Knowledge subordinates what is unknown to the known; and it subordinates the known to the knower. But when considered a revelation of all one can be, the world no longer becomes a field disciplines of knowledge can appropriate. Since the world reveals his inner life, the individual cannot subordinate it to what he already knows. He can only acknowledge the external world as he would a revelation of his inner life.

In Whitman's poetry the relation between the external world and an individual's inner life is that of a realized desire. When an object in the world acquires a relation to our inner life, it can lose whatever existence it possessed when considered apart from us, and be transposed, by delighting or inspiring us, into what we call our heart's desire. It ceases to be apart from us and becomes a part of who we are because it fulfills what we want.[60]

Usually it is through reflection that we manage this conversion of things in the world into images we want, or else we read poetry like Whitman's which manages the conversion our reflections could not. Whether reflecting upon our world or reading a poet's words, however, we more usually gain solitude than a "crowd identity." Instead of deepening our relation to the world, solitude intensifies our separateness. Through solitude we give the mental images our reflection has separated from things a home in the private medium traditionally called the soul.

What is surely most radical about Whitman's poetry inheres in his refusal to acknowledge the distinction between the individual soul and the United States of America. When Whitman writes, "The United States are themselves the greatest poem,"[61] and calls literature the "soul" of America, he means the observation quite literally. Like an image in a poem, the United States exists as a realization of desire; as the realization of Europe's wish to be a better world, America was from its origin the result of a reflection. America was what resulted when Europe's customs gave way to practices more answerable to the needs of her soul. In America, Whitman writes: "The soul or spirit transmits itself into all matter, into rocks . . . and can live the life as a rock. Into the sea . . . and can feel itself the seas."[62] As the fulfillment of Europe's desires, all things in America appear as they otherwise would only within the mind. The United States of America eradicates the distinction between the reflections within the mind and things in the world.

More precisely, America reverses the process of reflection. As the regeneration of the Old World, America does not "reflect" previous forms. Everything in America subsists within two simultaneous contexts: Everything is itself and is on the way to becoming all. In apprehending this world, individuals—or at least those in Whitman's poetry—do not reflect upon things but project them into what they can be, thereby extending what we more usually call memory, or the work of reflection, into the future. Unlike most acts of reflection, this projective activity takes place not within the mind, but in the world.

As what appears when individuals follow their deepest wish for renewal, regenerated things borrow from reflection the power to be memorable but throw away the need to attach that power to any single form. Regeneration divests the thing remembered of the power to hold the attention and reattaches this power to the process of becoming all. Consequently in a world organized according to the laws of regeneration no one can convert the world into internal reflections. Regeneration begins when reflection ends. Everything in America, Whitman believed, had already fulfilled what was wanted. So everything exists in an afterlife, where everything recollects forward what everything else can become—on the way to becoming all.[63]

These observations might become clearer if we imagine the law of regeneration stated as the following categorical imperative: "Everything in America should exist the way things do in a poem." For then we can conceive of America the way we do Whitman's poetic medium. America is the place where things in the world take on the life they more normally would within the mind.[64] As a poem, America is not a thought in the mind or a place on a map, but the medium through which everything passes on the way to becoming all it can be.

But while everything in America exists as if it were already within an inner life, not every American identifies that inner life with his own. Herein, Whitman believed, lay the task for the democratic poet, who should enable every American to recognize the United States as the revelation of the working of his inner life: "Without effort and without exposing in the least how it is done the greatest poet brings the spirit of any or all events and passions and scenes and persons . . . to bear on your individual character as you hear or read."[65] In asking Americans to experience America as if it were a manifestation of their shared inner life, the poet performs a duty more commonly performed by an orator. When we are held together in a crowd by the words of an inspiring orator, we share an inner life. The orator's words hold the crowd because they gratify the wishes the people hold in common. In holding the people together, the orator functions the way a law in nature does: he expresses a will common to all. He elevates things in the world into images of another world, a world everyone wants rather than the world everyone already has. In the orator's words, an inner life common to all the persons in the crowd become manifest. In *Leaves of Grass,* Whitman invites the reader to experience America itself as if it were spoken into existence by an orator.

Of course orators could spellbind a crowd by subjecting it to their own will rather than articulating the people's. And some of the greatest orators of Whitman's day had used the doctrine of natural law to serve private interests. That is why Whitman distinguishes the orator from the poet. The law of regeneration makes the poet's word principled rather than partial. This law also gives Whitman a way of putting political oratory to the test of nature.

On the issue of slavery Whitman had a test question for politicians: "Does this answer? or is it without reference to universal needs? or sprung of the needs of the less developed society of special ranks, or old needs of pleasure overlaid by modern science and forms? Does this acknowledge liberty with audible and absolute acknowledgment, and set slavery at naught for life and death? Will it help breed one goodshaped and wellhung man and woman to be his perfect and independent mate?"[66] When addressed by this question, a legislator could not put special interests—of the

Union or the states, of the slaveowners or the self-possessed—before "universal need." Whitman identifies liberty as the object of absolute acknowledgment because only one who acknowledges liberty absolutely—as the freedom of all others—can truly be said to act in accordance with the principle of liberty. In order to be absolute, acknowledgment must replace perception and cognition as means of communicating with the world. Knowledge of the world becomes absolute acknowledgment of its liberty only after knowledge of the world becomes absolutely indistinguishable from self-knowledge. The only thing most people acknowledge absolutely is the sanctity of an inner self. So to look out into a world one can acknowledge absolutely would be the same as looking into oneself.

Such a world had clearly not yet appeared in 1855. It also had not appeared in 1776. To make this world apparent in 1855—the year of *Leaves of Grass*—he had to restore natural liberty to its proper place within the psyche of the founders and remove whatever would impede its later appearance. Whitman claimed regeneration as the principle authorizing this restoration. As the means of releasing everything to all it can be, only regeneration could reveal its future implications to a moment in the past: "The greatest poet forms the consistence of what is to be from what has been and is . . . he says to the Past, Rise and walk before me that I may realize you . . . he places himself where the future becomes present."[67]

New World Nature and *Leaves of Grass*

Earlier I claimed that Whitman wrote *Leaves of Grass* to renew America's relation to her founding principles. Now I have made a different claim, namely that Whitman changed the nature of the founding covenant, reestablishing America in the principle of regeneration, the most fundamental law of nature. To make clear my rationale for this new claim, I need to reiterate the steps leading to it.

In the preface to the 1855 edition of *Leaves of Grass,* Whitman transferred the principle of liberty from one tradition of natural law to another. The great debate over slavery led many legislators to define liberty as a natural right guaranteed by the social contract, by which they meant that it was a right man exercised in the savage, prepolitical nature we entered culture to leave behind.[68] When properly exercised, liberty secured mastery over savage natural conditions. Property, whether in the material form of real estate or the psychological form of character, resulted from this exercise. Consequent to this "natural" association with property, natural liberty sanctioned diverse cultural institutions: the frontier and land speculation in the West, the market and salesmanship (or speculation in oneself) in the East, and slavery in the South. All of these institutions depended on "free" agents acting within competitive conditions. When successful, these "free" agents "mastered" those conditions.

In this tradition, liberty existed not as a principle within nature but as a power over nature, at least if nature was redefined as the frontier. It is not difficult to see how easily a freedom based upon the exercise of mastery could lend itself to a defense of a master's rights over his ("savage") slaves.[69]

To distinguish this Hobbesian natural liberty from the liberty he experienced in nature, Whitman could not simply oppose Hobbes's definition. Any opposition to this theory would simply be one more reenactment of the rebel's reaction to a tyrant, the frontiersman to a frontier (the slave's to his master). So instead of opposing the theory Whitman followed out its natural development. That is, he placed natural law in a context where it proved irrelevant to prevailing conditions. As the realization of the ideals at work in European history, America's liberty could not be defined as prepolitical or protocultural. America had *returned* European man to nature—not the nature he discovered in the New World and protected in the social contract, but a second nature, one that he had passed through culture to regain. This nature was not innocent of European history: it is what developed out of European history. As the power at work in this development, liberty, Whitman suggests, cannot be equated with an opposition to natural conditions. Development is the condition of nature's existence in America. By fulfilling Europe's laws, America released itself to a new development.[70]

As what had been developed to a point beyond European history, America could not continue to follow those older laws, but had to follow the law that led her out of history and into a new age. Whitman, as we have seen, identified the principle at work in Europe's development as regeneration. He further identified the force at work in the law with the forms produced by the law—all the forms.

In establishing regeneration as the natural basis for the nation's bond, Whitman used nature in a way almost the reverse of the way it is classically used in ideology. Ideology uses nature to make social institutions sound natural. The savage condition of the frontier, for example, enabled Americans to experience their relation to marketplace conditions as natural. But at the time Whitman wrote, no social institution had as yet appeared that would enable Americans to experience the law of regeneration as the nation's compact. *Leaves of Grass* enabled Americans to experience the law of their development as nature's. He did not write to sanction already existing social institutions. Most of them, Whitman believed, were inherited from Europe's history. So he redirected America's vision to what remained to be developed out of those institutions.

In redirecting America's vision away from its past, Whitman reminded Americans of their status as revelations. Their lives revealed what the founders meant by terms that had no precedents. More than anyone Whitman insisted on the distinction between a nation with a history and a nation without. A nation without a history had no precedents. Like nature, such a nation could only make visible what can be. Instead of representing "what was," everything in America participated in the process of becoming all it could be. And regeneration made this process principled.

Whitman and the Other World

Whitman's poetry, by being without reference to any prior development, by itself including all, leaves no place for the other. And I can think of no precedent for this omission in Western culture. But Tzvetan Todorov in his book *The Conquest of America* found a similar omission in a nature Spanish conquistadors discovered in the New World. So I shall use his discussion of the Aztecs as a point of reference for Whitman's poetry. Unlike the savage nature the Europeans would reform in the natives and recognize in themselves, the Aztecs' view of nature had no precedent in Europe. When the conquistadors encountered this unprecedented feature, they recorded it as a sign of the culturally primitive, "a certain inadequacy" in the natives' conception of each other. Later they used the Aztecs' inadequate development of "alterity" as a rationale for their conquest.

For Todorov, the touchstone of social alterity "is not the present and immediate second person singular but the absent or distant third person singular." The Aztec language had no third-person singular, implying "a predominance of presence over absence, of the immediate over the mediated."[71] After discussing the implications for language of the natives' inadequate conception of otherness, Todorov offers a remarkable series of observations:

> Language exists only by means of the other, not only because one always addresses someone but also insofar as it permits evoking the absent third person . . . the very existence of this other is measured by the space the symbolic system reserves for him.[72]

I call these observations remarkable because in them Todorov designates what for a European constitutes the greatest social scandal about the Aztec culture. They have no sense of otherness. We can understand Todorov's reason for being scandalized by this missing other when we recall the role the savages played when imported to Europe. They made possible an "other" set of social distinctions, distinctions not inherited, as was traditionally the case, but achieved by overcoming the "savage" other within oneself.

By being from a world utterly unrelated to the feudal organization in Europe, the savage made it possible for Europeans to reevaluate their social organization. The longterm results of this discovery of their savage nature were civil wars and the social-contract theories resulting from them. And Europe's myths about the "war of all against all" reportedly waged in the natives' land would make the universal competition of the marketplace sound "natural."

The conquistators more than made up for the Aztecs' lack of a sense of otherness, for they not only recognized them as other, but conquered this otherness. Then they traded the conquered others for class, rank, and wealth in Europe. In overcoming the "other," they earned the social distance making their persons other than (superior to) those of most individuals.

When Todorov registers his shock, he does so in terms of the semiotic system: "Any investigation of alterity is necessarily semiotic, and reciprocally, semiotics cannot be conceived outside the relation to the other."[73] A language organized through the power of words or "signs" to replace things is of a piece with a society organized around the "other." In learning how to use a word to refer to a thing or to another person, an individual learns how to separate from persons and things. Representations and sign systems organized through the promise of a representable world break down a participatory relation with a world by rewarding the separation with words. And words enable an individual to master the loss felt in the separation by transforming his relation to the absent: instead of feeling victimized by their disappearance, he can choose to make things (and persons) absent through his use of words.[74]

In their conquest of worldly otherness, signs are related to the explorers' "conquest." Both conquests resulted in a new world of signs and "new men" to deploy these signs. In failing to signify the "other" in their culture, the natives more importantly failed to acknowledge Europe's basis for the conquest. Until they got to Europe, they did not know they were supposed to be the other.

But while the Aztecs did not know anything was missing from their system, Todorov clearly does. In an interpretive gesture that reconquers the Aztecs, Todorov associates their inadequate semiotics with the barbarities of cannibalism and human sacrifice. Listen for a confusion of tongues as Todorov attempts to reinstate the distance (between Aztecs and their world, between Todorov and the Aztecs) missing from their culture. "In the first place," Todorov begins resolutely, "the prisoner literally becomes the god." But according to the rules of semiotics, no person can become another person, so the prisoner does not become the god as the Aztecs claim but "represents him," as semiotics says he should. Having translated the Aztecs' "sacrifice" into *his* semiotics, Todorov attributes the resultant confusion to the Aztecs' conception rather than to his system: "At the same time they act as if they were confusing the representative with what he represents. What begins as a representation ends as a participation and identification; the distance necessary to the symbolic functioning seems to be lacking."[75]

Now, how can a distance that the Aztecs do not recognize be missing anywhere but in Todorov's mind, or in the system of semiotics supporting that mind? The Aztecs did not acknowledge distance between the "prisoner" and the god in whose spirit the prisoner participated. Nor did they acknowledge the difference, as anthropologists at least since Jane Harrison have pointed out, between that god and the life of the group. Because the life of the group preceded and partook of the lives of its individuals, no symbolic function was needed. Symbol systems insist upon a separation between the individual and the others that the participatory culture of the Aztecs simply did not acknowledge. To live within the Aztec community was to experience one's individual life as given to the group from birth. As do the men-en-masse in Whitman's *Leaves of Grass,* the Aztecs participated in each others lives.[76]

But there is a world of difference between Whitman's poetry and a culture organized around blood sacrifice. In blood sacrifice, the priests reenacted as a ritual what went on day to day in a community to make certain it continued. By the time Whitman wrote, Europe had reversed the process. They had sacrificed the group sense to intensify the sense of the individual. By elevating the symbolic function into the highest value of language, Europe mastered the world of living things by replacing it with their not so vital signs. Every sign user inherited a position of mastery over the world. And when, in the "savages," the European encountered persons who did not "master" the world but "sacrificed" their persons to it, the Europeans simply "mastered" them as well.

The natives identified themselves with a part of nature that European man's symbolic function enabled him to leave behind. But Whitman traded on a different claim: that America returned man to this nature. In order to make good on this claim, Whitman had to show how man could re-experience participation in nature differently after having passed through culture. We can acknowledge Whitman's sense of this difference if we imagine that things in nature have a memory, because Whitman wrote as if things in nature could recall him to his former participation in their life. While it is everywhere present in his poetry, Whitman is most explicit about this memory *in* rather than *of* things in section 32 of *Song of Myself.*[77]

"I think I could turn and live awhile with the animals,"[78] he begins rather wistfully. Then, after noticing qualities in horses he either already finds in himself or wants to develop, he changes his attitude. Instead of remaining separated from them, he says the horses "bring me tokens of myself . . . they evince them plainly in their possession."[79] Following this recognition of qualities of his inner life preserved in the horses' forms, Whitman wonders how they came to remember him in the first place. This wonder soon gives way to a feeling of being absorbed within their place in nature. And he protects himself from utter identification with them only by an evolutionary impulse accompanying him throughout his stay with them.

> I must have passed that way untold times ago
> . . . .
> Myself moving forward then and now and forever
> Gathering and showing more always and with velocity
> Infinite and omnigenous and the like of these among them
> Not too exclusive towards the reachers of my remembrancers
> Picking out here one that shall be my amie
> Choosing to go with him on brotherly terms.[80]

In these lines Whitman's persona ceases to occupy a cultural position—that of an observer looking at a horse—and becomes a natural process. And he manages this transference by providing a cultural commonplace—that horses are below humans on the evolutionary scale—with a temporal dimension. If they exist beneath us on the evolutionary scale, Whitman reasons, then they are us but in a different dimension.

Since the natural law of evolution oversees the development from the plant world into the human world, Whitman takes this law at its word and recognizes everything in existence as what is evolving into the human (and beyond). Everything in nature is human, but in a different dimension of time and place. If they can develop into man then man can return to this former life as one of them, and experience his evolution into himself through them.

We can begin to understand how Whitman manages this wonderful passage by noticing what he has done to the symbolic function of language. Here, words do not guarantee Whitman a separate and masterful relationship to the horse he observes. If they did, the horse could be stored along with other representations in his personal memory. Instead of allowing the transmutation of his form into a sign, the horse absorbs Whitman within the more inclusive process of evolutionary development. Whitman's encounter with the horse reverses the usual flow of language: his words do not move the horse's presence into the personal memory signs produce; instead, Whitman and the horse both turn into traces in the reflective mind of the evolutionary process. Evolution remembers its steps, Whitman suggests, in their forms. For Whitman, each form in the evolutionary process preserves an impression of man's former presence within it on its way into the human form. The difference between the horse and the man is that Whitman can experience the process of his own development while the horse cannot.

This is also the difference between Whitman's poetry and the Aztecs' blood sacrifice. Through blood sacrifices performed by their priests, the Aztecs remained unconscious of their development into individuals. Whitman's poetry exploits the consciousness of individual development made possible by the symbolic function by rediscovering this consciousness preserved in things. Just as the person develops a personal memory through the use of signs, so, Whitman suggests, the things signified can develop a memory of the person who gave them up for signs. That is why the things in nature can recollect mankind. They are prior developments of mankind waiting to recollect man back into them.

The Poet, the Orator, and the Law of Regeneration

This explanation may have permitted me to make the relationship between Whitman's nature and Europe's culture clear, but at the cost of contradicting some earlier observations. Earlier I maintained that Whitman's America had no precedents, that it put revelation in the place more usually occupied by representations. Now I have argued that the things words represent are themselves representations—they represent nature's memory of its evolutionary process. And I have concluded that nature's memory can restore man to his participation in this natural process.

But this entire account depends upon terms (memory, representation) I claimed Whitman did not depend upon. To clear up this contradiction, I should return to Whitman's America the way he did, by way of contrast with Europe's culture. The Europeans led the native Americans out of nature by replacing communal participation with symbolic representations. And they justified this exchange the way Todorov does. In the adventure narratives with which they returned from the New World, they argued that sacrifice of nature's things to a person's signs was more humane than the sacrifice of persons to natural processes. Whitman acknowledges the superiority of culture's representations over human sacrifice, but he also acknowledges the loss of participatory energies involved in the exchange. To repair this loss Whitman treats symbolic representations as participants in a more inclusive process of speech.[81] In Whitman's poetry, things and words lead the lives not of representations but of apostrophes. Like things in nature, Whitman's words exist as if they have been commanded into existence by a law. Whitman imagines everything spoken into existence, or rather uttered by the natural law of regeneration. Things, words, and persons all follow the dictates of this law. When following the law of regeneration, nothing can exist separate from anything else. As aspects of a regenerative process, everything is developing into everything else. Development necessarily involves what is individual in a universal activity wherein everything exists in order to develop into something better and for the sake of regenerating everything else.

The law of regeneration subjects symbolic representations to linguistic duties "higher" than that of sanctioning social distance and personalized individuality. Instead of parsed sentences, Whitman writes what he called speech floods. His streams of words submerge the individual parts of speech, involving every word in a process in which the parts cannot be distinguished from the movement they carry forward.[82] Like masses of people gathering into a crowd, the parts of speech in Whitman's sentences discharge their differences into the electric energies holding them together, and become equal participants in the life they produce.

I have associated the parts of speech in Whitman's sentences with the masses because Whitman does. Listen to this sentence pick up stragglers and passersby the way a mob would:

> The pure contralto sings in the organloft,
> The carpenter dresses his plank . . . the tongue of his foreplane whistles
>   its wild ascending lisp,
> . . . .
> The pilot seizes the king-pin, he heaves down with a strong arm,
> The mate stands braced in the whale boat, lance and harpoon are ready,
> The duck-shooter walks by silent and cautious stretches,
> The deacons are ordain'd with cross-hands at the altar,
> The spinning girl retreats and advances to the hum of the big wheel.[83]

The phrases in this sentence do not represent individuals—they associate them. They draw single, separate persons, otherwise silently passing each other by, into a larger movement. As these persons and the parts of speech with which they are associated gather mass, they do not remain separate but flood through each new "pick-up," their lives deepening with a multitude of other possibilities. As the means of making these persons part of a mass movement, the individual a part of the en-masse, this sentence cannot be articulated by any single individual within it. In going through its motions, the sentence surges through all of these individuals, as if flooding over into new outlets of energy and reticulating a network of tributaries in its overflow.

As it overflows, the sentence spills a multiplicity of possible selves out of each individual, involving each in an identity much larger than his own. Whitman identifies this greater identity of the democratic masses as democracy's replacement for the lineage of ancestors in feudal Europe. Like those ancestral lineages, the masses permit each participant to conceive of himself as the work of generations. But unlike a European this man-en-masse cannot identify these generational labors with a family genealogy. Instead, each individual within a mass movement can experience himself undergoing an "instant" evolution. As Whitman observes the variety of possible shapes his own form can assume, he conceives these shapes in the crowd as his ancestors and descendants. Whitman exclaims from within a crowd: "There was never more inception than there is now. Nor any more youth or age than there is now; And will never be any more perfection than there is now."[84]

These observations could justify an attitude of complacency. If there will never be any more perfection than now, then, we might conclude, we have no need to change anything. And this conclusion would sanction a world Whitman wanted very much to see changed. The different point Whitman wishes to make, however, is that if you can experience the masses as a form of instantaneous human development you will change your attitude toward the masses. And when your attitude changes so will the world.

Mikhail Bakhtin's observations about the incompleteness of any single individual provide a useful context here:

> The individual cannot be completely incarnated into the flesh of existing sociohistorical categories. There is no more form that would be able to incarnate once and forever all of his human possibilities and needs, no form in which he could exhaust himself down to the last word . . . no form that he could fill to the brim, and yet at the same time not splash over the brim. There always remains an unrealized surplus of humanness. There always remains a need for the future."[85]

I cite this passage because Bakhtin defines the individual the way Whitman does: as a form congenial to multiple developments. But the difference in Bakhtin's emphasis is even more instructive. He identifies these possible developments with the life span of the single individual, where they indicate a "need for the future." And this description holds onto the opposition between the individual and the masses that Whitman has learned how to do without. The reason the individual seems incomplete and needs the future in Bakhtin is for Whitman all the more reason for moving among the masses. An individual in a democratic nation cannot be opposed to the masses and believe in freedom and equality for all. Yet the masses, in setting their numbers up against any single individual, seem almost to demand this opposition. To break his culture's habit of experiencing the masses as opposed to the individual, Whitman devises an alternative way to experience life among the masses. In Whitman's poetry the masses do not impede but develop each member. Their movement originates not from a partisan program, but from the process of human evolution involving everyone. Whereas this process formerly occupied thousands of years, and took place within the privacy of an individual's family lineage, in Whitman's masses this development is available for every individual, and within the present moment. In life among Whitman's masses, each needs only to "merge in the general run and await his development."

Thus, Whitman redistributes bonds of familial intimacy to all the persons in a crowd. Involved in each other's evolution, every member of a crowd is as "kin" to everyone else as ancestors and descendants would be. And no individual feels threatened by a gathering of his ancestors and descendants, as he might be by a crowd.[86]

What differentiates this mass evolution from family gatherings, however, is the equality of each of the humans "developing" within it. When experienced from within a mass movement, individual differences dissolve into a shared process. Different persons do not call attention to their differences, because these differences are all put to use in "developing" the human form. When conceived of as leading to the perfect human form, no single development can be described as superior or inferior. The "perfection" of the human form depends equally upon all the parts contributing to it. That's what Whitman meant when he wrote that there will never be any more perfection than there is now. For him the full run of the masses developed all the potentialities for humankind, and they did so in every moment of time. Whitman provides the most cogent explanation of his love for the masses in the following lines from the 1855 preface:

> To these [the masses] respond perfections not only in the committees that were supposed to stand for the rest but in the rest themselves just the same. These understand the law of perfection in masses and floods . . . that its finish is to each for itself and onward from itself . . . That it is profuse and impartial.[87]

The participants in a mass movement are like "leaves of grass" in a field. Both the persons in a mass movement and the leaves in a field of grass participate in a process of evolution. And both are subject to laws: the leaves to the laws of natural generation, and the masses to the regenerating cadences of an orator. This relationship between natural phenomena held together by nature's laws and the masses held together by an orator's words was much remarked upon in Whitman's day, and led many to conclude that the orator's words put the laws of nature into cultural service.

We have already considered Whitman's reaction to this conclusion. He believed that in covenanting the American people to the Fugitive Slave Law, the nation's orators had broken nature's law. So in *Leaves of Grass* he claimed the democratic people already had a prior binding covenant with a different orator.

We hear the difference between the national leaders and the speakers Whitman claims as the nation's true legislator in Whitman's crowded sentences. No orator would try to hold a crowd with a sentence like the one I cited above. That sentence, filled as it is with unruly energies and unchecked developments, sounds the way a crowd usually does *before* an orator begins to bind it up into his cadences. But Whitman intends this sentence to mean that the masses "are already spoken for" and are in need of no further leadership.

His sentences associate the participants in mass movements with the "speech floods" expressing them in his poetry. The participants as well as the movements in which they participate result from a torrent of speech that sweeps everything up into it. These sweeping lines are for Whitman the workings of a law—not the law of generation which works in seasonal cycles but the law of regeneration, which renews those cycles.

Nature's Orator

To develop the implications of Whitman's conception, I need to cite those famous lines where Whitman experiences himself uttered into existence.

> Loafe with me on the grass . . . loose the stop from your throat,
> Not words, not music or rhyme I want . . . not custom or lecture, not
>   even the best,
> Only the lull I like, the hum of your valued voice.
>
> I mind how we lay in June such a transparent summer morning
> You . . . plunged your tongue to my bare-stript heart,
> And reached till you felt any beard, and reached till you held my feet.
>
> Swiftly arose and spread around me the peace and joy and knowledge
>   that pass all the arguments of the earth;
> And I know that the hand of God is the elderhand of my own,
> . . . .
> And that a kelson of the creation is love,
> And limitless are leaves stiff or drooping in the fields
> And brown ants in the little wells beneath them,
> And mossy scabs of the wormfence, heaped stones, elder mullen and
>   pokeweed.[88]

Earlier I suggested, as a metaphor for understanding Whitman's America, that all the things in America be imagined as if they were figures in the speech of an inspiring orator. For then everything in America would be apprehended as if fulfilling the listeners' wishes. In these lines, Whitman turns this metaphor into a literal truth, as he experiences himself and everything else spoken into existence. In a useful commentary on these lines, Allen Grossman describes them as Whitman's way of "curing the human colloquy":

> To loaf ["Loafe with me on the grass . . ."] is to exchange the posture of hermeneutic attention for the posture of receptivity, the unity of all things in the last sorting category of mere consciousness prior to interpretation . . . What follows, then, is the sexual union reconstructed as a moment of primal communication . . . What is obtained [from this communication] is an unprecedented trope of inclusion . . . The logic of presence . . . attendant upon the reduction of all things to appearance [is] the reduction of all things to univocal meaning . . . continuity figured as the hum of subvocal, absorbed, multitudinous, continuously regulated "valved" voice.[89]

We already know why Whitman needed to "cure" what Grossman calls the human colloquy. With everyone in the nation caught up in the debate over slavery, no one would have disputed the value of a knowledge that would "pass all the arguments of the earth." What many critics still do dispute, however, is the identity of Whitman's dialogue partner.

Grossman speculates on the identity of Whitman's companion when he says their sexual union results in "primal communication." A further step toward identification might follow by comparing this companion with others Whitman chose. The "dumb, beautiful" street boys he liked to pick out of the crowd share at least one trait in common with this companion. They too are what we might call silent partners. Only the quality of their silence differs. The boys were silent because they were "dumb" in the sense of both inarticulate and unintelligent. The dumber they were the more appreciative they were of his gift—of gab. But Whitman's companion here is not dumb in either sense. He brings a knowledge that surpasses argument. What he communicates to Whitman is silent only insofar as it is intimated ("plunged your tongue to my bare-stript heart") rather than mediated by words. This intimation like "absolute acknowledgment" permeates everything else. Unlike a companion who might give of himself, this one does not reach an intimate relationship *with Whitman but releases an intimacy in* Whitman that spreads until it intimates itself into everything else, as peace and knowledge.

When it becomes common and everyday, as Whitman says everything must, this extraordinary experience must lose its mystery, and the silent partner his mystique. To be common, this dialogue partner must be equally available to everyone in America. As it happens, peace is the only partner that can answer this criterion. Peace, by definition, is a universal communication. If it could have communicated itself in 1855 rather than 1865, peace would have returned everyone in America into a silent agreement on principles. And this agreement would have been acknowledged as "silent" because peace would have returned to American speech the dimension "that goes without saying."

We commonly acknowledge this dimension of speech with a sound—"mm hmm"—that answers to Whitman's "hum." This "mm hmm" or "hum" of agreement does not communicate a message; rather, it acknowledges what linguists call a *phatic* dimension of speech, the dimension we use whenever we simply want to let someone know we are on the same channel, or within the same medium of communication or climate of opinion.

In 1855, very few people were humming. The terms that could hum along with their speech had entered into the terms of the national debate. When, in this passage, Whitman turns these terms of dispute back into a "hum," he means to bring the nation's arguments back into harmony with the preagreed-upon principles.

When conceived in personal terms, this "it goes without saying" aspect of national speech appears in the "unconscious," the place an individual stores motives. But by 1855 these motives no longer were in the unconscious, but had passed over into the nation's debate. Debate separated the terms of agreement from everyone's inner life, thereby enabling Whitman to experience these terms as if they were separate entities rather than inseparable qualities of an American identity. Usually the contents of the unconscious are too intimate or too indirect to lend themselves to experience. But when they appear on the conscious plane, they become available as an intimate but indirect form of communication, one capable of returning everything with which they communicate to the phatic dimension we associate with the unconscious.

As "what goes without saying," this phatic dimension can be considered the principle of peace within human consciousness. As the "preagreed" upon, this level of speech cannot lead to debate. When principles within this dimension come into mind, they more usually put arguments to rest.

They are the terms we reach when we come to an agreement. By 1855 the need to return these principles back into the status of the "preagreed upon" was deep and pervasive. Only the recovery of these principles could heal the nation, and only their recovery as "unconscious" or already agreed upon principles could safeguard them from compromise.

The Cure of the Nation's Colloquy

To conceive of communication as a means of recovering unconscious motives rather than, say, of arriving at an informed judgment is somewhat uncommon. Many believe that when free discussion of issues gives way to an unconscious allegiance to principles, genuine democracy leaves as well. Whitman would have agreed. He certainly did not want to forego discussion, but he did very much want to distinguish between discussions that deepened America's relation to its founding agreement and those that violated its terms.[90]

By 1855 so much of American conversation had fallen into the second category that Whitman invented a new dimension for American conversations. Whitman's "silent partner," or at least the way Whitman impersonated him, provides the best way to imagine this new dimension of conversation. He liked to go to Pfaff's, a broadway bar with a mixed clientele, and sit between two persons, more often than not utter strangers to himself. Then he would become "rapt up" in their conversation. Even when urged to offer his opinion on their subjects, he would simply sit and smile, saying he preferred to "absorb" what they had to say. "My own greatest pleasure at Pfaff's," Whitman recalled years later, "was to look on—to see, talk little, absorb."[91]

In sitting, absorbed in their conversation, Whitman gave personal form to the ingredient missing from most conversations, the primitive agreement they were founded upon. By not entering into conversations, Whitman kept these terms of prior agreement out of them as well. As a silent witness, he provided the terms of agreement the discussants could not violate. When Whitman describes this dimension of communication, it is in terms of restoring a soul: "First *POEMS, Leaves of Grass,* as of Intuitions, the Soul . . . descending below laws, social routines . . . to celebrate the inherent . . . By degrees to fashion for these states . . . the permanent Soul that speaks for all."[92] Among the social routines he intended his poems to descend below were the arguments keeping Americans apart: "Souls of men and women . . . It is not you I go argue for and about . . . I own publicly who you are, if nobody else owns . . . and see, hear you, and what you give and take; What is there you cannot give and take?"[93]

The unconscious or "soul" dimension of a speech is not what enters into speech as its message, but what lends force to the "give and take" leading to a message, what makes it take hold in its listeners. We acknowledge this force when we say someone speaks with conviction. Conviction does not result from a conversation but precedes it and can only be deepened by it. As the silent witness to the conversations in a nation of compromise, Whitman holds the place of conviction awaiting a new voice.

When witnessed by the voice of conviction missing from them, the nation's dialogue partners lose their oppositional quality. For Whitman all need for opposition, whether that of rebels against tyrants, or that of persons with opposing views, disappeared with the self-evident principles of our founding. So when listening to other Americans he imagined himself the bond of agreement preceding all American conversations. In this way he could "witness" oppositional views in the same way as he could envision natural objects, as man in the process of developing into himself.

By treating the nation's conversations as means of recovering its founding agreement, Whitman also changed the nature of the conversation partners: like the natural things evolving into man, they were an inchoate form of this bond of agreement in the act of developing into itself. Or put back into our original terms, they were in the process of regenerating the nation's bond.

The Regeneration of Oratory

This silent witness performed a valuable cultural service in saving a place in the nation's conversations for the founding principles. But his distance did not help the situation of the nation's speakers. In fact, many of the orators involved in the great debate used "distance" as a rhetorical sign—of their social superiority and mastery of the subject of debate.

In conducting the great debate, the nation's most renowned orators— Webster, Clay, Everett—set the tone for the nation's conversations. Their mastery of the art of partisan speech encouraged a contentious attitude.

The greatest of these orators learned their skills in the fields and the open air, where they put nature's things into service as tropes. Another trope they made use of was a wild and primitive child, who took enough delight in nature's things to believe they were part of him.[94]

The orator's attitude toward nature—as something to be used—was not an isolated one. In a sense the orator elevated into the domain of high art a stance he shared with other prominent American characters. The industrialist who harnessed nature's energies to factory duties, the businessman who traded in her raw materials, and the frontiersman who conquered the western wilderness shared the orator's attitude toward nature. All believed nature a proving ground to test their will. Through the orator's words these other men of will could achieve the prominence in culture they already enjoyed in their own spheres.

In watching an orator work a debate, the American people could find in his high calling a confirmation of the social status of the businessmen, industrialists, and frontiersmen who were no less dedicated in pursuing their will. The American masses could also find a pervasive structure of social organization corroborated in the debate. As the debate approached its conclusion, the gathered onlookers could prepare to terminate this association the same way they did when they voted with a majority. After their orator proved his superiority to an opponent, the members of the audience could return to their separate spheres with a renewed faith in the authority of social distance.

An orator measured his powers of persuasion in the audience's reaction and only secondarily in his opponent's response. In defeating an opponent, an orator proved his power to argue, but when he held the crowd they elevated him into a leader, one of nature's aristocracy.

To understand the peculiar nature of Whitman's distrust of the orator's relation to his audience, we need to take up our earlier discussion of natural law where we left it off. Then we saw that the orators who compromised the nation's principles based their compromises on one way of interpreting natural law. According to this interpretation, freedom was a possession a man gained when he opposed either natural conditions or a tyrant's will. The orators lent credibility to this understanding when they correlated the unruly energies of the masses with forces in nature. Then they brought the masses within the rule of their will.

For Whitman, any orator who put the masses into bondage to his tropes supported slavery. The orator's mastery over the masses was of a piece with a monarch's or a slaveowner's. This tradition of natural law as well as the social organization it confirmed was a remnant from feudal Europe, where it confirmed the rule of monarchs. But Americans could not abide the rule of such a law. The law of nature Whitman invoked did not establish rule over multitudes but released each person to a multitude of possible developments. Neither did this law of nature distinguish the tropes in man's mind from the things in nature. When considered in terms of evolution (which for Whitman was the law of nature), everything in nature was simply one or another evolutionary stage of man.[95]

The opposition between man and nature formed the shadowy backdrop for the national debate. This opposition made mastery—whether over nature, over others, or oneself—necessary. The great national debate confirmed the opposition by producing masters—of the art of debate. But Whitman believed America had already put an end to masters, by ending the opposition between man and nature. So Whitman's poetry for America ended the opposition at work in what he called the nation's "colloquy" by returning the nation's speakers to nature.

Returning the nation's orators to nature did not entangle Whitman in any struggle against them—such a struggle would only initiate one more cycle of mastery and rebellion, and one more issue to debate over. But his program did entail releasing the nature at work within these orators. Earlier we suggested that the orator turned things in nature into tropes in his mind. An orator also proved his self-mastery by taking possession of a dimension of himself, one he identified with the unruly energies of nature, translating this potential identity into an internal representation as well.

To return the orator to nature, Whitman devised a form of speech that reversed the orator's program of self-mastery. His poetry released both the inner self and the other inner representations within the nation's orators back into the common life they shared with natural processes and the American masses.[96]

But these internal forms did not return to nature unchanged. As we have seen, the nature Whitman identified with America had learned a great lesson from its passage through Europe's culture. When Europe's explorers turned nature's things into their inner representations, they formed a life nature shared in common with man. When the American descendants of these Europeans returned to nature, so did these internal representations, establishing a continuity between the inner life of things in nature and the inner life of mankind.

I cannot overemphasize the importance of the national debate as a context for Whitman's coming to understand this development. Whitman's poetry utterly reverses the relation between the nation's orators and their audience. Here no speaker can bring the masses into submission to his tropes because the masses continued in culture the process of evolution begun in nature. When released to the freedom of nature, the nation's speakers were liberated into the full run of development America's masses made possible.

A Conversation the Masses Develop

This last point provides a key for understanding the most elusive aspect of Whitman's poetry. Americans were not self-sufficient identities for Whitman but participants in the process of developing a common humanity. As men-en-masse, individual Americans were to be valued not in and for whatever they were individually, but for what they made visible in the ongoing process of development men shared with Nature. That ongoing process was what Whitman called the me/myself, and what we earlier called the common self. By identifying the self with the evolutionary process, rather than any single individual, Whitman turned individuals into motive forces or what we could call variations on the theme of the self.

Each individual became a transitional force, a personal resource with which other individuals could identify on their way to becoming someone else. Everything and everyone in Whitman's America are free and equal revelations of the self in process. But only the masses in culture can allow this development its full vista.

Hence merging with the masses becomes for Whitman the equivalent of total self-realization. Usually we reserve the expression "self-realization" to describe what happens when an individual becomes all that he can be. But in Whitman self-realization more readily occurs through relations with the masses. The differentiations and variations taking place within the masses can realize all that any individual can be.

But like the individuals comprising them, the democratic masses cannot be identified with any single self. The self reveals itself through the masses by passing through all of its heterogeneous developments. When identifying with this transitive power in the self he shares with the masses, Whitman describes himself as both in the game and outside of it, waiting and won-

dering. He requires both the single separate person and the man-en-masse
to give free run to this processual self as it transits through him. The single
separate person forms one pole (which he calls the "Me"), the masses another (which he calls the "I"), and the process of self-development takes
place between them.

This process is designated by what linguists call the middle voice of the
verb. We use the active voice to express an individual's power to act upon
the world. We use the passive voice when an individual is acted upon by
forces within the world. But in such expressions as "I celebrate myself and
sing myself and what I assume, you shall assume," the "I" is both active and
acted upon.[97] "I" cannot be separated from the activity which "I" celebrates. The "I" who celebrates is both the effect of this activity and its
agent. Only the middle voice could do justice to the participatory process
Whitman called the American man-en-masse, for only the middle voice
permits Whitman an accurate way to express the relation between the individual and the mass.

As an effect of the process of self-development, the individual cannot
separate himself from the masses. They realize the self the individual takes
part in developing. Self-reflection reestablished the opposition between an
individual and the masses, and this cultural attitude identified freedom as
an inner property an individual alone could possess rather than a motive
force inherent in the self Americans share in common. To effect a reversal
in the individual's relation to the masses, Whitman offered the individual
not a different way personally to experience liberty and equality, but a different way to experience personal separation: an American need not separate himself from the masses in order to look within himself.

The Individual

More precisely, in what would later become section 38 of *Song of Myself,*
Whitman identifies himself with the experience of separation common to
cripples, beggars, the diseased, and many other individuals the democratic
masses quite commonly exclude from membership. Unlike an individual
who can choose to distinguish himself from the masses, these outcasts do
not choose their alienation. They reverse the more usual relationship between the individual and the collective self, and this reversal permits Whitman to devise an unusual persona in his *Song of Myself.* Prior to his identifi-

cation with one of the urban poor, Whitman claimed a power to "become any presence or truth of humanity."[98] He earlier called this outline of endless embodiment the "spirit" of crowd life. While impersonating this "spirit," Whitman makes his outline available to whatever form appears before him. When embodied by these forms, Whitman usually experiences a gain in self-awareness. When the urban outcasts "embody themselves in"[99] him, however, Whitman loses consciousness of the "spirit" of crowd life. Identity with an excluded individual necessarily separates him from the spirit of the crowd. Then he articulates his experience of being embodied by these outcasts in terms of a loss of consciousness:

> Somehow I have been stunned. Stand back!
> Give me a little time beyond my cuffed head and
>   slumbers and dreams and gaping.
> I discover myself on the verge of the usual mistake.

The self who says "I" here is not one of the outcasts, nor is it Whitman's personal identity. It is the crowd spirit that loses consciousness of its common self when embodied by urban outcasts.

In this section of "Song of Myself" Whitman conflates two quite different ways of experiencing a separate self into a common scenario of loss. As the section makes clear, the separate self is the locus for not a gain in self-consciousness but a loss of collective identity. The individual, whether an urban beggar or a self-reliant man, is what results when the common self becomes forgetful of its identity with the mass of mankind.

In the remainder of what will become section 38 the speaker recovers consciousness by losing his need to remain separate or, as he puts it, the need either to regard himself with a "separate look" or to regard others with a "separative" look. Only when he abandons the need either to exclude or to feel excluded can the common self "remember" who he is.

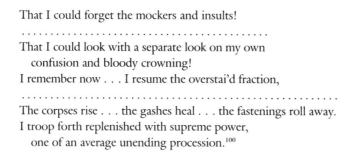

> That I could forget the mockers and insults!
> ....
> That I could look with a separate look on my own
>   confusion and bloody crowning!
> I remember now . . . I resume the overstai'd fraction,
> ....
> The corpses rise . . . the gashes heal . . . the fastenings roll away.
> I troop forth replenished with supreme power,
>   one of an average unending procession.[100]

What enables this speaker to remember cannot be distinguished from the unending process of human development, the "spirit" of the recuperated mass movement that does the remembering. Like the agent of all the other locutions in Whitman's poetry, the subject of these sentences is involved in a process taking place in the middle voice. "He" is remembered by the potential for further self-"development," the "crowd spirit" in which "he" participates.

In this section, Whitman does not reaffirm his faith in the democratic masses at the expense of the individual, but comes to terms with the greatest complaint directed against the masses by the single, separate person. In experiencing all the pain accompanying democracy's outcasts, he implicitly questions the power of American democracy to make good its claim to treat all as equals. As if to legitimize the outcasts' claims of inequity, Whitman experiences his merger with them as a loss of equality and identity with a common self. But this merger quickly gives way to a democratizing power. In a remarkable turn, Whitman transforms the exclusionary impulse into a social energy only a crowd can enable a man to give up. Whitman recovers relation with the democratic masses by sacrificing the exclusive sense of self his identification with the outcasts engendered to that more inclusive self an "unending" urban crowd makes available. As it turns out, urban crowds can enable Whitman to give up that exclusive self these same crowds produce in urban outcasts.

Death and Development

For Whitman the processes of species development cannot be differentiated from an individual's capacity for self-development. So when Whitman writes, "I hasten to inform him or her it is just as lucky to die, *and* I know it,"[101] he speaks from the perspective of potentially infinite self-development where all that any man can be takes priority over any individual development.

By positioning the total process of self-development of a species before the individual's, Whitman turns an individual's death into a stage in the self-development of the species. But this replacement of the logic of the person by the logic of the species changes the way a man represents his world and himself.

I indicated the consequences of this transformation for the nation's speech earlier when I claimed that persons and things in Whitman's poetry lived the life of apostrophes and vocatives rather than representations. I also suggested a rationale for their leading this life. As participants in a natural process, they could not be identified with any single moment or location, as their potential for further development took priority over whatever they may have already become.

Representations permit words to take the place of things, but in Whitman no one thing is possessed of sufficient self-identity to be replaced; everything is instead in the process of developing into and through everything else. Unable to be any one thing, everything becomes everything else—but through a very specific process. Earlier we identified America as Europe's memory turned inside out. When turned inside out, all the representations within Europe's memory lost their need to imitate what was, and acquired the power to motivate what could be. Everything in America is released from identification with a single representation—into unending development.

Consequently, relationships between Americans must be described not as confrontations between persons but as exchanges of political energies akin to the relation between motive and act. Instead of representing their identities, other persons function as motives for the further development of an individual. An individual then exists the way a motive does, as a goad to future action. And relationships between individuals become opportunities for mutual motivation, and further development.

This redefinition of personal relations performs political duties; it recovers the possibility of peace. No one person can pose a threat to another because no one person possesses a personal claim on another's existence. Informed by the logic of species, rather than individual development, Whitman's man-en-masse develops through the developments of other persons even as his own existence develops them.

Things in Whitman's world call forth potentials in other things in the way projects do in a psyche, and apostrophes do in a speech. Living apostrophaically entails living for the sake of the activity which the apostrophe calls forth. An apostrophe has no existence apart from the activity it motivates. Hence death can have no dominion over it. When one has no personal identity to lose, death cannot be experienced as a loss in this world.

An identity appropriates the world in representations best preserved in a personal memory. They compensate the individual for his anticipated separation from a world that will go on without him. An individual's represen-

tations mark his efforts to master his own future disappearance from the
world. Through them he takes possession of things, thereby mastering his
recognition of their separation from him and his separation from them.[102]
There are no individuals in Whitman's world but only "presences," what
he calls "eidolons" who call for further development to and for other
presences.

By treating America as if it were Europe's memory turned inside out,
Whitman completes the conversion of representations into apostrophes.
Through the use of apostrophe, everything in the outside world is permeated with qualities developed by memory. As externalizations of formerly
internal memories everything in Whitman's America is possessed of an associative, binding energy formerly associated with memory.

This last point is worth emphasizing because it is the source of the energy permeating the "body electric" of America's masses. When things and
persons in the world are indistinguishable from the intimate connections
at work in memory, they possess all the depth, and infinite associative
value, of impressive memories.[103] Instead of reactivating internal memories
to secure an individual against the loss of past perceptions, every percept in
Whitman's external world makes a demand on consciousness formerly reserved for internal memories. In Whitman's poetry, the individual speakers
are absorbed into the object of perception as if they were being remembered by it.

Again an analogy with individual memory can prove useful. When we
say a memory is too deep or traumatic to be recalled, we act it out rather
than remember it. Things in Whitman's poetry reverse the direction of
memory, projecting it into the future, and "act" the individual out of his
existence and into their processes. An individual cannot see such things, if
seeing means converting them into visual representations, but becomes
them, or rather becomes absorbed in what remains to be made of them.

Which is another way of saying that in Whitman's world things do not
represent what is absent but call forth what can be. Speaking without
benefit of representations entails an individual in becoming what he apprehends rather than remembering it, or standing apart from it.[104]

Longing and Speech

The psychic economy underwritten by representational discourse sustains
a sense of ever-renewed longing for a presence that can never be achieved.[105]

But, as we have seen, Whitman acts upon an utterly different potential in human speech. In experiencing his power of speech as a participation in a prior speech act—that is, nature speaking—Whitman reevaluates the psychic effect of language use. In his poetry, language affirms satisfaction rather than longing. As a personification of the power of speech calling him as well as everything else forth, Whitman experiences language not as a deprivation but as a plenipotential force. Insofar as he as well as everything else in existence has already given form to this provocative force, he fulfills a linguistic imperative by his simple presence. He is the form called forth by nature's ongoing apostrophe, the evolutionary process, so whenever Whitman refers to his experience of personal existence it is in terms of satisfaction. The self-sufficient motive force of liberty in nature expresses itself as his human form.

As Whitman makes clear in *Song of Myself*, this experience of self-gratification is utterly perfect:

> Welcome is every organ and attribute of me . . .
> Not an inch nor a particle of an inch is vile . . .
> I am satisfied.[106]

As the same section of the poem makes equally clear, however, this experience of satisfaction is not grounded in the self by itself but eventuates through a relation.

Unlike merely personal apostrophes, nature's speech does not exhaust itself fully in the personal energies it arouses. Whitman experiences its imperatives as the need to assume all forms. He experiences two different qualities in the liberty he embodies: not only does it satisfy him perfectly but it leads him to endless developments. He describes this second quality as longing, but a different kind of longing from a personal one based on "lack." Longing in Whitman is grounded in the experience of the masses of possible developments within each individual and is the motive for entering into them. It is a longing grounded in fullness rather than need.

In Whitman's poetry, longing does not result from social distance but is expressive of communal intimacy. In an early section of *Song of Myself* Whitman gives expression to the relationship between longing and communal intimacy by adopting the persona of a lonely young woman who watches twenty-eight young men bathing naked in a river. The power in this scenario derives from the unusual work to which Whitman puts this young woman's loneliness and longing. For she does not indulge in regret for what she cannot have. Her longing does not, as it would in Hawthorne or Poe, intensify our sense of her separateness. Instead the intensity of her longing fills in the distance between these young men. She fills the spaces separating the men with the fullness of her longing for all of them equally. As her eyes touch and caress the men, her vision claims an intimacy with the bathers greater than the intimacy with each other disclosed by their nakedness. Her intimacy with them is similar to that of nature:

> Little streams passed all over their bodies.
> An unseen hand also passed over their bodies,
> It descended tremblingly over their temples and ribs.
> The young men float on their backs,
> Their white bellies swell to the sun, they do not ask
>   who seizes fast to them,
> They do not know who puffs and declines with pendant
>   and bending arch,
> They do not think whom they souse with spray.[107]

Placed alongside what Whitman would call the "men's "insouciance," the woman's longing does not call attention to what she lacks; it reveals what these men do not (and perhaps cannot) know. Only her longing is intense enough to disclose the "connectedness" at work in the scene. These "unseen" relations, the intimate compact the men did not know they shared, becomes visible only through her sight. Her longing invests the men's associations with an intimacy more profound than their separateness.

By the end of the scene, the woman has not returned to her isolation. When she "seizes fast" to the men, her act of beholding is in deeper possession of them than is their consciousness of themselves. While they look at one another, the bond holding them together remains unseen. But when she beholds them, all the intimacy in their nakedness becomes visible.

Through this woman's longing Whitman makes visible an "unseen" power of speech. She sees the men the way a voice would name a thing into existence. Like a beckoning word, her sight invests the air bathing these men with bonding energy. Her sight makes visible the union to which her invisible caress aspires. In caressing each of the men, her eyes supply the bonds of intimacy holding them all together.

Re-Union

Whitman's redefinition of America as the universal medium through which everything passes to realize its full potential sounds like a form of personal mysticism, but for Whitman such a conception of America was a political program as well—the only one capable of realizing America's founding principles. In *Leaves of Grass* he turned liberty, equality, and justice into motive forces, and made these motive forces available once again to the internal lives of all the American people.

Whereas the nation's debate set liberty at odds with national union, Whitman's poetry made the liberty of full human development indistinguishable from union, which he defined as participation in the common process of human development.

He released liberty from its place within the mind of separate individuals and returned it to the full range of human existence. In so doing Whitman enabled individuals to experience liberty, equality, and justice as available motives, common to all experiences. Whitman identified them as the sources of those moments everyone knows when he feels most alive. Whitman takes such a moment—when what one is gives way to what one can be—and defines it as the ever-present and endlessly developing moment of American democracy.

At a time when Americans found their personal conversations filled with dissension and opposition, Whitman located a dimension of speech speaking through every other speech act—he called it nature's speech. When nature spoke, Whitman suggested, she uttered liberty, equality, and justice, the nation's founding principles. If they listened rightly, Americans could hear themselves uttered by nature speaking, as well. And if they entered into common voice with that speech, they could recover the harmony missing from their own lives. As forms of nature speaking, Americans could enter into relations with each other, in the same way they entered into relation with the thoughts, emotions, memories in their own minds. They could apprehend one another as a way of developing more of themselves, and they could acknowledge one another as silently and intimately as they did the most private reflections taking place in their minds, the ones that reminded them how they could become better.

Chapter Five

Edgar A. Poe: The Lost Soul of America's Tradition

> *If we respond to our world sensibly rather than speculatively, we feel that by nature men differ from one another and do so hierarchically, some being stronger, more beautiful, or more intelligent than others. The recognition of these distinctions and the building upon them are what is meant by civilization, and are what elsewhere and earlier made art possible. To say, as Americans now do, that equality is the system of nature is to affirm the theory in the face of contradictory evidence. Democracy, the political result of a blind, abstract assertion, is a system nowhere observable in nature save, perhaps, in a village of prairie dogs.*
>
> *—Edgar A. Poe*

Whitman believed he could include almost anyone in America's masses. But when considering the significance of Edgar A. Poe, the man as well as the artist, he relegated him to a character in one of his dreams, in a boat about to be swept out of America by a storm at sea.[1] Poe, in his markedly self-involved attitude toward everything, had already positioned himself apart from everyone and everything else in American life. Whitman, in his dream, only recognized the consequences of Poe's chosen alienation by seeing him on his way out of America—to someplace else.

But the late twentieth century has witnessed the return of Poe to America, after a lengthy stay in France. In a debate over Poe's "Purloined Letter" engaged in by a series of notable critics including Jacques Lacan and Jacques Derrida in France, refereed by Barbara Johnson and Joseph Riddel in America, and commented on by such notable younger American critics as John Carlos Rowe and Louis A. Renza, Poe has found a passport back into the United States, and a crucial place in the American canon.[2] The controversy engaging these critics has turned Poe's corpus into an opportunity to illustrate the theoretical resourcefulness of a new critical method.

The method is called deconstruction, and it involves exonerating a work's words from any claim to representational value, and exposing as false any claims for a self-present world for these words to represent. Poe, who was formerly a much discredited presence in American culture, has, in a weird inversion of cultural duties, helped legitimize this new and somewhat dubious French practice.[3]

Throughout this chapter I will argue that the use to which the French poststructuralists have put Poe is opposed to his own project. He did not, I will maintain, look forward to deconstructing a Western tradition. In the mid-nineteenth century, America was a country without a tradition, and Poe believed an artist very much needed a tradition in order to write anything worth preserving at all. Poe envisioned mid-nineteenth-century America as a modern world, and for Poe, living in a modern world meant being dispossessed of a tradition. By inventing the literary persona of a dispossessed aristocrat, Poe found a way to experience life in the modern world as a terrifying loss—of place, past, lineage, and position.

Poe actually had more in common with the work of French aristocrats of the time than with their twentieth-century descendants. Like Count de Tocqueville, these aristocrats needed to believe a democratic revolution could produce a cultural tradition. Hence they went to America to gather evidence for this belief. The French poststructuralists' rebellion against the logocentric tradition, and Count de Tocqueville's nostalgia for a lost French tradition, should, I hope, provide an informing context for Poe's own attitude—which differs from both of theirs.

The Return of Edgar Poe

With the reevaluation of his work, Poe has acquired renewed prominence as a literary figure. When we consider the use to which the French have put him, however, Poe seems less an author the French deem worthy of lengthy analysis and more a tutelary spirit capable of sanctioning new directions in French culture. This should not surprise anyone aware of the history behind the appropriation of American culture by the French.[4] In the early nineteenth century, Frenchmen traveled to America to confirm the success of their revolution. The observations about American manners, customs, and politics appearing in the journals, letters, and memoirs provided

France with a needed history for its revolution. For example, Alexis de Tocqueville, in that famous memoir of his travels in America, *Democracy in America,* recorded two different attitudes toward the American Revolution. One set of his views of American democracy fulfilled the wishes of those French revolutionaries who fancied democracy an ideal. They could read *Democracy in America* as a realization of their political aspirations. But those aristocrats who had been dispossessed by the French Revolution could use *Democracy in America* as what Freud would call a "screen memory." When the book was so used, its surface content gave way to a lengthy, aristocratic reflection on all that democracy displaced.[5] Those aristocrats who knew democracy only as "destruction, anarchy, spoliation and murder" could read *Democracy in America* in accompaniment with Tocqueville's other historical study, "France before the Revolution," as a joint historical lesson instructing an entire nation on how to give up its past.

As Bruce James Smith has reminded us, those aristocrats who lost their privileges and power in the Revolution were preoccupied with remembrance of all they lost.[6] And they could find few consoling prospects for the future. For them, *Democracy in America* was a work of cultural mourning, a long letter written by a disinterested French count and addressed to other aristocrats sharing his loss of a shared past. In *Democracy in America* Tocqueville turned his attention away from the world he had lost, and toward the possibilities opened up by the Revolution. The real trouble according to Tocqueville was that at the time of his visit to America, France had still not gotten the Revolution behind it.

American democracy seemed to have a history, even a tradition. In America Tocqueville believed he could discover the salutary historical consequences that should follow a democratic revolution. The Tocqueville who traveled to America needed to find a history for democracy capable of settling the disruptive events produced during the French Revolution into a meaningful sequence. By writing *Democracy in America,* Tocqueville invented for the French Revolution a historical memory his nation very desperately needed.

His historical account has been read as a direct, exhaustively researched series of insights into America's polity and manners. But in France these same observations served an unusual cultural duty. They became a means of reflecting upon historical conditions bereft of any other historical association. Tocqueville elaborates on the resources for cultural replenishment the New World made available for France in *Journey to America:* "The French of America . . . have preserved the greater part of the original traits of the national character, and have added more morality and more simplicity. They, like them [the French in Europe], have broken free from a crowd of prejudices and false points of departure which cause and will cause all the miseries of Europe. In a word they have in them all that is needed to create a great memory of France in the New World."[7] In such passages as this one, Tocqueville, the American traveler, strikes an unusual cultural bargain. He agrees, while in the New World, to give up as "mere prejudice" all the rich cultural inheritance that revolution at home had already lost.[8] But in exchange he must see America as that cultural past, that newly empowered democratic tradition, France so urgently needed to inherit.

Travel to America, then, does not really fill Tocqueville with nostalgia for all that he left behind in France. Instead America enables him to possess France's future as a peculiar kind of memory—one coming to France from America, her future prospect. Tocqueville produces a historical memory for a France that lost hers during the Revolution. In remarks such as the one about the French in America, he emphatically does not wish to be considered for citizenship in the United States. Through his reflections, written with vivid attention to details, their interrelationships and complications, he lets go of France's actual past by discovering a new past for France—just as arresting, equally rewarding, perhaps more inspiring—in America.

Tocqueville's travels to America produce cultural reserves he then sends home to post-Revolutionary France. These impressions of America, when qualified by the refined taste, discriminating judgment, and occasional hauteur bred in Tocqueville by his aristocratic lineage, cease to be "American" and become a cultural resource worthy only of France and her aristocratic tradition. When seen as a work of cultural mourning, *Democracy in America* seems less a history and more a romance with history for a nation without one, similar to what we earlier saw in Hawthorne's work. Like Hawthorne, Tocqueville thought that uncovering the "pathos" in historical events was more important than their mere transcription. The emotions and sentiments accompanying a culture's recollection of persons and events supply the memorable associations necessary to bind together a nation's persons and their actions. Both Hawthorne and Tocqueville discover an archaic reserve in America, a mnemonic chain capable of accommodating "new" events. Making the New World old gave the moment duration in Hawthorne; making America memorable enabled Tocqueville to endure what had become new in Old World France.[9]

The Other French Poe

While Tocqueville may share similarities with Hawthorne, he bears little resemblance to those recent French immigrants who have entered America with their commentaries on Poe's work as a visa. Far from desiring a memory or tradition for the French Revolution, these critics celebrate a revolutionary cultural force greatly superior to the one needed to overthrow the ancien régime in Tocqueville's era.

In a sense the recent French immigration to America has restored those historic losses Tocqueville traveled to America to get out of France's history. In affirming no cultural position more durative than the tracing of what Jacques Derrida calls a "*différance*"—a minimal distinction, an endless deferral of presence, a way to forget the past without reservation—poststructuralism is not so much the latest in modernisms but the ideology of modernity itself, one associating what we earlier called the cultural operations of "the new" with endless revolution. The French poststructuralist translates the endless displacement effected by the "shock of the new" into an inevitable and seemingly permanent revolutionary linguistic project. In a typical "deconstruction," apparently meaningful utterances get reduced to the differences among their signifiers. During a "deconstruction," the need for significance emerges as a recidivist symptom, signaling the residual anxiety of the reader. Any wish to attach the signifiers to signifieds, to make meanings of their differences, is identified as a reader's nostalgia for the most ancien of régimes—the entire Western tradition.

In its rhetoric poststructuralism describes itself as a late-twentieth-century version of the French Revolution, able to reenact the earlier revolution through the revolutionary eventfulness reputedly at play in language. Practitioners of French deconstruction generalize a reign of linguistic terror, condemning the desire for meaning, presence, or memory as aristocratic recidivism. Following an elevation of seemingly any linguistic utterance into a revolutionary event, poststructuralism is able to read any defense of literary tradition as a loss of the revolutionary power of language.[10] While they generalize the Revolutionary moment, however, French poststructuralists also reenact what Tocqueville found most disturbing about the French Revolution: its power to remove French culture not simply from an aristocratic past but from any past whatsoever. Without a past to which it could refer, France was unable to get the Revolution out of its history. By reducing the complex activity of Western culture to a "tracing" operation that erases cultural memory, poststructuralism relieves those attached to the Old World of any pain accompanying their memories of a lost past. For when reduced to these traces the lost past can be forgotten without too much regret.

When the French poststructuralists use Poe as a passport authorizing their entrance into America, however, they should not forget the actual pain Poe endured when he felt forgotten in the culture of nineteenth-century America. Poe has returned to America, but only after a one-hundred-year exile in France, a country that adopted him as a means of coming to cultural terms with the consequences of its revolution. Consequently, in reclaiming Poe, America should at least honor the distinction between the cultural duties to which the French have put Poe and what Poe made of nineteenth-century American culture.

The poststructuralists have implicitly turned Poe into a way of remembering a nineteenth-century America quite different from that of either Poe himself or their countryman, Count de Tocqueville. A reflection that did not find its way into *Democracy in America* but did appear in a letter Tocqueville wrote to another aristocrat, Count Chabrol, permits us to distinguish these three quite different versions of nineteenth-century America: Picture to yourself, my dear friend, if you can, a society which comprises all the nations of the world—English, French, German: people differing from one another in language, in beliefs, in opinions; in a word, a society possessing no roots, no memories, no prejudices, no routine, no common ideas, no national character."[11] This remark records Tocqueville's distress upon encountering a nation with no revered past upon which it can ground its convictions. In the recognition preserved by this remark, Tocqueville rediscovers in America the loss of a cultural past he left France to forget. Writing *Democracy in America* several years later enabled him to forget about this recognition by supplying America with all the memories, prejudices, rituals, and national character it needed. In doing so, however, *Democracy in America* differed from *The Collected Works of Edgar Allan Poe*.

Poe complained of America's cultural impoverishment and did not qualify this complaint with the vision of either poststructuralism's permanent revolution or Count de Tocqueville's "progressive democracy."

Liberalism as an Impulse without Ideals

Situating Poe within America's past rather than France's tradition reminds us of his problematic status within the American canon. The other American writers who appeared within the "Renaissance" moment in American literature founded a lineage for their labors within that moment. And each subsequent generation proved the value of this cultural legacy by failing to exhaust its wealth, no matter how liberally some later heirs might have distributed it.

Precisely because of its failure to be utterly incorporated within any present generation's terms, the "Renaissance" moment of our literary tradition remains intact. Unlike that of the other canonical figures subsisting within the "Renaissance" tradition, however, Poe's work always threatens to be exhausted upon a single reading. Acting less like a cultural resource and more like cultural debris, Poe's work sometimes threatens to communicate its inherent tendency toward cultural obsolescence to other works within the canon. Other works in the tradition display their cultural superiority by refusing to be outmoded, acting like some archaic resource in the midst of a thoroughly modern world. Cultural symbols for what surpasses the merely passing moment, these canonical works sustain what we have called the culture's collective memory. Because they cannot be replaced, they must be remembered.

Both in his work and in the literary principles supporting it, however, Poe insists on his cultural expendability. Indeed, Poe elevates the procedures of cultural obsolescence into a necessary criterion for taking the measure of his literary merit. Each of his principles of composition presupposes a distracted mass readership, an audience with so many other things on its mind that it should be able to have a work and be done with it, in a single sitting.[12] Reduced to their essential demands, these principles do not confirm the cultural superiority of a literary work, but align it culturally with technological artifacts. The literary qualities in these works can with a single exception also be found in labor-saving devices. Like literary works such devices are constructed for a single unified effect (a use value), and their "denouement" (how they should be used) is foremost in Poe's (or the inventor's) mind. The single difference separating Poe's literary work from a labor-saving device is that, unlike Poe's literary work, labor-saving devices do not exhaust their usefulness in a single sitting.

In adopting technical criteria for literary works indistinguishable from principles of technological efficiency, Poe subjects his literary artifacts to those modernization procedures Hawthorne wrote *The Scarlet Letter* to evade. If anything, Poe was more aware of the cost of modernity than was Hawthorne. The literary strategies each adopted differed so completely, however, that Poe might be called the cultural opposite of Hawthorne. The weird inversion of their cultural personae becomes most distinct when we juxtapose the manner of Poe's actual death with Hawthorne's "figurative" death. While in the Custom House, Hawthorne experienced the effect of the cultural substitution at work in the spoils system. Displacement followed by revenge for the displacement: these were the standard operating procedures of cultural representation in Hawthorne's Custom House. Poe did not lose any public office; he never had one to lose. But in his last week alive he impersonated one of a mob of voters in Baltimore, not unlike the majority whose collective submission to opinion Hawthorne held responsible for his "ejectment." After the votes were counted, Poe was found outside a polling station, dressed in the clothes of someone else, in a drunken stupor apparently paid for with the money he gained as the price of his vote. Shortly thereafter, Poe passed out of life as ignominiously as he entered it.

Indeed, Poe's curriculum vitae reads as the record of one violent displacement after another. First there was his illegitimate birth to an actress. Then, following her early death, his adoption by the wealthy Allan family of Virginia. But upon Poe's reaching majority, John Allan in his turn dispossessed Poe, leaving him to seek his fortune as a man of letters. Poe then passed from one literary periodical to another, his reputation in literary circles always attended by an air of scandal or corruption, until his death made final his displacement.

Whitman in his development of a cultural surplus of binding power and Hawthorne in his rediscovery of a cultural reserve both promoted the transmissibility of cultural energy. Everything about Poe, however, insists on a recognition of cultural disconnection, threatening the feasibility of the notion of cultural transmission I have been developing. A literary figure disaffiliated from both a cultural past and a future, whose writing insists on its availability to immediate consumption, Poe exhausts what we have been calling the liberal impulse (the sheer wish to be free from any cultural associations at all) by perfecting it. Whereas Emerson and Whitman might have idealized the negative freedom of this impulse into an emulable self-reliance, Poe reduced it to a force expending itself in the motion of displacement.

The Allegory of the Instant

In their design, Poe's tales construct monumental cultural disconnections. Narrated by murderers, thieves, "ennuyés," these tales all can be called allegories of the instant. A moment ago we remarked on Poe's critical demotion of the literary to the level of obsolescent technological gadgets. His narrators convert those activities we earlier argued produced obsolescence—the interrelated activities of repetition, displacement, and revenge—into the informing energies of their lives. Through the narrators of such tales as "Hop Frog," "The Cask of Amontillado," and "The Black Cat," the sheer negative mark of novelty, the transformation of "what is" into a "has-been," assumes the temporal dimensions traditionally afforded a tale. The revenge motivating each of these narrators turns each into an impersonation of the movement of the "new." Revenge commands these narrators simply to repeat in reverse, in an endless "has-been effect," what has been done to them. As the sheer force of displacement but replayed backward, an action performed out of revenge breaks down a narrative's tendency toward successivity even as it borrows on a narrative sequence for its informing shape. In its operation, revenge denies the substitution effect narrative sequence depends upon. In place of the smooth replacement of one action with another, such revenge plots as the one executed by the narrator in "The Cask of Amontillado" conflate all the action into the simultaneity of a nongenerative scene of origin.

Poe's revenge narratives spread out the simultaneity of action and reaction effected by revenge into a sequence, thereby lending the instant of revenge the appearance of an enduring moment. This appearance of duration, however, is truly that: a mere appearance. Through revenge, the punishment—the reversal of what has been—fits the crime. But in the case of Poe's tales, the crime is that of temporality—or, rather, modernity itself—the modern instant's production of has-beens. Without a character's revenge to replay their disappearance in slow motion, such modern moments as the ones preserved in Poe's tales would disappear without a trace.

When considered as allegories of the instant, these tales can be brought into closer relation to the subjects of Poe's poetry. Poe declares that he finds ideal subjects for poetry "in the waving of grain fields—in the slanting of tall Eastern trees—in the blue distance of mountains—in the gleaming of silver rivers—in the repose of sequestered lakes—in the star-mirroring depth of lovely wells."[13] All of these visionary forms derive their beauty from the elusive, evanescent, fleeting quality of their appearances. In foregrounding their apparitional as opposed to their representational qualities, Poe's poetry appears under the aegis of its own disappearance.

Withdrawing themselves from sight almost as rapidly as they offer themselves to the eye, these apparitional objects really demand to be remembered rather than perceived, and need the protection of representation. The imminent displacement of these forms always threatens to overshadow the delight evoked by their appearance.

Poe's tales, as we suggested, elaborated upon the allegories of the negated moment effected by the production of the "new." But his poems translate these negated moments into another realm, one populated by figures that either cannot pass over into the culture's representations or have already passed out of them. Unike Hawthorne's twice-told tales, Poe's allegories of the instant interrupt cultural transmission. In accounting for an instant of change unrelated to any previous or subsequent moment, Poe's tales violate a culture's collective memory. Productive of forgettable instants rather than renewable memories, impulses without either a personal or a collective memory upon which to impress themselves, these tales represent change as a sheer disruption rather than a force of progress.

As effects of the forces of cultural and temporal displacement, Poe's allegories differ radically from Hawthorne's. Through the allegorical figuration at work in Hawthorne's twice-told tales, the culture displayed its "exemplarity," the imitability accompanying persons, places, and things. In Poe's works, however, imitability is precisely what has been displaced. Hawthorne's personifications of the exemplary give way to Poe's impersonations of impulses that declare their difference from every other impulse. Persons exist in Poe's tales only to displace other persons, not to model themselves after another's example. Through allegory, Hawthorne places the significance human beings have for one another before the meaning they possess for themselves. But Poe reprivatizes allegory, stripping away signs of any meaning other than what Paul de Man has described as "its distance in relation to its own origin."[14] "Renouncing the nostalgia and the desire to coincide [with meaning]," in Paul de Man's elegant definition, allegory "establishes its language in the void of this temporal distance."[15] Existing only to name this void, Poe's writing allegorizes the loss of Hawthorne's cultural memory.

Cultural Change and *The Narrative of A. Gordon Pym*

To put the matter into terms that will make psychological sense of these abstractions, we might equate the allegory of the instant with what we earlier called cultural oblivion: the inability to be and to remember what one's being carries forward for a culture. This analogy makes the relation between Poe's work and cultural forgetting explicit. In anticipation of a later refinement on the point, we might here risk the assertion that Poe's work represents the oblivion cultural change effects. In order that we do not lose this rather abstract formulation, we need to locate it in a specific work. Both the content and the form of *The Narrative of A. Gordon Pym* concern the breakdown in a line of cultural succession. Since this narrative also gives dramatic emphasis to other themes and strategies at work in Poe's corpus, I will use Pym to organize this discussion of Poe, paying special attention to the attitude toward adventure, which differs fundamentally from Melville's in *Moby-Dick*.

As a narrative about a young American who abandons home for a life at sea, *The Narrative of A. Gordon Pym* stands in a long line of adventure narratives. And at its outset it seems to share their cultural function. In the nineteenth century, America had a vested interest in maintaining the myth of an endlessly open frontier. Purveyors of this cultural myth used adventure at sea and westward migration as equivalent settings for Americans to exercise their self-reliance. Crowded by the settled life of Old World America (which New England had become), a young American could realize independence by conquering a new frontier, whether in the West or at sea.

This correlation of a cultural "new man" with the effects of conquest had a tradition beginning in the Old World. America itself (which began as a confirmation of Old World ideology) shaped, through its presentation of wonders and facts without precedent in the Old World, a subjectivity independent of Old World belief. While many adventurers may have begun their journeys equipped with diaries to record the correspondences between Old World beliefs and New World revelations, most adventurers ended them with a record of observations without any analogue in either the predictions or the beliefs shaped in the Old World. Such unprecedented adventures constituted the ideological grounds for a validation of change in and for itself.

Presented with secrets and wonders antithetical to the subjectivity sustained by Old World beliefs, such adventurers assumed an unprecedented cultural role. While at sea, they opened themselves to adventures and experiences for no other reason than that they were available. Then, after returning home, they reshaped these wondrous perceptions into reflections, converting adventures in the New World into occasions for the "education" of the human soul and the "progress" of culture.

The autobiographies resulting from adventurers' reflections soon became numerous enough to change the relationship between human subjectivity and Old World life. Since the "new" subjectivity recorded in the adventurers' diaries could appear only after New World exploration, the New World became the ideological base of operations for the appearance of a man who could progress. Progress, change, and individuality merged into a mutually sustaining partnership. William C. Spengemann concludes: "Romanticism is only accidentally a congeries of conventional subjects and attitudes. It is essentially an acceptance of change—of movement, time and process—as an ineluctable dimension of reality, and hence the ground upon which reality must be apprehended . . . In a very important sense, the discovery, exploration, and settlement of America created the world that Romanticism was invented to deal with, the world of change." [16]

Among the values of this account of adventure in *The Adventurous Muse* is Spengemann's sense of the historical exchange at issue. In a way Spengemann's account fills in the picture sketched out by Stephen Greenblatt's analysis of the relation between Old and New Worlds. Whereas Greenblatt's "improvisational self" reshaped the ideological beliefs of New World natives to fit his own purposes, Spengemann's "new man" could abandon his Old World ideological beliefs but only after discovering a self shaped by his new experiences. Whereas Greenblatt's "improvisational self" took advantage of the new, Spengemann's adventurer replaced the collective belief of the Old World through his experience of the New World.

But it was not, as Spengemann suggests, "change" that became the valuable cultural commodity. Rather it was the new subjectivity produced by experience in the New World that underwrote the transition from the Old World to the New. Having granted cultural power to a self in the process of being formed by new experience, adventure in the new world released the explorer from his Old World beliefs. But the explorer had to compensate his culture for this exchange of an old for a new self with an account of his explorations. After returning home, the explorer became a narrator. His narrated reflections converted the sensations, wonders, and mysteries of the traveler into a stock of personal discoveries he could distribute to other persons who were also in the process of becoming "new."

According to the logic of cultural compensation underwriting adventure, the adventurer's increased subjectivity satisfied the Old World's cultural demand. He recorded this increase in subjectivity through the reflective consciousness which had been silenced following separation from home, but that he reactivated upon return. When applied to *The Narrative of A. Gordon Pym,* however, the logic of cultural compensation loses explanatory force. Cultural compensation cannot explain Pym's narrative consciousness. In *Pym* no reflective consciousness is able to convert an excess of sensational incidents into subjective experiences. Pym's perverse need for renewed sensation displaces his faculty of reflection, and the shocks resulting from each sensational incident refuse assimilation into the coherent explanations of reflective commentary. Without reflective commentary to record his reactions to life at sea, the Pym who disappears at the end of the narrative cannot be described as having undergone psychological development, nor can he be designated a changed man. Instead of changing or developing, he has simply been propelled from one incident to the next through an ever-ungratified and compulsive will for adventure.

Pym's will for sensational incidents preceded Pym's adventures. This perverse will did not quite proceed from his subjectivity; more accurately stated, his perverse will impersonated Pym's subjectivity. If we define subjectivity as what achieves cultural difference through experience, we cannot truly claim a subjectivity for Pym at all. Pym's will for adventure did not originate in any impulse from within his psyche; Pym had no desires of his own, but wanted what others wanted. And it was his relation to others' wants that put him into a compulsive relation to his world so unlike that of other adventurers.

Without the reciprocal interplay of changing mind and changing scene, without the inward change that should result from these adventures, Pym has no way to make good a cultural claim on them. Without the reflective act crucial to converting adventuresome incident into geographical or psychological information, the incidents remain just that: sensational events utterly unavailable to either culture or persons. What takes the place of the adventurer's psychobiography is a will to adventure recast in the drive to do what threatens both a culture and its persons: the perverse desire to do what Pym knows he should not.

This perversity utterly disrespectful of persons or their psyches comes into clear focus in the preface to the narrative proper. The tale of an adventurer who will not survive his own appearance within it (the chapter recounting Pym's final adventure is "missing"), *The Narrative of A. Gordon Pym* does not transmit an account of a return home from adventure but transmits a perverse will for continued adventure to the reader. This faculty of perversity in transition from Pym to Poe back to Pym and in turn to the reader is the true subject of *The Narrative of A. Gordon Pym.*

According to Pym, he hesitated to publish the narrative out of a fear that he lacked the literary ability to do the narrative justice and a doubt that the public would ever believe a story as wonder-full as the one he would write. But at the very instant Pym gives himself over to despair about the crediting of all he shall tell, Edgar Poe in his position as editor of the *Southern Literary Messenger* appears and urges Pym to go on with the unpolished account. Pym's very lack of sophistication, "Poe" argues, will lend needed credibility to the narrative. As if to prove his point, "Poe" publishes the first two accounts of Pym's tale under the "garb of fiction." [17] Yet in spite of the "air" of fiction, "the public were still not at all disposed to receive it as a fable" (248). As a result of the public's reaction, Pym quickly learns an unspoken lesson that he will not forget throughout the entire length of his narrative: no matter how wildly inconceivable a tale of adventure might seem, it cannot be written about and not be believed.

Strengthened by this understanding and perhaps in order to forewarn the reader of things to come, Pym prefaces his tale with a perverse act of will prefigurative of the many to come: he reappropriates his narrative from Poe by exposing Poe's fiction as his own truth. In so doing, Pym displays a knack for compressed expression that will not reappear until the end of the narrative. But even this expression has a tactical function. In the short compass of the preface, he coopts any tactic to expose his narrative, thereby preempting the prerogatives of any reader's will over his personal account. In beginning by exposing not the fictiveness of fact but the factuality of fiction, Pym establishes the need to displace one will with another (whether the will of a person or the will underwriting the way persons appropriate the truth of their world) as his reality principle. In recording his fears over the public's incredulity Pym does not merely anticipate but identifies with public skepticism as another appropriate persona for his perverse will; or rather he identifies with it just long enough to realize that skepticism is too ordinary an attitude to assume when confronted with a life of adventure. He dissipates doubts by identifying with them until doubts themselves dissolve into Pym's will to write a narrative unbelievable enough to pervert doubt into the will to believe.

In dramatizing the struggle between his will to write his narrative and the doubt that it will be believed, he evokes a correlatively perverse will in the reader. Then he indulges that will with a matching narrative. Instead of supplying psychological developments, geographical information, historical documentation, Pym justifies his adventure by identifying it with his readers' simple compulsion to believe in what will grant the greatest excitement to the will. Inserting a wedge between what a reader does in fact believe and what a reader wants to believe, Pym invests this space between him and them with a promise of shocking excitement that becomes its own justification. The desire to believe becomes so compelling as to turn excitement into its only ideal. And since the ultimate form of this excitement is absolutely disrespectful of the lives of persons, it is no wonder that in the preface the act of taking possession of a person's life (Pym's by Poe) become indistinguishable from dispossessing another of it (Poe's by Pym). Once a personal life becomes identified with the will to risk it, that personal identity belongs to no person. It passes through persons as a force capable of taking away their lives.

A New Self-Reliance

Put differently, in *Pym* the "subjectivity" adventurers put forward as the enabling justification for the loss of their Old World simply did not materialize. The perverse will to adventure reduced subjectivity to an excuse for the existence of the faculty of perversity, then displaced it altogether. The adventurer in Pym did not, upon return "home," give way to a narrator whose reflections would discover valuable experiences to be shared with the rest of his culture. The struggle between Pym and Poe over the "truth" of the narrative did away with the need for such a personal transformation in Pym, thereby turning the relation between narrator and adventurer into just one more occasion for excitement.

Despite Poe's relegation of the culturally uncompensated status of adventure to the space of a brief preface, I want to pause over it. For the insufficient value accrued either for "progress," for home, or for the self reveals the peculiar cultural status of the displacement at work in *Pym* and the rest of Poe's work. We might best ascertain the significance of *Pym* for Old World culture if we imagine Count de Tocqueville reading it. In the French Revolution, Tocqueville had already lost a past to a perverse will to adventure comparable to Pym's. And since he came to America to discover a post-Revolutionary tradition for French culture, *Pym* would have truly frustrated him. For *Pym* reactivated that same endlessly perverse will that destroyed the count's old world, and threatened the entire lineage of post-Revolutionary French culture.

Unlike Count de Tocqueville, who came to America to discover a tradition of progress reminiscent of an ancien régime, Poe imagines noblemen like Roderick Usher, who descend into a past world utterly separated from their present one. The preface to *Pym* prefigures and parodies the cultural transmission that should be at work in this genealogical descent, for in that preface Poe dramatizes the disappearance from America of the scene of the transmission for what we have called a cultural memory.

As we have suggested, the return home of the adventurer should permit him to add his incidents to the store of a culture's memory. Indeed, as Washington Irving makes clear in the following passage from his *Sketch Book,* adventure at sea produced in the adventurer a strong memory of home: "The land . . . now vanishing from my view which contained all that was most dear to my life, what vicissitudes might take place in me before I should ever visit it again." [18] With the possibility that he might not ever return home, the adventurer secrets home into the place of memory, and with it his reflective self. In an implicit cultural contract, the reflective narrator agrees to appear only after the return home, whereupon he converts the sensational incidents at sea into meaningful experiences. His reflecting consciousness does not reflect upon experiences while undergoing an adventure. Such reflections would detract from the intensity of the adventure. But he produces significant experiences by literally domesticating adventure, after returning home.

Guided by the terms of the adventurer's cultural contract, we can recognize a subjectivity quite different from Pym's in this quotation from Henry Dana, the author of *Two Years before the Mast,* which, published two years after *Pym,* was the most popular adventure narrative in Poe's day: "I could not but remember that I was separating myself from all the social and intellectual enjoyments of life. Yet, strange as it may seem, I did then and afterwards take pleasure in these reflections, hoping by them to prevent my becoming insensible to the value of what I was leaving."[19] The permanent loss of home feared by the speaker of these lines only heightens his need to remember home. His fear turns his personal memory of his homeland into a moral faculty capable of preserving the values at work in his national culture. Only memory can preserve both the homeland and the adventurer from the extinction always risked during an adventure. His continuous reflections upon the homeland he has "lost" safeguard the "homebody" in the adventurer. Along with the memories of his home accompanying him throughout his journeys, an adventurer conceals a person within his memory who will, on the return home, develop the ability to be at home with any of his adventures, by remembering them for his homeland.

Unlike other adventurers Pym can remember neither his home nor his adventures, and he persistently disassociates his narrative from the workings of "mere memory" (247). Instead of recollecting his life at home or reflecting upon its incidents, Pym separates the impressions, the "powerful influences" his narrative will induce from a "minute and connected" chain of human memory (247). In place of a faculty of memory, Pym exercises a faculty of perversity: a compulsion to displace persons, events, and things from their places within a chain of memorable recollections. Without a memory upon which they can be impressed, Pym's incidents surge up as one overpowering impulse after another with nothing more lasting to sustain them than the perverse will for another.

As Dana's statement makes quite clear, only through a vivid memory of the past can one experience anything at all. As the site for a cultural loss without the protection of a memory, the preface to *Pym* dramatizes the loss of any connection whatsoever with a past. And in place of an adventurer's reflective record of his experiences, Pym's account is finally of nothing more enduring than his own disappearance from it. An adventure story making total the oblivion at work in every act of his will, *The Narrative of A. Gordon Pym* is not an adventurer's account but a narrated instance of the obliteration of a person.

So *Pym* does not corroborate the cultural usefulness of the adventurer's narrative, but exposes its cultural limits. Earlier we suggested that the adventurer's narrative sustained the culture's belief in self-reliance. As accounts of the individual's freedom to act in a realm independent of others, these adventure narratives worked in mutual relation with the political doctrine of western expansionism. Usually, however, the independence of these adventurers was not total. Recollection informed by nostalgia for the place of birth customarily kept the "self-reliant" western adventurer in "reflective" relation to the East. In utterly disconnecting the adventurer from the rest of culture, however, Poe severs the relation between these two worlds. The incidents resulting from this severance untouched by recollection surge up as shocks of excitement whose extraordinary status signals their utter "disrelation" to anything else. In this sense we might read *Pym* as the critique of the doctrine of self-reliance underwriting the form of the adventure novel. Self-reliance carried to its extreme, *Pym* exposes the negative freedom underwriting the doctrine as "absolute irrelation,"[20] a total cultural oblivion endemic to the "shock" of the new.

The Loss of the Spirit of Place

Pym, who leaves home without regret, has no sense of any past that could be threatened by the new. Throughout the rest of Poe's tales, however, many characters seem to have returned to present life from out of some lost past. Speaking an unplaceable aristocratic dialect, they always seem slightly indignant over the inadequacy of the cultural milieux in which they presently find themselves.

In our introductory chapter we discussed the ways in which Washington Irving and others reabsorbed the discontinuity of the American Revolution into the continuities of place and time. Rip Van Winkle, for example, by his visionary encounter with Hendrick Hudson, the founder and guardian spirit of the locale, carried into new America the approval of old America, enabling Tarrytown to drop the Revolution out of its history and restore its continuity with the past.

In tales like "The Masque of the Red Death," "Metzgenstern," and most particularly "The Fall of the House of Usher," however, Poe's narrators react to the oftentimes violent disappearance of a genius loci, a tutelary presence who safeguards a culture's place. Now the notion of a genius loci is itself rather archaic. When revived from the cultural reserves, it is usually as a quaint poetic superstition rather than a cultural fact. Or, as Geoffrey Hartman cogently demonstrates, the genius loci remains to remind us of the ways romanticism did not adequately compensate the ancient world for the loss of the classical tradition. When confronted by the genius of a man of letters, "the *genius loci* can rival Genius as an influence, for it suggests the possibility of a more natural (unselfconscious) participation in a pre-existent or larger self. England as Gloriana and America as Virgin Land are visionary commonplaces indistinguishable from an 'idol of the tribe' or 'collective representation.' Though bounded by period and place, the *genius loci* is as all-pervasive in its domain as a climate of opinion." [21] Through the confrontation with this genius loci the present can so blend with the past as to bring both present and past forward into the prospect for a future.

Our discussion of Whitman disclosed the ways in which America realized the spirit of the past. In our discussion of Hawthorne we considered the ways in which he recalled the spirit of the past to the present age. But unlike them, Poe in his tales rehearses the utter disconnection of the spirit of the past from his age. Much of the terror in his tales derives from their power to render absolute the disconnection of the new age from a past. [22]

In *The Narrative of A. Gordon Pym,* Poe disclosed a need for the new as the compulsion underwriting Pym's narrative. This compulsion impersonates a human form and survives him in the reader. The absence of a reflective consciousness guarantees the continued existence of this compulsion. In its "shock," the compulsion for the new obliterates reflection. Without such a reflective consciousness, however, no past can be brought forward into the present.

"The Fall of the House of Usher" eerily dramatizes the terror in this loss. When Roderick Usher summons the narrator to witness the disappearance of his entire lineage, he addresses a man utterly disqualified to restore the tradition of the house to cultural memory. As the last of the house, Usher needs a cultural witness to transmit its legacy. The friend, however, cannot do the work of cultural memory—for he is under the dominion of what we have called the modernist compulsion. So he treats the summons as an occasion to relieve the "dreary" boredom of an otherwise uneventful life. After reading Usher's letter he notes only its "wildly importunate" quality, so different from the "reserve" of one upon whom has fallen the duty of the "undeviating transmission" of the "time-honoured" House of Usher(97). The unusual turn in his friend's character does not lead the narrator to reflect on what is worthy of remembrance in this lineage. Instead, it becomes an occasion for the narrator to "feel the vivid force" of a new sensation made possible by "a pestilent and mystic vapor" (103).

However insistent on not understanding his friend the narrator may be, Roderick Usher makes explicit his reason for calling upon the narrator in the song "The Haunted Palace." In this song Usher records both his lineage's past ("once a fair and stately palace" in a happy valley) and the loss of the past in the present ("And travellers now within that valley" see "a hideous throng rush out forever") (103). In this poem Usher has stored the tradition of his house within a cultural form he wishes the narrator to preserve and pass on. Like Hendrick Hudson in his apparition to Rip, the spirit of democracy addressing Count de Tocqueville, or the scarlet letter appealing to Hawthorne in the Custom House, Roderick Usher wills that his friend the narrator pass on the spirit of his lineage. In his response to this plaintive appeal, the narrator distinguishes Usher's need for the preservation of a cultural patrimony from his own more urgent need for present excitement. More accurately, his need for excitement enables him to separate his present world from Usher's last wish. Unlike Rip, Tocqueville, or Hawthorne, Poe's narrator does not carry the spirit of this presence from a past world forward but utterly disengages his own present needs from the spirit's demands.

Listening *with* his need rather than *to* Usher's words, the narrator has ears only for the despair in Usher's tone, the abandon with which Usher delivers himself of speech: "I lack words to express the full extent, or the earnest *abandon* of his persuasion . . . The result was discoverable, he added, in that silent yet importunate and terrible influence which for centuries had moulded the destinies of his family, and which made *him* what I now saw him—what he was" (104). Usher wants the narrator to lend him his memory, where his lineage can be stored before the total decay of his house. But the narrator hears the request for his reflective consciousness as a thrilling speculation on the "sentience of vegetable things." And his refusal to provide the reflection on the past Usher so urgently demands continues until the tale ends. But it never enters either into the tale's theme or into its narrator's consciousness. Even Usher's death, when recast into an event no different from those in one of the thrilling narratives the narrator reads as Usher dies, turns into an occasion for excitement. Nowhere else in American literature is the alienation of the past by the present represented so starkly. And no one else in American literature expresses so clearly the horror involved in securing the spirit of the past to the need for present excitement.

Hawthorne Twice Reviewed

Throughout Poe's work there are figures—Ligeia, Helen, Berenice come to mind as immediate examples—whose present existence depends upon references to "lost" civilizations, epochs and aeons separated sufficiently from Poe's present to have no memorable shape whatsoever. Characters with eyes "fuller . . . than the fullest of the gazelle eyes of the tribe of the valley of the Nourjahad," a chin resembling that of the "god Apollo revealed but in a dream to Cleomenes," with complete beauty like that of "Nicean barks of yore" exist without reference to the present conditions of any living reader.[23]

Poe's penchant for looting temporal periods contemporary culture must invariably leave behind provides him with a frame for understanding his own cultural position. Authorities in the American canon customarily borrow from the psychologists' models of human development to find in Poe an example of adolescent American culture, whose lurid tales must be left behind as a sign of achieved literary maturity. When Yvor Winters called Poe vulgar, F. O. Matthiessen relegated him to his footnotes, T. S. Eliot declared him permanently adolescent, and Henry James pronounced his audience unreflective, they displayed the maturity of their own judgment.[24] These later arbiters of cultural taste had plenty of predecessors in Poe's own day. Not the least eager to discredit him as disreputable for culture was the man Poe prepared to transmit his work. The executor of his literary estate, Rufus Griswold, a man whose work was the subject of more than one of Poe's scurrilous reviews, warmed to his task with the energies of a narrator in one of Poe's tales. Bent on revenge against a man who had insulted his achievement, Griswold seemed more eager for the obliteration than the preservation of Poe's estate.[25]

Nonetheless, one figure within Poe's culture shared many of his concerns. And Poe recognized this similarity with sufficient acuity to make Hawthorne's "Twice Told Tales" the subject of two remarkable reviews.

Poe neither explicates Hawthorne's work nor quite carries forward Hawthorne's vision, but uses the review format to stage a perverse reenactment of the loss of cultural memory we found at work in "The Fall of the

House of Usher." What transpires in the reviews is a displacement of the aesthetic at work in Hawthorne's tales by a version of Poe's philosophy of composition. Whereas twice-telling was Hawthorne's means of entering into relation with the past, the critical repetition at work in Poe's two reviews reneges on the possibility for any relation with time other than forcible displacement. So whenever a narrator in one of Hawthorne's tales effectively restores a present relation to a past, Poe's *re*view reduces the tale to an "example" of "novelty." Whereas Hawthorne attached the material trace of the scarlet letter onto a memory capable of preserving it, Poe transfers every person, place, and fact into sites that never could exist anywhere but within Hawthorne's tales, where they become self-contained sensations, utterly disconnected from the present, existing only to be used up, then forgotten, by readers.

Following his reduction of Hawthorne's tales into momentary impulses separated from any reflective consciousness capable of preserving them, Poe did not have to reflect upon Hawthorne's work, but produced a literary way to forget them.[26] In short, Poe's reviews became a cultural opportunity for Poe to separate the faculty of collective memory from Hawthorne's work, replacing it with his own theory of instantaneous consumption. Once it was converted into the "double" of Poe's philosophy of composition, Hawthorne's work could become as forgettable as one of Poe's tales.

This displacement by Poe of Hawthorne's faculty of memory becomes clearest during his discussion of Hawthorne's allegory. When he considers those moments in Hawthorne's allegories when the past reappears, Poe quickly blocks the place of its return. Instead of recalling the past as Hawthorne does, he treats Hawthorne's recollective accounts as if they were allegories of the instant, "with no stronger tie with the past than a ghost has with the present: having *never more* of intelligible connection than has something with nothing, never half so much of effective affinity than has the substance with the shadow" (445).

Nevermore

Now, what is most striking to the ear of any student of Poe is the presence in this review of the words "never more." In Poe's most popular work, "The Raven," "nevermore" functions as a dissonant sound, the resonance of a noise coming from somewhere and something else. Uncalled for by the speaker yet what must somehow return to his thoughts, the sound of the word carries all the force of the loss of his lover Lenore. In the poem the sound separates the speaker from his need to remember his dead lover. Appearing within Poe's second review of Hawthorne, at the moment when Poe discusses Hawthorne's literary relation to his past, the word has the curious effect of exempting Poe, like the speaker in "The Raven," from any need to reflect on the past.

What takes the place of reflection in Poe's review of Hawthorne is what takes the place of reflection in "The Raven," i.e., the word "nevermore." Through the inclusion of this sonorous word, Poe relocated Hawthorne's work within a work of his own. Unlike Hawthorne's tales, Poe's works kept the past out of the present. His two reviews removed a past from Hawthorne's work as well, enabling Poe, who could find no justification for his contemporary age at all, to destroy the collective memory, the element in Hawthorne's work capable of providing the present with a cultural rationale.

Mourning and "The Philosophy of Composition"

Without benefit of the faculty of memory, Poe's entire corpus reads like an unsuccessful work of mourning. In Freud's terms, the work of mourning is an intrapsychic process occurring after the loss of a loved one. When successful, this work permits a person to detach from this object. But the process can be long and difficult. Through mourning, a person comes to terms with life and death, the absolute limits of human existence. When successful, mourning separates the dead from the living, converting the dead into memories the living can *choose* to recall. Another dimension of Poe's work appears when interpreted within this context. Since in "The Philosophy of Composition" Poe reflects upon a poem whose subject is a work of mourning, we can encounter this other dimension there.

When the speaker in that essay distinguishes his work from that of other writers, he confirms his rational, even calculating control over his material, thereby demonstrating the power of his will as a principle of composition.

> Most writers—poets in especial—prefer having it understood that they compose by a species of fine frenzy—an ecstatic intuition—and would positively shudder at letting the public take a peep behind the scenes, at the elaborate and vacillating crudities of thought—at the true purposes seized only at the last moment . . . at the wheels and pinions—the

> tackle for scene-shifting—the step-ladders and demon-traps—the cock's feathers, the red paint and the black patches, which, in ninety-nine out of the hundred constitute the properties of the literary histrio. (454)

Should we reduce this manifesto to the barest statement possible, we find in it an intention to bring the reader backstage and expose the merely performative, the literal as opposed to the literary, quality of a literary work. But this analytic statement cannot be distinguished from a performance in its own right. When we consider the iteration, then the reiteration, of the elusive qualities of the artifact he is about to describe, we find that the speaker wishes not to reflect upon the poetic process but to act out an analytic exercise. In announcing his decision to expose the "staged" quality of his work, the speaker has staged and then performed this very announcement. Consequently, his glimpse backstage provides not a "critical" perspective, but only another staged version of the same activity resulting in "The Raven."

To see "The Philosophy of Composition" as only a melodramatic rehearsal of "The Raven" is nonetheless to miss an important difference between the two versions. For this variation violates the time and import of the action of the original enough to make it read as a parody. Moreover, this rehearsal violates the very effect the essayist claims he aspired to in the poem. After the speaker isolates "Beauty" with its "intense and pure elevation of soul" as the purpose of the poem, he reduces the activity eliciting this effect to the mechanical operations of a "sonorous" refrain. His need to continue hearing this "resonance" leads him to a decision to use "the long *o* as the most sonorous vowel, in connection with *r* as the most reproducible consonant (460). This description of an elevation of soul attained through the mechanisms of rhyme is not the only reduction of emotional response this analysis brings about. The death of the beautiful Lenore, the apparent "cause for the melancholy of the speaker in "The Raven," itself becomes a mere excuse for the sonorous refrain "nevermore." By reinterpreting the death of Lenore as a mere excuse for resonant vowels and consonants, the speaker has seemingly overturned the stipulated table of values in the poem.

I say seemingly because the "mechanism" informing the analysis does bear a subtle resemblance to the mourner's attitude in the poem. Like the speaker in "The Raven," the analyst in "The Philosophy of Composition" wishes to separate the sounds in the poem from their source. In separating grief from its object, both speakers, on second thought, wish to lose touch with the actual cause for mourning. Like the "analyst," the speaker in the poem needs to treat mourning as a pretext for another action. When we follow the lead of this similarity, however, we become uncertain about which is the original and which the rehearsal in these two works. For the speaker in the poem, when he, too, begins with only the raven's sonorous and somber repetition of the refrain "Nevermore," seems upon our reflection not to be distracted so much as calculating, not at a loss but sufficiently composed to reenact the procedures of the analyst:

> Then, upon the velvet sinking, I betook myself to linking
> Fancy unto fancy, thinking what this ominous bird of yore—
> What this grim, ungainly, ghastly, gaunt, and ominous bird of yore
> Meant in croaking "Nevermore." (38)

Still, there is the stark fact of the beautiful lady's death (which Poe has elsewhere described as the ideal subject for poetry). And her death releases enough pressure to make us hear the dissociation of the sound from its significance as the desire—on the part of *both* speakers—to forget that the lady has died. Both speakers act upon a wish to release the memory of her death from the fact of the corpse and attach it to a beautiful resonant word. In both the poem and the essay, then, the memory of Lenore gets attached to the word "Nevermore." When so attached this memory ceases to recall her actual person and becomes instead an echo—of the word "Nevermore."

This startling transference of mnemic qualities occurs most clearly in the poem. Following the climactic "Nevermore," the speaker shrieks,

> Be that word our sign of parting, bird or fiend . . .
> . . . .
> Leave my loneliness unbroken!—quit the bust above my door!
> Take thy beak from out my heart, and take thy form from off my door!
>   (39)

When the speaker issues these commands to the bird whose response is already a foregone conclusion, he simultaneously demands the opposite result. Or rather, he splits the figure he addresses into the raven and its sound. He displaces the loss he felt in the death of Lenore onto a wish for separation from the raven, and doubles his attitude toward separation. The speaker can hear in "Nevermore" the denial of separation he mourns rather than wills. Through the raven's "Nevermore," the speaker discovers a way to desire the separation he did not want.

"Nevermore" affirms yet denies Lenore's absolute separation. It functions as both a repression of her death and a return of the repressed material (in the echo of "Lenore" in "Nevermore"). In reaffirming its status neither as a sign nor as a referent but as a resonance, "Nevermore" never stops being an echo of another word, "Lenore," a proper name which has lost its living referent. Thus the word "Nevermore," in the series of transformations it undergoes through the stanzas of the poem, becomes not a word but an echo, the audible equivalent of a "memory of a memory."

By the poem's conclusion, the speaker becomes absorbed enough in this scene of memory to seem less a detached observer of it than its shadow. So again he seems to differ from the analyst who never hesitates to treat the scene as a spectacle available for analysis. In commenting on the final scene in "The Raven," the analyst writes, "The reader begins now to regard the Raven as emblematical—but it is not until the very last line of the very last stanza that the intention of making him emblematical of *Mournful and Never-ending Remembrance* is allowed to be seen" (463). Now this gloss on the lines rings true enough. These lines, in their transformation of speaker, scene, and raven into mere signs of memory separated from any significance, do indeed bespeak an endlessly "returning" or echoing quality of an always forgotten memory. But the speaker's need to repeat these lines from the poem within another context is somewhat startling. Throughout his analysis of the poem, the speaker has not, as he promised, given us a backstage glimpse that translates the poem into verse props. Nor has he quite replicated the mental condition of the poem's speaker. Rather, in reducing any potential significance suggested by the poem to the mechanical activity of refrains, sonorous sounds, and repetitions, he has in his analysis reenacted the role of the raven.[27] The analyst, like the raven, has reduced potentially dangerous repressed material to the level of mere sounds. Moreover, the analyst has repeated the bird's sonorous refrain not as its sounds but as his own insights. The eyes the speaker of the essay brings to rest upon the poem are not the eyes of a critic who would deliver the poem over to significance. In their relentless exposition of the repetitions, their echoes and refrains, the analyst's eyes never see into the actual meaning of the poem but only see what the speaker in the poem hears: the teasing, tantalizing pretense, the "Nevermore" quality the poem provides instead of a meaning.

Like the raven's, the analyst's eyes also "have all the seeming of a demon's that is dreaming." Moreover, his function, like the raven's, is not to interrupt but to repeat and even perpetuate the dream of Lenore. That is why the critical essay finally seems less an explication of "The Raven" than a context in which "The Raven" can repeat itself; or, rather, the poem and the essay truly provide each other with contexts. When seen from this perspective, the poem interprets the essay, for the poem provides the only context in which the purely mechanical, "ravening" activity (what we could call the "Nevermore" quality) of the essay can *seem* to make sense. We cannot quite say, however, that either the essay or the poem ever quite manages to make sense of the other. Each instead functions as a "mournful and never-ending remembrance" of the other.

The Detective in the Philosopher

If the speaker in the essay reenacts "The Raven" while pretending to explain its significance, he does not fundamentally differ from the narrator in Poe's tales of terror, who also acts out rather than reflects upon his relation to the situation.

He is less obviously similar to the narrator in Poe's tales of ratiocination who, as a permanent witness to Monsieur Dupin's remarkable powers of deduction, manages to repeat the crimes to be solved. A crime, like a tale of terror, intensifies the sensational quality of existence. Everyday events lose their routine quality and partake of the sensational nature of a crime. As possible clues, everything becomes charged with potential significance. Following a crime, and the intensity attending the search for the criminal, the everyday world almost turns into a memory of the criminal event. Like every other memory in Poe, the everyday world then turns into raw material for his work of forgetting.

This reduction of the world to the dimensions of a memory explains the urgency in the need for a solution to the crime. Only the solution can restore presentational rather than representational value to the everyday world. In Poe's tales of ratiocination, however, Monsieur Dupin does not acknowledge the inherent value of everyday life. Hence he does not need to restore its presentational aspect. In "The Murders in the Rue Morgue," the narrator's need to solve a lurid crime, complete with stabbings, animal screams, and throat slashings, barely disguises his need to ward off the boredom of his existence with sensational incidents. Monsieur Dupin's acts of ratiocination do not diminish the narrator's (and, by extension, the reader's) will for sensation but provide it with a rationale: through Dupin, the narrator's need for excitement is preserved, but proceeds under the cover of a rational pursuit of a criminal. When, however, Dupin's intellectual activity uncovers an orangutan who is even more responsive to the impulses of the moment than the narrator, his discovery does not result in a return of the world to the realm of reason. The orangutan's motive for murder cannot be distinguished in any meaningful way from the narrator's (or the reader's) need to solve (and by extension repeat) the crime.[28]

If there is any real criminal at all, in other words, it is the will to sensation at work in both the narrator and the reader (and the orangutan). And while we might add that such a will informs all detective novels, it is customarily displaced onto and punished in a criminal. Upon apprehension, the criminal atones for the reader's criminal need to indulge his own will in the pursuit of extravagant sensation. Without the apprehension of a punishable criminal, the reader of Poe's detective stories is left to contemplate his own complicity in crime, constituted by the very act of reading.

Aristocratic Writing

Poe's tales neither "reflect" the organizing principles of a world independent of them nor enrich the cultural world, as romances usually do, with a realm existing alongside of it. Instead these tales become sites where the world, by coming to nothing, can be forgotten.

As Poe makes clear in his "Philosophy of Composition," however, when this world comes to nothing something else begins. I say begins advisedly. For an intimation of this something else arises with Poe's description of the creative process at work in the tales. Poe says he begins with the effect his work will have on the reader. He locates the shaping design for the work in the will of a reading public which demands instant gratification. He does not designate himself as a causative agent with an intention all his own.

Through the process of writing, however, Poe establishes two quite distinct realms: that of the reading public whose need for immediate sensation is both acknowledged and, as we have seen, obliterated; and that of Poe, the writer who recovers touch with an irredeemably past world that cannot become present in this work, but whose effects can be experienced as he writes it.

Insofar as the words he writes are for the readers, they gratify their demands. Insofar as they stand over against the readers' world, they produce another one. When writing according to the imagined effect he will have on a reader, Poe imagines an effect unsupported by a causative principle.

He identifies this unsupported effect with the world supporting his read-ers' existence.[29] And he makes this identification for a specific reason: a world reduced to the play of "effects" cannot cause Poe's own existence within it. In beginning with an effect Poe begins with a presupposition: that his readers' world was already fully "effected" before he wrote. In keeping with the temporal implications of this presupposition, Poe need not write according to the strictures of a preterite time sequence. Poe can move backward into a past the work effects as he writes. Instead of remain-ing in the present world, Poe writes in alliance with a past able to obliterate the present instead of being made past by it.

The dissolution taking place through the process of writing repeats itself within the tales the process produces. Characteristically in these tales of terror the narrators record their own impending disappearance. They do so, moreover, within the confines of a narrating consciousness denied the possibility for present reflection. Without the intervention of reflection, the narrative conveys only the immediacy of the event narrated. Then the narrative permits its immediate consumption.

In reading these tales, Poe's mass audience, subjected in everyday life to shocks intense enough to separate it from reflective consciousness, can re-discover a pleasure in what is shocking. Moreover, it can interpret the sepa-ration from reflective consciousness as the necessary precondition for the intensity of present existence. Pleasure, sensation, intense excitement, shock—all rise up in the place of horror, that space of imminent disap-pearance into oblivion we formerly identified as the "allegory of the in-stant." As shocks of the new, these sensational fictions unsupported by re-flection constitute a relationship between reader and writer as sudden and oblivious as those usually struck up within a crowd.

Poe's Uneventuating Cultural Reserve

But the temporal reversibility implicit in the act of writing these tales qualifies an earlier description. In the discussion of Poe's "allegory of the instant," we said these tales produced oblivion. But now it is difficult to ascertain whether the tales obliterate the present moment or whether Poe's present world is simply forgetful, in its constant need for shocking distrac-tions, of itself.

Like the action through which they take possession of their existence, Poe's narrators, in dress, language, and attitude, seem out of place in their time. Like Count de Tocqueville they seem emigrés from a time and place no longer able to exist under present conditions. Dispossessed of the means whereby they can be presentable either to themselves or to others, these characters haunt the scenes of their present existence with a sense of their pastness. The air of pastness surrounding them exceeds what we might call the presentational power of the moment, the moment's ability to make persons presentable within it. Temporally past but not made past by the present, such characters as Roderick Usher seem as if they are about to disappear into another time.

These narrators deserve to be contrasted with Hawthorne's in a way other than the one Poe effected in his reviews. Hawthorne wrote with the same sense of disconnection from a past. But he wrote in order to recover the living spirit of the past for and in the present. Full of pathos for what his present age had left behind, Hawthorne reunited the present with a living past. But Poe, after acknowledging the same disconnection, works in the opposite direction. Instead of relating the past to the present, he identifies with a lost lineage from the past, then generalizes this disconnection into the basis of all present relationships. Experiencing the separation of a pastness from the present as he writes, Poe identifies himself with a past aristocratic lineage but beyond the power of his age to bring into present existence.

Earlier we suggested a common linkage for the liberal impulse, the self-made man, and the illegitimate child: all three are instances of cultural disrelation. As an illegitimate child Poe found no satisfaction in the cultural ideal of the self-made man. Consequently, he never shared his culture's need to assert absolute independence from others. Poe needed to establish a legitimate claim on a cultural lineage. So he calls attention in his work to the cultural discontinuity produced by a nation of self-made men. In transmuting the self-obliterating shock effects of everyday life into the form of his literary tales, Poe separates himself from a self-referential modern world even as he writes himself into relation with the "absolute irrelation" [30] of a cultural lineage modern America has utterly lost.

Language and Mourning

Here let me take up the relation between language and the work of mourning once again to emphasize Poe's motive for constructing these forms. According to the psychic bargain struck in most works of mourning, the mourner agrees to let go of the person mourned in exchange for a memory. Referential language, insofar as it presupposes the absence of a person from the word representing this person, socializes separation. But Poe's writings do not agree to this substitution. Representational language performs a necessary cultural task. It permits a separation from other persons that results in individuals.[31] Representations permit persons to confirm their independence from one another by displacing one another's presence with words that make actual presence unnecessary. In Poe's works, however, words disintegrate into letters, sheer material impressions bereft of their power to represent. Poe thereby breaks the verbal contract constitutive of a culture of individuals. In the process of writing, he produces words without the power to refer and persons without the power to reflect and thereby empties persons and characters out of the actual world and into a world of memory. Instead of establishing a cultural contract with the world, Poe destroys the grounds upon which all other cultural contracts base their claims, leaving only the faculty of perversity in the wake of this dissolution.

To prove the incompatibility of memory and world, Poe replaces characters capable of being preserved as persons in memory with doubles. A reflective consciousness performs the cultural task of storing and transmitting the representations language produces. Without such a reflective consciousness, existence can be experienced only as an immediacy without duration. "Doubles" represent such an immediacy.

What takes the place of enduring representations in Poe's tales is a monumental reduction—the reduction of existence to the level of an absolute disconnection. The "unitive" effect dictating his process of composition is really nothing more than a non sequitur, the mark of what breaks a temporal sequence. The mark of this break permeates all the words in his prose, disintegrating them into letters, significant of nothing. Such decomposing words materialize the disconnections at work in the world, instead of representing the world's permanance. What these tales finally narrate is the inability of the human form to hold onto its personhood, and human words to uphold life. And what his tales leave in their wake is the apparition of a world long past, utterly unavailable for present reflection.

This irretrievably past world, however, communicates itself on two different planes. In gratifying the public's need for the immediate pleasure of watching a world come to nothing, this lost past becomes part of a pleasurable activity, one that is exercised and then used up in the reading of the tale. A more intimate relation with this past can result but only through the activity of writing. Reading produces oblivion, but writing produces a realm of pure memory, a sense of a past that is so irretrieveably past that it cannot come into presence except as an unrepresentable memory. Like the word "Nevermore" in "The Raven", this past world perdures only as a memory of a memory.

Read forward, these tales discharge themselves utterly into the allegory of the instant. But read as written—that is, read beginning with the effect but not affected by it—they recover their status as effects of what Poe calls pure memory. Bereft of the reflective consciousness in which they can appear as representations, they sustain themselves as psychic forces no representation can displace. Unable to be without being temporally past, they overturn the immediacy of their disappearance with an "it was" that "was" before they disappeared. Made past by a prior pastness rather than by the present, the temporal lineage supporting these tales haunts present time with a "time immemorial" quality unbeholden to the modern world's short-term cultural memory.

Affirming the irretrievability of their pastness rather than the power of the present to make them presentable within it, these tales produce a past; a past productive of its own pastness and temporally superior to the "primitive" demands of the present. Read as they appear from within the activity of writing, these pure memories give expression to an archaic past's revenge against the new. Unable to appear within the modern world, they obliterate its instants by gratifying the modern reader's need for the immediate.

By considering these memories in the context of a blood lineage, we might say that Poe's works are engaged in a blood feud against present conditions that made the continued existence of an ancient lineage impossible. Poe, the illegitimate child, experienced life in mid-nineteenth century America as an incessant reminder of the noble lineage he was born without. He did not write for nineteenth-century America, however much he may have impersonated the techniques capable of making a writer popular. He wrote for an ancient lineage, the tradition life in America denied him.

And herein lies the major reason for the French appropriation of Poe in the nineteenth century. Poe wrote as if he were coping with the problems a post-Revolutionary period posed for France. Writing as if he were in a line of American nobility that America's Revolution had dispossessed, Poe—in such tales as "Ligeia," "Morella," and "Berenice"—created settings where fallen nobility could recover relation with someone or something lost. Like

Count de Tocqueville in his travels through a new world, Poe's characters customarily experience themselves as displaced from some noble past. Unlike Tocqueville, however, the narrators do not find comfort in American democracy. Instead of accommodating themselves to prevailing conditions, they attempt to displace their present world by acting according to the demands of an archaic and infinitely more powerful past.

Imagination and Memory

Unlike other writers within the postrevolutionary romantic tradition, Poe did not elevate imagination above memory. In his famous Drake Halleck review, Poe took issue with Coleridge on the absolute originality of imagination.

> "Fancy," says the author of "Aids to Reflection," (who aided reflection to much better purpose in his "Genevieve")—"Fancy combines— Imagination creates." This was intended and has been received, as a distinction, but it is a distinction without a difference—without even a difference of degree. The Fancy as nearly creates as the imagination, and neither at all. Novel conceptions are merely unusual combinations . . . What man imagines, *is*, but *was* also. The mind of man cannot imagine what is not. (12:37; see also 15:13, n. 2)

In place of the imagination romantically corroborative of "independence" from a past, Poe elevated memory into the fundamental principle of composition.

Imagination elevates the shock of the new into the realm of absolute originality. Memory, on the other hand, insists on the writer's awareness of his situation within a renewable tradition. At the time Poe wrote, America did not have a recognizable tradition. But Poe wrote as if it had lost a tradition. Unable to take their place within a tradition, the narrators of his tales recall the loss of an ancient tradition. They invoke the energy of a betrayed cultural memory to revenge themselves against the cultural amnesia of modernity.

Reading Poe's work sanctions present circumstances, but in his lengthy analysis of his work, Poe "suggests" the presence of another realm. He distinguishes events in a tale that are supervised by present circumstances from events that could be possible in another world—not another world "reflective" of the inadequacies in the present one, but a world in which what could not take place in the tale haunts the tale with events capable of undoing it.

In writing *from* the effect he would have upon his present world, Poe estranges himself from that world, establishing not quite a separate realm but a relation to separation. In the activity of writing, he establishes relations apart from this world. He does not thereby become part of another world (that would only turn him into a representable form). Unable to appear within a reflective consciousness, his separation (like the echoing refrain "Nevermore") assumes the shape of a perpetual returning. It is a memory, but a memory reduced to its fundamental, abstract motion, that of a return.

This past exists as a cultural reserve, but one without use in the present. It is a form of time occupying a peculiar temporal dimension. Unable to be made past or absent by the present, yet not made present by it either, it can continue its existence only by perpetually returning upon itself. A past inaccessible to the present, it is nonetheless kept, preserved in a realm of memory Poe refers to as "ideality." Here it appears much more temporally dense than the present because it is interlaced with a surplus of eventfulness the present simply does not possess. These reserves of uneventuated archaic possibilities are saturated with memories dense enough in their demand to become presentable to obliterate a present that has forgotten them. While Poe's tales satisfy the modernists' need for instant gratification, the act of writing them perpetuates an archaic time lineage, and preserves a place where a long-forgotten tradition can continue as the memory of what cannot presently appear in the world.[32]

Poe's tales give the people what they want, but the activity of writing them, in bringing what the people want to nothing, takes it back. In declaring his "principles" of composition, Poe recovers the noble bearing and manner of the lineage, whose spirit has been denigrated by the reading public. But writing was the only cultural activity in which Poe could recover this noble bearing. Writing developed for him intimations of an irretrievable past, a cultural reserve so utterly contemptuous of the needs of the present as not to deign to appear within it.

The Spirit of the New and the Spirit of the Past

While this irretrievably past world does not appear in any of Poe's tales, it does appear in *Eureka*, a metaphysical treatise Poe wrote shortly before he died. In *Eureka* Poe perfects the attitude of the dispossessed nobleman by returning all the world to the realm of memory. Not a separate metaphysical tract so much as the philosophy of composition restated in absolute terms, *Eureka* is where Poe rediscovers his principles of composition: in the divine will. Like Poe in his activity of writing, the divine will also begins with a sensed unity of effect. But for the divine will the unity is much vaster, including the created universe as a massive, already effected unit. Like Poe, the divine will begins with this already effected universe and follows it backward through its decomposition into an "absolute irrelation," an irrelative unit Poe calls the "lost parent" of the universe (16:220).

In reducing all the universe to an "irrelative unit," then generalizing that irrelation into infinity, Poe recovers the metaphysical realm of pure, "ever present Memories." Here an endless lineage of memories slips through infinity like rhymes through representations. This "moral embodiment of man's abstract idea of time" (16:218) is a realm where recollection purifies itself of any dependence upon presently existing forms. As a "mere consciousness of existence without thought" (16:219), this realm stands alone, as a pure pastness, a cultural reserve of what was extended to infinity.

Eureka makes Poe's separation from the present absolute by establishing an infinite dimension for his apartness to occupy. In imagining this realm of pure pastness without a dimension through which to become present, he imagined a spiritual realm for what we earlier called a cultural reserve. In *Eureka* Poe justifies his failure to bring these reserves into his present world by aligning his separation from the world with the will of God, the only reflective consciousness expansive enough for a past absolutely dissociated from the present.

Freud's slippery notion of what he calls primal repression provides the best gloss for the realm of pure memory Poe imagined in *Eureka*.[33] Like Poe's pure memory, primal repression describes a process in which a force of memory subsists, but with no form through which it can become memorable in the present. Freud designates the place where primal repression stores its memories as the unconscious. The unconscious is also the place where the cultural reserve is preserved in the individual. This reserve appears in the individual unconscious after it loses a cultural locus guaranteeing the preservation and continuity of its reflections. The primary process Freud finds at work in every individual unconscious stores memories that could not have been part of the life experience of any individual. Much more ancient than any individual's lineage, the origin for a cultural line whose patrimony extends beyond that of any known genealogy, the primary process preserves the collective memory of that irretrievably lost parent Poe recalled in *Eureka*.

Despite our association of it with a premodern past, recently Freud's primary process has been invoked by French poststructuralists as their means of returning Poe to modern America.[34] They have used the locus of primary repression in the same way as they have used Poe's work; as a scene on which to elaborate their method. Unlike Tocqueville, the French poststructuralists have come to America not in order to discover a past for the French Revolution but to generalize the disruptive force of a revolutionary event into the nature of signification itself. What Derrida calls "the play of *différance*" is actually the impact of the shock of the new upon language formation. What Derrida calls *différance* is what Poe would call the "ghost" of the new.

When pressed to designate a locus for *différance*, Derrida attempts to install it within a peculiar temporal dimension he discovers in the Freudian unconscious: "With the alterity of the 'unconscious' we have to deal not with the horizons of modified presents—past or future—but with a 'past' that has never been nor will ever be present, whose 'future' will not be produced or reproduced in the form of presence."[35] Derrida here is distinguishing between the "trace" of *différance* and the protention/retention operations supervising an individual's memory, hoping to enrich *différance* with the reserve power produced within an individual's unconscious by what Freud calls primary repression. But the realm of primary repression cannot be displaced by *différance* any more than it can become presentable in ordinary memories. Derrida needs to invoke this primally repressed reserve for quite specific reason. This vast cultural reserve haunting the present with the sense of what it has lost becomes in Derrida's writing the "logocentric tradition." And it is only by its displacement of the entire logocentric tradition that *différance* can be detected. But Poe's attitude to the tradition was the reverse of the poststructuralists. He wished not to repeat its loss in the displacements at work in his language, but to recover relation to the lost tradition, in the process of writing.

The Narrative of A. Gordon Pym

According to the poststructuralists, the revolutionary power inherent in the "shock," the *différance*, of the "new" had the ability to lay waste the entire Western tradition. While we are indebted to the poststructuralists for clarifying the relationship between the loss of a tradition and the spirit of the new, it was the loss of this tradition rather than an alliance with the new that moved Poe to write. And while the French poststructuralists may have returned Poe to America under the tutelage of a permanent revolution, we can rediscover a different Poe when we understand what he can tell us about living in an America without a tradition to claim its citizens.

Unable to perpetuate itself within the present, yet not displaced by the present, a traditional past can be experienced as an unmet demand. When New World adventurers insisted upon the value of personal experience independent of its allegorical significance, they changed the traditional mode of cultural transmission. As we have seen, change—the promised effect of adventure in the New World—became a cultural asset. After the adventurer returned home, his reflections upon his experiences became a potential addition to the culture's reserves.

Autobiographical reflection, or what we could call a memory of one's contemporaneity, was the price paid to the Old World for adventure. Through the autobiographical accounts of their adventures the adventurers' experiences became a cultural surplus available to many members of the culture. The adventurer's "new," in turn, dislodges the unquestioned authority of a culture's traditions and customs. Upon the appearance of the "new," these customs can be designated as dead habits, and buried in its past.

These habits and customs displaced by the new do not disappear. They must remain as cultural memories from a past; otherwise adventurers would have no way to elaborate on the cultural effects of the new. Without these customs, habits, and established orders as the necessary background against which the new can display its distinctness, adventure would again appear indistinguishable from the random movement of mere chance. Without the routines and rituals of everyday life as a constructive context, no one would be able to experience an adventure as either a gamble or an admirable risk. And without admiration as an anticipated response to his risks, the adventurer would have no guarantee that he would produce an impressive effect upon his return to culture.

Without an Old World chain of recollections capable of turning chance adventures into the wonders and rarities a culture saves, exchanges, and transmits, these adventures would simply pass out of consciousness altogether. Thus the Old World supervises an orderly transition to a New World. After this transition the experience of the eternal made possible by participation in cultural allegory gives way to the promise of the infinite made possible by the new. The prospect of an endless supply of cultural novelty makes it possible to conceive of the development of any individual as potentially infinite. And this infinite capability, when affiliated with the opportunities for cultural exchange associated with a rising entrepreneurial class, more than makes up for the overthrow of a noble lineage.[36] Inheritance from an ancient past depended upon the preservation of a single cultural line—that of the royal family—but the establishment of a New World trades upon the possibility for renewal of all existing lineages.

But without the accompanying guarantee of infinite novelty or the persistent proof of this guarantee, the new could not justify its displacement of the old. Instead of replacing the old, the new would turn into what it does in Poe; that is, a forgettable instant, an impulse threatening to the cultural reserves it falsely promises to replenish to infinity. Without an Old World memory to negate, in other words, New World adventure could itself be consigned to oblivion.

Aware of its threat to their cultural positions, many of the Old World nobility from the fifteenth through the eighteenth century believed oblivion the appropriate cultural reward for adventurers. But Edgar Allan Poe was the first New World author to relegate the true subject of an adventure narrative to cultural oblivion. Unlike other authors of adventure narratives, Poe never valued the urge for adventure. Like Old World noblemen he considered the adventurer's urge to be a threat to the cultural memory, or at least he assumed the attitude of a dispossessed nobleman as an appropriate cultural posture.[37]

Because his *Narrative of A. Gordon Pym* reads quite differently from any other narrative in its genre, I am going to elaborate on this proposition by returning to *Pym*. For Pym never manages the return home necessary for the cultural transformation of the adventurer into the narrator. Without this transformation his adventures read as mere novelties, sheer discontinuities unsalvageable by any reflective consciousness. Poe focuses on the determinant precondition for adventure—its disregard for those customs and habits preserved in the adventurer's cultural memory—but only to renege on the adventurer's consequent claim to cultural prominence. In *The Narrative of A. Gordon Pym*, the "new" grounding the "progress" of Pym's adventures is neither infinite nor inexhaustible. From the very beginning Pym is driven to leave home by a very specific itinerary of desired adventures: "of shipwreck and famine, of death and captivity among barbarian hordes, of a lifetime dragged out in sorrow and tears, upon some gray and desolated rock, in an ocean unapproachable and unknown" (257). And upon completion of this itinerary, Pym's narrative ends.

It ends, however, with the same impulsive abruptness as did many of his adventures. As if to consign the adventurer to a final scene utterly compatible with his desire for sensational incidents, Poe ends Pym's narrative with an uncompleted adventure. This unfinished adventure underscores the fundamental contradiction at work in any culture's adventure with the new. Only an incomplete adventure can maintain the promise for an utterly open, hence infinite supply of novelty, but the incomplete adventure without any adventurer left to complete its narration reveals the difference between the infinity claimed for adventure and the finite condition of the adventurer.

The adventurer's finite condition, in its turn, insists upon reflection, the labor the adventurer owes to the culture, as the necessary precondition for any life of adventure more lasting than the shocking impulse of the instant. Without reflection, adventure appears as finite as is the adventurer. By reflection, however, the adventurer violates the fundamental claim of adventure: that it exists independent of any memory. Poe thoroughly exploits this contradiction within the adventure narrative.

Knowing that reflection would qualify the wonder in adventure, Pym cannot reflect upon persons or events. Without a reflective consciousness in which to store his percepts, Pym's narrative does not represent other persons, places, or things but indicates what is passing irretrievably out of present consciousness, including Pym himself. Divorced from a reflective power necessary to convert persons into representations of themselves, Pym cannot perceive others as others. He sees other persons as threats to the only person his consciousness can ever presently experience, namely, himself. Unable to substitute representations for other persons, and unable to recall them in memory, he must become them. Since his own person is the only point of reference Pym has, he refers all others back to himself by literally impersonating them.

This impersonation begins on the *Ariel,* the skiff belonging to Pym's friend Augustus Barnard. Here Pym does not act on his own but echoes and mirrors Augustus' need for adventure that has become so desperate that it must pass over into dream for its gratification. When Pym discovers Augustus Barnard in a drunken dream state, he identifies with the elements in the situation that will perpetuate Augustus' dream. Thus, after tying Augustus to the bottom of the skiff, he renounces his home, pledges to follow a wild destiny at sea, and commends himself to God. As if in response to this surrender of his will, Pym hears a series of loud screams, "as if from the throat of a thousand demons" (253), destined to resound as a chorus throughout the narrative.

These screams launch Pym on a narrative quest grounded in his need for what he has not yet actualized as his. Since Pym falls into a swoon at the first sound of these yells, his miraculous escape from death by drowning cannot be called part of his narrative. It remains the tale of a group of sailors on board a ship call the *Penguin,* who rescue Pym and Augustus only after rebelling against their leader, Captain Block. Apparently to emphasize the exclusivity of their adventure, Pym overhears in their account of "having run down a vessel at sea and drowned some thirty or forty poor devils" (257) only the elimination of himself from it. Perhaps to assert the priority of his own claim on his first scene, Pym will repeat it in subsequent adventures, thereby denying his difference from all the other participants in it. Once he identifies with or refers to himself all the other characters, they implicitly become identical to himself.

Unable to recall or reflect upon them, Pym must repeat those first actions even when they are inappropriate to the events that immediately confront him. Each element of that initial scene will be repeated in a subsequent episode; in effect, Pym will continue to write his narrative until he has neutralized any otherness in that scene by quite literally incorporating all of its parts. Thus the same Pym who seemed at first solely to mirror Augustus' actions will have an entire repertoire of parts to play. Pym will by turns identify with the nearly drowned Augustus, the mutinous sailors, the image of death itself, and the tyrannical Captain Block, until all the characters who threatened his life become identified with his narrative. In other words, Pym begins by imitating another's will and ends by absorbing all others into his narrative.

In order to make his policy of identification with and incorporation of others as eventful as possible, Pym envisions a life filled with a catalogue of disasters dazzling enough to overshadow Augustus' dream. As a result of Pym's wish to make Augustus' dream his life, Pym's longing for adventure coincides with Augustus' loss of his ego: "Augustus thoroughly entered into my state of mind. It is probable indeed that our intimate communion had resulted in a partial interchange of character" (289). Moreover, to maintain the integrity of his reclamation of Augustus' dream in his narrative proper, Pym sets the facts, observations, and perceptions—the public's share of an adventure narrative—in a style and tone clearly separable from it. While digressions upon the meaning of such terms as "laying to" might partially justify Pym's adventures by grounding them in a historical context, the manner in which he manages these digressions—with its countervocabulary and tone of nautical expertise—only underscores the intensity of Pym's personal narrative. More importantly, however, Pym places these unexciting details in a context separable from his narrative, so that he will be able to forget them. By compartmentalizing these details in an alienable form, Pym compulsively asserts their separation from his narrative and the self identical with that narrative. After he has divided mere detail from an exciting incident, he is free to ignore the details and repeat the incidents.

In fact, three different expository styles coexist in *The Narrative of A. Gordon Pym:* the reportorial style in the log, the factual style in the digressions, and the lurid style in Pym's narrative. Pym casts events into the style of the log when he wants to forget or erase them; uses the digressive style when he needs to gain credence and justification for his narrative; and writes over the prior two styles to assert the prerogatives of his own adventure narrative.

Pym's use of diverse narrative styles underscores the dilemma in his narrative. He does not wish to surrender the immediate benefits of his adventure to any agency other than himself. But he cannot engage in adventure and return to society without such social justifications for his narrative as the style of history or the informative style of geographical observation will provide. Pym's alienation of the historical and informative styles from the narrative proper indicates his need to keep his person separate from social-symbol systems altogether.

Indeed if we argue that the fundamental prerequisite for reentrance into any social world includes the agreement of the self to cease being simply and immediately present to and for itself and to become representable for others, we can say Pym refuses to sign this agreement. Utterly without the reflecting capacity necessary to convert his person into a representation, Pym experiences other persons not as representations of themselves but as his person embodied in them.

Being unable to reflect means being unable to acknowledge the difference between other persons and his person. Since he himself is the only reference for persons that Pym can acknowledge, Pym cannot accept others as different from him. So instead of acknowledging others in their representations, he participates in them by acting as if their persons were his own. Taking the American self-reliant man to an extreme, Poe exposes Pym's need for immediate unrelated adventure as the inability to be in relation with anyone other than oneself.

But without another through whom it can be experienced as a reflection or a representation, the self cannot be differentiated from a ghost. Pym demands immediacy; this means Pym cannot accept words for persons but must have their unmediated presence. In a world without referents or substitutions, however, persons, places, and things are inseparable from apparitions, which are in their turn immediate presences but without representable forms. As might be expected from his pattern of behavior, Pym recognizes his likeness to an apparition all right, but only after he impersonates one:

> The isolated effect produced by the sudden apparition is not at all to be wondered at when the various circumstances are taken into consideration. Usually, in cases of a similar nature, there is left in the mind of the spectator some glimmering of doubt as to the reality of the vision before his eyes; a degree of hope, however feeble, that he is the victim of chicanery, and that the apparition is not actually a visitant from the world of shadows. It is not too much to say that such remnants of doubt have been at the bottom of almost every such visitation and that the appalling horror which has sometimes been brought about, is to be attributed even in the cases most in point, and where the most suffering has been experienced, to a kind of anticipative horror, lest the apparition *might possibly* be real, rather than to any unwavering belief in its reality. But in the present instance, it will be seen immediately, that in the minds of the mutineers there was not even the shadow of a basis upon which to rest a doubt that the apparition of Rogers was indeed a revivification of his disgusting person, or at least its spiritual image. (307–8)

In impersonating a figure whose death has separated him from any proper referent, Pym acts out the implications of what it means to live in a world without representations through which the individuals can mediate his existence: he cannot be distinguished from an apparition ungrounded in anything more permanent than the sensational response provoked in another apparition.

Put more starkly, in a world where no substitute formations can be acknowledged, absolutely no difference can be sustained between those who are actually dead and those who remain separate from us because of the words we use to refer to them. Without faith in representations, Pym treats the living the way a ghost returned from the dead might: as embodiments of his missing person.

Moreover, in dying within rather than outside his narrative, Pym violates the social terms sanctioning the adventurer's return to society. Ordinarily, in becoming a narrator who recalls, hence mediates, his formerly immediate adventures, an adventurer symbolically dies in order to be symbolized, reborn as a narrator. Owing to his refusal to exchange the immediacy of adventure for the social mediation of language, Pym cannot exchange immediate death for symbolic death. He dies within a narrative that has not paid its social debt, the acceptance of the social-symbol system guaranteeing entrance back into society.

The greatest irony in Pym's refusal of reflection pervades the conclusion of his narrative. After having acted out all the adventures motivating his departure from home in the first place, Pym literally exhausts the resources of his character. Dying into his adventures rather than into their representations, Pym can subsist only within a memory he exists to deny. The consequences of this perverse turn of character become clear in his penultimate adventure, his "captivity among barbarian hordes" on Tsalal. Here, instead of reflecting on his previous adventures, Pym is compelled to watch as the natives repeat them—as the only way of sustaining a relation to any action at all.

The Tsalalians repeat all of Pym's narrative actions: shipwreck, burial alive, death by drowning, mutiny, tyranny, and threat of drowning. The Tsalalians also subtly reenact a less obvious action. When Tsalemon hides from his reflection in a mirror, he repeats Pym's earlier fear of his own (unreflecting) reflection. We might elaborate the narrative logic concealed in this action with a proposition: when Pym hates and fears the Tsalalians, who are made in the image of his own unreflective immediacy, he fears his own unreflective existence—but through them. In their repetition of everything Pym has already done, these barbarian hordes repeat the terms, quite literally in black characters, of his narrative.[38] The Tsalalians' narrative, however, with no other action left for immediacy to engage, threatens to engulf him (whether as cannibalism or burial alive) in its literal characters.

Thus, at the end of the narrative, Pym regresses to his position at the beginning. Having achieved a coherent identity, Pym perceives this identity as a loss of immediacy. In order to recover immediacy, he reverts to his earliest tactic, but with an important difference. At the beginning of his narrative, Pym came into his own by acting out the desires of another person, Augustus Barnard. After their shared adventure, Pym became himself by acting out the parts of all the others involved in that adventure. But since Pym became himself by impersonating the actions of others, each attempt to discover his identity became quite literally an act of self-evasion.

The logic here is as perverse as Pym. However, once Pym, in Tsalal, finds his impersonation of all the others involved in that first scene embodied in the form of characters who threaten to bury him alive, he can no longer desire to be these others. Having absorbed and enacted all of these possible roles, Pym exists without any part left to play. Alone and with no person left to impersonate and no adventure left to act out, on Tsalal Pym experiences his self not as an immediate presence but as a mediated "has-been."

On its most fundamental level *Pym* presents the psychology of an adventurer as that of the man who perpetually wards off the insistent threat of boredom (and the death it conceals) by filling up each moment with an incident even more sensational than the one before. Pym begins his narrative with a primordial, even primal, death-defying adventure, and he desires to master this close call with death by mastering all its parts. But the very thoroughness of his mastery brings him face to face with the ultimate master.

Pym concludes with the log of the sighting on March 22: "But there arose in our pathway a shrouded human figure, very far larger in its proportions than any dweller among men. And the hue of the skin of the figure was of the perfect whiteness of the snow" (405).[39] Having exhausted the resources of novelty supervising his narrative, Pym encounters a figure whose person he can neither convert into an adventure nor act out of his narrative. With this conclusion of adventure, Pym disappears from present consciousness as completely as did one adventure when displaced by another. Unable to represent himself in a form of social memory, Pym disappears from immediate perception. At the conclusion, an "it was" permeates his "it is" as a powerfully alien force, a wonder but a wonder whose form is not appropriable as an adventure. Pym disappears, then, with the recognition of the ghostly, apparitional form an unreflective existence assumes. In apprehending a presence without any representable human form, Pym rec-

ognizes the figure of unreflective human existence itself. Like Pym this figure can only be the sign of its own disappearance from any memorable
form whatsoever. And this disappearance of the New World adventure
from any memorable form is the final revenge of the spirit from a past the
"new" world has erased from its memory.

Chapter Six

Emerson and the Law of Nature

They have difficulty in bringing their reason to act, and on occasion use their memories first.

—*Ralph Waldo Emerson*

Throughout this book, I have invoked Emerson as a tutelary presence. But the topic I invoked him to guard over had more in common with a specific theme I have written this book to develop than with a specifically Emersonian doctrine. To be faithful to his presence, I must now distinguish my theme from his doctrine. Let me begin with a disclaimer. When I equated Emerson's doctrine of self-reliance with a predisposition shared by masses of post-Jacksonian Americans to separate themselves from both kith and kin, I remained faithful only to the letter of Emerson's doctrine.

Emerson was, if anything, more opposed to democratic majorities than were any of his contemporaries, except possibly Edgar Poe. In his animus against the masses, he never quite equaled Poe, who characterized mass opinion as "the most odious and insupportable despotism that ever was heard of upon the face of the earth." [1] But after watching a politician work a crowd for its votes, Emerson tapped a vein of invective certainly contiguous to Poe's. Unlike Poe, however, Emerson usually used his journal entries, rather than tales of terror, as the appropriate place to discharge indignation.

> Here, thought I, is one who loves what I hate . . . I hate numbers . . .
> He cares for nothing but numbers and persons. [2]

When in need of a moral doctrine to justify this distaste, Emerson turned to self-reliance. This doctrine enjoined all Americans to share Emerson's contempt for the masses. A self-reliant American could be what none of Jackson's common men could ever quite manage to be—independent of a majority holding the same opinion.

This recovery of a free inner existence from the claims of majority opinion was a fairly representative need for mid-nineteenth-century Americans.

Many of Emerson's contemporaries found in his prose a way to separate themselves from the contentious demands of partisan politics. Some others turned his doctrine into another weapon in the growing arsenal commanded by the party of compromise. Emerson, however, did not condone this usage. Indeed, when he saw the spirit of compromise at work in Daniel Webster's support of the Fugitive Slave Bill, Emerson attacked this spirit with the most partisan address of his career.

Emerson made this speech as part of a campaign for the Free Soil candidate in his congressional district, John Gorham Palfrey. Emerson would not tolerate any compromise on the question of liberty. Whether or not this compromise would preserve the Union was for Emerson not to the point. For him, union was the external form of the nation's compact, and had no meaning apart from the principles—of liberty, equality, justice— agreed upon in the compact.

Emerson's response to the Fugitive Slave Law provide a good example of Emersonian self-reliance at work. Popularly understood, self-reliance emphasized the priority of the individual's rights over the society's; it substantiated a negative interpretation of liberty, defining it solely as a freedom from any constraint. But in fact Emerson's doctrine does not place the individual's rights above the society's. Self-reliance directs the individual as well as the culture to a vision of the innermost principles underlying both. When he opposed the Fugitive Slave Bill, his person became transparent so that the principle of liberty could speak all the more forcibly through it.

To distinguish his merely personal interests from nationally shared convictions, Emerson had to exercise self-reliance. When exercised effectively, it resulted in a revelation: of the moral convictions informing the inner life of every American. Self-reliance became a means of making the person transparent before the principles his person represented.

The popular understanding of the doctrine consigns value to what Emerson himself denies is valuable—the individual's reliance upon his own person. The faculty of self-reliance permits the individual to discriminate the person's transitory interests from the unchanging principles upon which his person relies. An individual could then put those principles into practice, as Emerson did when he opposed the Fugitive Slave Law.

We began this chapter with an acknowledgment of an undiscriminating association of terms. Throughout this book Emerson's doctrine of self-reliance has been treated as a synonym for rugged individualism. In his own speeches, Emerson himself was not careful to distinguish what he meant by self-reliance from what the term was popularly understood to mean. His essays and orations exploited the confusion between what he meant and what the public understood. Only the listeners' exercise of self-reliance as a moral faculty could definitively clarify the confusion between these terms. Indeed the ability to discriminate the doctrine from the faculty was the best indication that a person's self-reliance was at work.

What this discrimination cannot adequately explain, however, is why Emerson believed the nation needed this new moral faculty. Part of the explanation is personal and appears throughout his early journal entries. There Emerson records a struggle that will eventuate in the need for this faculty. In the long entry dated April 18, 1824, Emerson distinguishes what he inherits from others—his parents and his culture—from what he is in himself. This self-examination concludes with a sentence full of overtones: "I judge that if I devote my nights and days in *form,* to the services of God and the War against Sin, I shall soon be prepared to do the same in *substance*."

In later journal entries as well as in the essays Emerson will compose out of them, this basic distinction between form and substance will yield new oppositions: freedom and fate, idealist and materialist, society and solitude are some. Traversing all these oppositions however, is a fundamental and pervasive resolve: to be in substance what reveals itself through every noble human form.

Underlying this resolve is an unstated misgiving. Emerson felt overshadowed by the achievements of his ancestors, his brothers, his predecessors, and his culture. For the young Emerson, life in culture felt like a moral rebuke. Moving among the inspired works of his religious tradition, Emerson often felt himself incompetent and uncreative. A single discrimination, however, recovered for him all of his creative energies. We can hear his need to make the discrimination in the early resolve: "I shall soon be prepared to do the same [as his renowned ancestors] in *substance*." In this sentence, Emerson distinguishes the power resulting in his ancestors' achievements from the ancestors' persons. Once separated from the persons through whom they acted, these powers could move to other persons, who were adequate to their epoch. Without forms appropriate to the needs of the age, these powers would simply replicate models from the past. The faculty of self-reliance performed two fundamental duties: it discriminated the power giving rise to an achievement from the achievement itself, and it indicated the timely work—what Emerson called the "duty of the day"—to which these powers were to be devoted.

An Emerson Tradition

In order to awaken these powers in his listeners, Emerson asked them to treat the popular urge for self-reliance in an unusual way: not as a demand to be fulfilled by personal isolation but as a means of distinguishing what was self-sufficient within them from what was not. This distinction would permit every American to contribute to the life of the culture, which relied on the same self-sufficient principles.

Sensitive to the debilitating effects of historical forms, Emerson believed his entire age was burdened by the memory of the Revolutionary fathers, rather than inspired by the founding powers. Like Hawthorne, he believed the Revolutionary mythos had emptied present existence of all value, but unlike him he did not turn to the collective memory for a cure.

We have already considered why Hawthorne turned to the collective memory as a moral faculty with redemptive social powers. To understand Emerson's need for self-reliance as a moral faculty we might contrast Emersonian self-reliance with Hawthorne's collective memory. Hawthorne was as unsympathetic to the faculty of self-reliance as Emerson was to the collective memory. Self-reliance was a doctrine he left the commune of Brook Farm to get behind him. He believed self-reliance was a principle persons invoked when they did not wish to do something routine, like milk a cow, or sow seeds, or shovel manure—or when they did not wish to be a part of the community.

Hawthorne distrusted the humanity of any person who claimed self-reliance as a ruling princple. Like the displacement procedures at work in the Custom House, the doctrine of self-reliance made possible a complete devastation of an antiquated way of life, without even a retrospective glance.

Individual self-reliance disabled the work of human memory. Hawthorne's entire project was grounded in a restoration of what we might call commemorative perception: the ability to perceive a person as at once himself and a communally sustained account of him. Without a communal memory to preserve them, persons, for Hawthorne, could not be distinguished from ghosts. As a means of securing a shared human context for a person's movement through time, memory socialized perception. But self-reliance dispensed with memory on the grounds that it was representational. Memory put a person in mind of what he had done: self-reliance put a person in mind of what he could do.

Of course, self-reliance and memory can be placed on much friendlier terms. A dose of self-reliance can seem a healthy cure for an excessively self-reflective consciousness. Anyone familiar with Emerson's early journals can trace the development of self-reliance as his personal way of recovering from self-consciousness.

While memory cannot be reduced to self-reflection, these two separate acts of consciousness do work in relation to one another. Memory preserves what self-reflection produces. It also preserves what self-reflection cannot produce, representations of persons whose proper referents (their names, bodies, personalities) have been destroyed by death. Emerson's memory was filled with both of these productions. Recollection of his dead brothers, his first wife, close friends took their place alongside reflection on his personal shortcomings, inadequacies, failures of resolve.

And Emerson did not devise the doctrine of self-reliance without reflecting on its consequences for memory. If anything, Emerson considered memory a tyrant, rather than—as did Hawthorne—a beleaguered servant. Again unlike Hawthorne, he thought the age excessively retrospective, too enthralled with the lives of its founders to accomplish anything on its own.

But Emerson could not overthrow the faculty of memory without putting another in its place. Self-reliance usurped at least part of the work usually assigned to the faculty of memory: it acknowledged previous cultural achievements but only the better to separate the power (whether physical, perceptual, intellectual, moral, or emotional) leading to the achievement from the achievement itself. Self-reliance produced an enabling amnesia. Emerson separated the power informing the memorable form from the form itself. Inspired by the power, he forgot about the form.

Emerson did not reserve his exercise in amnesia for his memories of persons (though he quite programmatically separated his brother Charles's accounts of his life from the powers at work in his person) but extended it to locales, things, even memorable quotes. Only by detaching the forms (of persons, places, and things) from the powers that made them memorable could Emerson imagine his own life sufficiently empowered. The powers which passed through all truly impressive forms were not beholden to any one of them, Emerson believed. Utterly self-sufficient, these powers enabled persons to act rather than react, to live memorable or, as Emerson put it, representative lives rather than, as Hawthorne would have it, to commemorate others' lives.

Hawthorne believed that he carried forward the memorable spirit of the past in his own person. He also believed that only memory could induce man to provide institutions adequate to common rather than merely private needs. But Emerson believed that the enabling power self-reliance released included all Americans rather than a single individual as its appropriate vehicle. He invokes the moral faculty of self-reliance as a means of reminding his contemporaries of their power to make a truly free world. Insofar as it depends upon a prior need to be free from past accomplishments, the faculty of self-reliance begins its work with a negation, but unlike the doctrine of rugged individualism, it puts this negation into the service of future accomplishments for the commonwealth. Nevertheless, defined as what makes forms (whether persons or their actions) memorable rather than as what preserves them in memory, the faculty of self-reliance justifies the separation of actions from any reflective consciousness capable of preserving them.

We have already considered the consequences of this separation for Hawthorne. He considered the exercise of self-reliance indistinguishable from a wish to enter a state of oblivion. It took Poe, rather than Hawthorne, to provide this oblivion with the horrific cultural context it deserved. Poe treated self-reliance as an excuse for detaching persons from presentable cultural forms. Without appropriate cultural memories to preserve them, the persons in Poe's tales of terror regularly decomposed into the unrepresentable; and the words meant to represent (or remember) them disintegrated into letters, the linguistic remains of traces of words on the way to oblivion. When Emersonian self-reliance replaced memory as a faculty of human acknowledgment, it empowered (at least for Poe and probably for Emerson) the premature disappearance of persons.

Emersonian Tradition, Modernity, and Memory

In fact, Poe was more indignant over the cultural privileges granted forms of instant gratification than over Emersonian doctrines. When he suggested that pertinent issues of a popular transcendentalist quarterly be thrown to the pigs, Poe correlated the transcendentalists with other beings who lived for the instant.

In a recent review of the Library of America edition of Poe's collected works, Harold Bloom discusses Poe in a context that can shed light on our own. Bloom compares Poe's project with Emerson's: "Poe (like Emerson) desired to be the American Coleridge or Byron or Shelley, and his poetry, at its rare best, echoes those High Romantic forerunners, with some grace and a certain . . . plangent urgency."[3] But whatever anxious relation to their predecessors Emerson and Poe may have had turned into an excuse for Poe's hostility toward Emerson. "Poe, a true Southerner, abominated Emerson, plainly perceiving that Emerson . . . was not a Christian, not a royalist, not a classicist. Self-reliance, the Emersonian answer to original sin, does not exist in the Poe cosmos, where you necessarily start out damned, doomed and dismal."[4]

Bloom contrasts Poe and Emerson to make clear the terms of his preference for Emerson over Poe. Like Poe, Bloom feels a traditionalist's need to be revenged against modernity's version of human time. Unlike Poe, however, Bloom does not limit the power of a tradition to its ability to choose the terms of its oblivion, but displays the tradition's power to return to a modern age as the memory modernity has repressed.

Bloom does not not rely on a more powerful form of producing a past in order to overcome the obsolescence procedures of literary modernity, as Poe did. Instead, Bloom lets the tradition happen forever again in the mind, as a repressed memory. In his "modern" version of a scene of election from the Jewish tradition, Bloom redefines the "instant" of modernity as a repression of the fact that modernity originated in an enduring moment. Acting with the authority of the modern speech act of repression, Bloom can restore as much of the past as he wishes, as what has been repressed by modern originality. In his criticism, Bloom exercises the revenge of a tradition of memory against a regnant modernism, and uses Emerson rather than Buber or Freud as the authority for his method.

Emerson's doctrine of self-reliance sanctions this use. For as we have seen, self-reliance corroborates the fundamental modernist wish to be free of all precursors even as it calls attention to the inability to forget them.

> Emerson's beautiful conclusion *is* beautiful because the conflict is emotional, between equal impulses, and it cannot be resolved . . . He asks for a stance simultaneously Dionysiac and self-reliant, and he does not know how this is to be attained, nor do we . . . He believed that poetry

came from Dionysian influx [i.e., "the poet's return to his subsuming precursors"], yet . . . preaches an Apollonian self-reliance while fearing the individualism it would bring.[5]

In his Library of America review, Bloom suggested that self-reliance was Emerson's answer to original sin. And now we understand why. Emerson's failed quest to be original restores psychological depth to his relations with his ancestors. His wish for originality, when equated with a repression of cultural precursors, turns repression into a kinship bond as effective in its interrelational effects as was the theological notion of original sin for Hawthorne. Emerson's wish to be original, in Bloom's poignant interpretation, turns out to be a disguise for his culturally unspeakable need to remember (i.e., modernistically repress) his precursors. And his failed repression leads to as many cultural associations as Bloom's recollections of the Western tradition can manage to make presentable.

In treating Emerson's wish to be *causa sui* as a repressed memory, Bloom restores Emerson to communal relations with the rest of the Western tradition. In this way, Bloom's psychological faculty of repression performs tasks for modern culture similar to those performed by Hawthorne's collective memory; both restore a communal sensibility to a modern culture.[6]

However resourceful it may be in providing us with a means of being recalled by premodern cultural relations, and however consonant it may be with Hawthorne's (and even Poe's) versions of Emerson, Bloom's theory does not yet begin to do justice to Whitman's cultural relationship to his "master." If he were true to Bloom's theory, Whitman would have felt the need to repress Emerson's influence on him. But in "paying his respects" to Emerson, Whitman does not deny that Emerson influenced him, nor does he fail to recognize that Emerson himself was influenced. Whitman believes Emerson may even have been overinfluenced by inferior predecessors: "I see he covertly or plainly liked best superb verbal polish, or something old or odd—Waller's 'Go lovely rose,' or Lovelace's lines 'to Lucasta'—the quaint conceits of the old French bards, and the like." After having acknowledged the figures who influenced Emerson, however, Whitman concludes with a recognition of Emerson's singular power. For an appropriate sense of this recognition, we must keep in mind its context. The concluding remark appears under the journal heading "Emerson's Books (The Shadows of Them)." And it concludes a line of thought including meditations on poets who influenced Emerson as well as the extent of Emerson's earlier influence upon Whitman. But Whitman completes this meditation on his literary heritage with an unusual observation: "The best part of Emersonism is it breeds the giant that destroy itself."[7]

This observation differentiates the influence of the "master" from the figures who influenced Emerson. Unlike theirs, Emerson's influence is destined, Whitman suggests, to destroy itself. When we give full cultural weight to this description of the protocol Emersonian influence follows, we cannot, as Bloom would, subject it to the discourse of repression. Another Emerson scholar, Richard Poirier, provides an understanding of Emerson's influence more compatible with Whitman's version than Bloom's.

Poirier, unlike Bloom, does not turn to Emerson in order to be recalled to America's past, although he is just as alert to the contradictions of modernity. Poirier turns to Emerson for a premodern accommodation to the obsolescence procedures of modernity. When considered as the result of an "influx of vehicular power," modernity, in its power to displace inherited structures, can be praised as akin to Emerson's style:

> The invisible and therefore the most unavoidable and voracious instrument of inherited culture was language itself. That, I think, is what Emerson means by the wonderful phrase "this riddle of liberty." He was ready to teach us, long before Foucault, that if we intend ever to resist our social and cultural fate, then we must first see it for what it is, and the form of that fate, ultimately, is the language we use and by which we learn to know ourselves. Language is also, however, the place wherein we can make our most effective inflection of dissent. These consist of acts of writing, reading, speaking by which language gets modified to individual purpose. Through such acts as these, more than by directly political actions, consciousness might be altered and, if only on occasion, a truer self or "genius" might be discovered.[8]

Like Whitman, Poirier finds a genius at work in Emerson's writing, a "giant" that, in resisting the structures of language through which it is fated to appear, destroys them to become a free power. Emerson's style, "by its own forever unsatisfied anticipations, at once creates, passes through and banishes the solidified aspects of the work."[9] In distilling Emerson's cultural duty to that of representing the genius of language—its appearance, transmission, and perpetuation—Poirier emphasizes an important effect of Emerson's work: it puts every reader in mind of his own genius.

I wonder, however, if literary genius would insist on this power to be unlocatable everywhere except in a modernist's context. Writing in a premodern America, Whitman did not need an "unlocatable" power. For him, Emerson's genius was needed the way a regenerative force in nature was: to develop a new generation of Americans. Once Emerson's genius fulfilled this task, it could disappear. For the persons his genius had evolved itself into could carry on the process of evolution on their own. Emerson's "final influence," Whitman writes, is "to make his students . . . cease to believe in anything outside of themselves . . . when one needs the impalpably soothing and vitalizing influences of abysmic Nature . . . they will not be sought for." [10]

While Poirier hears in Emerson's style an unappeasable desire to be free of every literary form in which genius materializes, Whitman inherits from Emerson the power to be regenerated by the forms through which nature materializes her powers. In Poirier's version, all of the moral maxims through which Emerson took the measure of his passage through culture become instances of a Nietzschean will to power over any and all forms—including the human form itself. For Whitman, however, the full force of Emerson's genius derived from its power to remind every man of his natural genius. Unlike Poirier, Whitman found in Emerson a reaffirmation of what he called the law of nature, the revelation to mankind of the imaginative power creative of nature.

Modern and Premodern Americans

In a sense Bloom and Poirier reduplicate, in the context of literary modernism, the premodern solutions of Hawthorne and Whitman to the encroachment of modernity. In response to the willed shortening of memory at work in literary modernism, Bloom puts the speech act of "repression" to unusual duty. In his criticism, "repression" removes itself from the psychoanalysts' enclave and enters the world of modern poetry, where it enables a modern poet to assert his originality by repressing his precursors.

In Bloom's criticism, "repression" trades upon the ambivalence attending a modernist's wish to be original. His wish to be free from his literary precursors turns out to be indistinguishable from the simultaneous wish for them to return through the words of his poetry. The speech act of repression translates the modern poet's wish to be original into its opposite—the desire for the return of the precursors.

Bloom's work turns Nietzsche on his head. Bloom turns Nietzsche's "active forgetting" into a repression of cultural memory. By setting Nietzsche's insistence on the willful separation of the superman from culture into a cultural context of its own, Bloom undoes the cultural use to which Nazi anti-Semitism put Nietzsche's doctrines. He revives the value of a Jewish culture of memory the modernist movement of Nazism tried to destroy.

In Bloom's criticism, the modern instant is extemporized into anxious relations with a past. His notion of the anxiety attending literary expressions enables him to archaicize modern poetry by deliberating on its lineage. Like Hawthorne's collective memory, Bloom's notion of literary anxiety calls attention to the repression of communal relations in a modern world. And like Hawthorne's collective memory, Bloom's repression permits a recovery of communal relations by deepening their basis in time.

Emerson's *Nature*

Unlike Bloom, Emerson lived at a time when it was possible to believe the culture needed to remember nothing but its Revolutionary beginnings. Consequently he did not need to revive the cultural value of memory. But neither did he affirm his contemporaneity the way Poirier does. Poirier uses style as a principle of negative freedom able to release literary figures from existing cultural forms, but Emerson's age wanted the power of natural liberty able to release the genius in every citizen.

To direct the nation's attention to its natural liberty, Emerson turned to the scene of the nation's founding. We have already seen how such orators as Daniel Webster derived all their authority by claiming that scene as the cultural locus for their speech and action. In claiming that scene they were implicitly claiming the founding principles as the motives for their actions. We have also seen that practically no one else in the culture presumed to speak or act from these principles, and we have considered Webster's compromise on these principles and Emerson's response to that compromise.

But we have not as yet considered why Emerson should find it so important to respond to Webster personally. As it happens, Emerson began his public career as a man of letters by using Webster's 1825 speech at Bunker Hill Monument as a point of departure. Emerson called Webster a "natural genius,"[11] thus indicating his belief that Webster spoke with all the force of nature's laws. Consequently, when Emerson wrote his *Nature,* an essay he hoped would make the laws of nature available as a moral resource to the nation, he turned to Webster as an embodiment of those laws.

When he wrote the essay, America had, in Emerson's mind, lost relation to the laws of nature, converting them instead into forms of self-interest. Emerson believed the nation was founded upon these laws, and that the nation's finest men embodied them. That is why he always described Webster in terms borrowed from scenes in nature. That is also why he began *Nature* with reference to Webster's Bunker Hill speech—he wanted to identify his essay with the same motive powers from which Webster spoke.

But there was a rather important difference between Emerson's conception of the availability of nature's laws and Webster's. When Webster spoke at the Bunker Hill Monument in 1825, he addressed his listeners as a "race of children" who, while "standing among the sepulchres of our fathers," must feel themselves looked down upon by the fathers.[12] After having reminded his listeners of their continued debt to their Revolutionary fathers, he commanded them to defend and preserve the fathers' creation.

What Emerson found most powerful in this speech—Webster's ability to speak with all the living power of the Revolutionary moment—he also found most debilitating: Webster's identification of this power with his person and the dead fathers' bones rather than the "race of children" he addressed.

In Emerson's mind this power did not come from the Revolutionary fathers or from Webster but from nature. And he wrote *Nature* in order to restore nature's power rather than the fathers' watchful eyes to the American people. To achieve his purpose, Emerson returned to the foundation scene upon which Webster based his speech. But once there he founded a compact between the people and their principles different from Webster's. Emerson's visionary compact educated the American people in the use of self-reliance, a faculty of their own that would enable them to turn their founding principles into motives for their actions.

Unlike Hawthorne, Emerson did not want to return the American people to a vision of the shared collective life they achieved in the past. Only the founding principles could permit them to act according to nature's laws. Those laws and the nation's principles were, for Emerson, the same.

His visionary compact founded on the faculty of self-reliance differed most dramatically from Poe's breach of the cultural contract, founded on the faculty of perversity. For Poe, as we have seen, any culture that based its actions on a Revolutionary mythos disconnecting it from any continuing relation to its past was indistinguishable from oblivion.

Like Poe, Emerson recognized the problem with the Revolutionary mythos, but he also saw cultural benefits. In the persistent presence of the founding scene, Emerson found a way to give cultural validity to moral principles that would otherwise be considered mere idealizations. That founding scene was for Emerson the cultural equivalent of the nation's soul. The faculty of self-reliance enabled Americans to rely on that soul when they could no longer depend upon the politicians' compromises. Living at a time in which the people were extremely aware of the difference between the politicians' compromises and the nation's principles, Emerson like Whitman underscored these differences to salvage the principles rather than the compromises.

Unlike Whitman, however, Emerson grounded the faculty of self-reliance in the whole self, or the collective within (rather than, as Whitman did, in the masses outside) the individual. Whitman's man-en-masse claims the same moral principles as does Emerson's self-reliant man as the justification for his actions. But the man-en-masse performs actions *in* the world instead of contemplating the self-sufficiency of the principles.

When Emerson wrote *Nature,* he needed to address what was whole and unified within all Americans in order to prevent them from feeling part of that "race of children" to which such orators as Webster reduced them. In addressing the whole self, Emerson hoped to make the listener whole and the nation healthy.

The Law of Nature

Addressing the whole self, however, made it necessary for Emerson to acknowledge what threatened its wholeness. Emerson numbered actions separated from their principles, individuals apart from the self, things detached from their thoughts, among the threats to wholeness. He also envisioned the laws of nature as the answer to these threats. In Emerson's essays, a law of nature cannot be distinguished from a spiritual law. A spiritual law establishes indissoluble connections between thoughts and things, individuals and the self, actions and their principles. Instead of prescribing rules, a law of nature works the way a spiritual proverb does. It never stops making connections between an individual's experiences and his understanding of them. Like a tried and true proverb a law of nature can apply to an almost infinite number of situations, all of which can be understood on its terms.

Throughout *Nature,* Emerson will use two figures who are more usually thought of as utterly separated from one another, an idealist and a materialist, as his way of revealing how nature's laws work. Nature encourages both the idealist, who wants the world converted into ideas, and the materialist, who wants ideas converted into useful things, to realize their will. It does so, Emerson suggests, because nature works best when all the things that can be realized from thoughts, and all the thoughts that can be inferred from things, are simultaneously achieved. Nature's law might best be described as the relation, the ever-enlivened relation, between thoughts and things. To have the one compensatorily releases the need for the other. All the vitality in the law inheres in the transition from the thought to the thing or the thing to the thought, for that is the ever-moving course of nature.

At a time in which the Revolutionary mythos was organizing America into factions, Emerson wrote to bring opponents into reciprocal, transitive relationships with one another. In returning a thing to a thought or a thought to a thing, a human being experienced the life of things and thoughts in terms of a separative connection. And the experience of separative connection was the experience of the law of nature. Through an experience of the connection relating what would otherwise remain separated, an individual could know the whole of existence rather than identify with any of the parts. So to return persons to the whole, Emerson began *Nature* by separating them from what made them feel partitive—such as the bones of the dead founding fathers, or their scrutinizing eyes, or their overshadowing deeds.

To disconnect his listeners from what made them feel ghostly by comparison, Emerson addressed what made them feel whole again. He spoke to the whole self when he asked, "Why cannot we also enjoy an original relation with the universe?" That question dissolved all the past into the felt power to begin anew: what Martin Buber has described as the "soul's part" of a deed—not an achieved action but the will to achieve it.

> Imagine a man, who breaks off his deed, who lives only the soul's part of it, who feels that nameless spark, that kinesis through which the deed from being the life experience of an individual becomes a happening given to all; is he not similar to the doer and yet before all his counter-

part. For this fragment of the deed that he lives receives the autonomy of a whole.[13]

Writing at a time in which Americans lived a life of deeds split off from the enlivening motive forces for action, Emerson restores the priority of motives and principles over any particular action. *Nature* exists as a thought experiment Emerson intended to be used in a specific way: to dissolve a world of disconnected agents and dissociated actions back into their source in the nation's principles, which are nature's laws.

Nature has recently been described as Emerson's reaction-formation against the influence of the founding fathers. By reading *Nature* through this modern resistance, I hope to indicate the power of the law of nature,[14] and how nature's law—which in Emerson's view was not the regenerative power we found in Whitman, but the experience of an original relation with everything in the universe—manifests itself in Emerson's use of language.

A Point of Departure

On one level (and this is particularly true in the case of *Nature*'s relation to the death of Ellen Tucker), Emerson's essays do relate to a lost past and can be considered sustained works of mourning—in Freud's sense of the working through of the loss of a love object.[15] From this perspective the speaker of these essays attains an identity through his internalization of the lost objects. But whereas Freud describes this "working through" solely in terms of such an internalization, Emerson goes a step further in his doctrine of compensation.[16] This doctrine is expressed most succinctly in the sentence "Though defeated all the time, to victory I am born." As is implicit in this expression, Emerson considers compensation not as a mere reaction to defeat and loss, but as a demand for them as prerequisites for an expansion in power. Power, for Emerson, results from an increased capability, and capability increases for him through an awareness of what is possible. Since what is actual suppresses the possible, the loss of what is actual marks for Emerson the return in principle of the power of possibility.

When we follow out the implications of this process for Emerson's essays, we find his already actualized utterances to be the suppression of possible ones, which is one reason why Emerson's essays always seem in the act of self-revision. In his self-revisions, Emerson always suggests a knowledge just beyond the reach of any single conceptual representation. Metaphor is the literary figure expressive of this reach beyond the grasp of a concept. For Emerson representational thinking represses a language able to signify beyond the reach of conceptual formulation.

Hence in *Nature* Emerson's doctrine of compensation works on two contradictory levels. On one level, an idealist's discourse "works through" a traumatic scene like the one mentioned at the end of the "Nature" section, where "contempt of the landscape" is experienced after the loss "by death of a dear friend." Two different losses threaten the idealist in this traumatic scene: his friend's death and the seeming loss of nature's sympathy. The idealist protects himself from the first loss in the "Discipline" section when he turns the death of a friend into a sign of an already completed idealization. After their transformation into the "solid and sweet wisdom" of their constituent ideas, the idealist can permit his friends to be "withdrawn from our sight." The idealist protects himself from the loss of nature in the section of the essay entitled "Idealism." There, after he "postpones" nature into the "empire" of his thought, he can reduce physical nature to an "outcast corpse," and no longer fear her withdrawal of sympathy. Yet no sooner does he complete this conversion of nature into a corpse than a second thought intervenes: "I have no hostility to nature but a child's love of it, I expand and live in the warm day like corn and melons."

On the level of the child, the idealist's defenses are experienced as an even more profound loss—that of a precognitive relation to nature. Whereas the idealist seeks to possess man and nature in his idealizations, the child is equiprimordial to nature. The child's materialistic demands of nature are irretrievably opposed to the idealist's.

Two conclusions follow: the idealist's conceptual activity represses the child's more materialistic relation to nature. But only through such a repression can nature be represented at all. Which means that Emerson uses the repression we usually associate with law and the ego as the mental constraint required before representational thinking can take place.

In *Nature,* each of the idealist's formulations "takes" a natural object and replaces it with an abstract expression, thereby recalling the melancholy scene at the end of "Nature" the idealist wants to forget but the child cannot forget. In partial recognition of this dilemma, the idealist, in such pronouncements as "Even the corpse has its own beauty," cultivates a taste for the beauty of the morbid. Through such refinements of his perceptions, the idealist tries to reexperience the earlier "contempt" he felt in the landscape after the death of his friend as a "hidden" beauty. Following this mental revision, even the "natural" contempt of a wintry landscape can seem beautiful. "Leafless trees" can turn into "spires of flame" and "dead calices" into stars—all this to the accompaniment of the "mute music" of "withered stems and stubble."

But it is not long before the idealist, having made the desolate itself appear beautiful, further displays the abstract power of his thought to make the beautiful itself disappear.[17] For, he explains, "this beauty of Nature which is seen and felt as beauty is the least part." The idealist's entire discourse, begun with the question "to what end Nature?" (itself ambiguous with its concealed linkage of death and purpose in the word "end"), proceeds through a progressive dematerialization of the objective world, as nature is transformed successively into "Commodity," "Beauty," "Language," "Discipline," until finally, in the "Idealism" section, the "end" of nature turns out to be her ability to come to an end. Throughout *Nature* the object of the idealist's discourse, the teleology of objective nature, subtly conflicts with the idealist's means of articulating this teleology, which dematerializes objective nature.

But if the "real" purpose of the discourse of idealism turns out to be this dematerialization, all its utterances derive their cognitive value from this act. Before we can acknowledge the loss of nature resulting from this activity, however, we need to hear the complaints of the materialistic child who wants to recover nature, but as a loss of idealism.

Involved in a discursive economy based on an excess of demand yet a deficiency of response,[18] the child and the idealist mutually oppose yet also complement one another throughout *Nature*. Possessing what the other lacks, each serves as a point of departure for the other. The child wants an immediate relation to nature devoid of any articulation; the idealist wants the "splendid labyrinth" of his own ideas voided of a grounding world. Ideally, of course, the child's things without thoughts and the idealist's thoughts without things should come together in a realized metaphor. For as the idealist argues in the "Language" section, "a material image, more or less luminous," should arise in the mind of a real thinker "contemporaneous with his every thought." But this stricture only exposes the inadequacy of idealism, which has come up with ideas unable to be grasped except through the very things idealism must dematerialize in attaining its ideas.

The discourse of idealism implies that the idealist "possesses" no ideas but only performs this dematerialization. Consequently if his identity depends on this act, he is always on the verge of becoming reflective enough to dissolve even his own identity into its constituent ideas. Peculiar to this "ultimate" self-realization, though, is the idealist's recognition that reason is "not mine, or theirs, or his, but we are its; we are its property and men."

Nature will soon convert this recognition into the metaphor of the transparent eyeball. For now, we must understand that nature cannot be adequately represented in either the child's precognitive relation or the idealist's abstractions. It can appear only in the separative connection between them, as what remains unthought and unspoken in each.

Although it does not do so explicitly, *Nature* reserves a place for just such unthinkable thinking—in the section marked "Spirit." In keeping with the unthinkable value of "Spirit," its positioning in the text is more informative than any of its statements, for "Spirit" appears only after the intended purpose of *Nature*—the discovery of the "end" of nature in "Idealism"—has been completed. In coming after the end of nature, "Spirit" serves as a postreflexive afterthought[19] to the earlier understanding of nature. By redefining nature as "God projected into the unconscious," thus reenvisioning nature as the actualization not of clear ideas but of unthought or at least unconscious thinking, "Spirit" moves beyond the discourse of idealism. But if "Spirit" is the name for this thinking outside the context authorized by the idealist's philosophy, then all those unassimilable thoughts, and revisions of earlier thoughts by later ones, at work in the composition of *Nature* turn out to be the work not of idealism but—in its broadest definition as an afterthinking—of "Spirit." Or, put as starkly as possible, the essay *Nature* is, from the beginning, a work of "Spirit."

A Spirited Start

Idealism, though, should not be seen to precede spirit in any formally causal sense; otherwise the notions of causality and sequential progress inherent in idealistic discourse could be used as adequate descriptive terms for spirit. "Spirit" not only appears after the idealist's discourse reaches an impasse, but has been in the idealist's discourse from the beginning. For nowhere does an unbridgeable gap become more evident than in the opening paragraph of *Nature:*

> Our age is retrospective. It builds the sepulchre of the fathers. It writes biographies, histories and criticism. The foregoing generation beheld God and nature face to face; we through their eyes. Why should not we also enjoy an original relation to the universe? Why should not we have a poetry and philosophy of insight and not of tradition, and a religion by revelation to us, and not the history of theirs? Embosomed for a season in nature, whose floods of life stream around and through us, and invite us by the powers they supply, to action proportioned to nature, why should we grope among the dead bones of the past or put the living generation into masquerade out of its faded wardrobe. The sun shines today also. There is more wool and flax in the fields. There are new lands, new men, new thoughts. Let us demand our own works and laws and worship.[20]

Anyone reading these lines hears Emerson achieve his characteristic tone through the conversion of pathos into self-command. Taken together, the first three sentences register a feeling of belatedness, then reiterate that sense until the declarations of dependence shift into a tone of self-assertion. Each sentence seems expressed with enough finality to declare its independence from the next, even before that independence asserts itself rhetorically through Emerson's characteristic avoidance of transitions. The elliptical form of the first three sentences only underscores their tension, a taut opposition growing tighter with each unresolved reiteration—as if each sentence carried the urgency of a will before it became speech. Moreover, the absence of either transitionals or subordination confers the intensity of an "insubordinate" opening statement upon each sentence. Then the repeated opening construction—"it builds," "it writes"—suspends the sense of succession. Each of these three sentences returns to the same point but with renewed force, as if they existed simply to indicate the power to generate expressions rather than to express anything in particular.

In its ostensible rhetoric of defensive reaction, this opening paragraph could be pointed to as an example of Emerson's susceptibility to repression. (It does after all set a later generation against an earlier one.) But such a view would have to ignore the way that Emerson uses the force of this opening conflict between generations as an enabling energy.

Instead of being immediately discharged into meaning, these opening sentences remain suspended in possibility. Their putative subject, "we," is literally defined by an undischargeable belatedness felt in the clause "we through their eyes." According to the logic of defensive reaction, this is exactly where "our" problem arises: "We" cannot convert the potential energy of discontent into the actual content of a new world independent of "our" reaction to the old. In the apparently revolutionary question "Why should we not *also* enjoy an original relation with the universe?" the "also" implies a repetition if not an imitation at work in the very wish for independence, as if "our" wish were first the fathers'. Moreover, any attempt to enact the policy commanded in the ringing exhortation "Let us demand our own works and laws and worship" will inevitably substitute a second nature or culture for this "original relation." The entire paragraph reacts against the fathers but in a tone commanding enough to be a father's. Consequently when the tone of the paragraph finally eventuates in a command, it turns out to be one that demands that "we" do precisely what we feel compelled not to do, repeat the desires and actions of the fathers.

The complex tone of this passage calls for independence in a way that implicates independence in the logic of a double bind. and it does so in a language itself dependent on a preexisting discourse of independence: when the passage rings true at all, it does so precisely because it echoes previously formulated declarations of independence. "We" do not speak this discourse so much as we are spoken by it, as a plurality not of first but of third persons—for if we long for our independence in a replication of the expressions of the fathers, "we" cannot be distinguished from them.[21]

All of this only suggests that Emerson begins *Nature* with the recognition of an impasse, an introduction going noplace but where "we" were in Webster's Bunker Hill Monument speech—longing for independence in the language of the fathers.

This is not to say, however, that the introduction lacks force. Emerson will reactivate the shifts and revisions necessitated by this opening opposition between generations as a textual strategy throughout the remainder of the essay. But he will convert the generational difference into the opposition we have already seen between the idealist, who thinks in one set of categories, and the child, who feels in another. The presence of this later opposition in the initial generational conflict can easily be grasped once we place that final (idealistic) command to begin a new culture directly in front of the first question. For such an idealistic command to build a culture will inevitably lead to the child's demand to recover an original relation with the universe.

The rest of the introduction only elaborates on the implications of this contradiction. First the idealist's culture (wherein the "most abstract truth" is the "most practical"), then the child's nature (which reduces culture to so much "chipping, baking, painting and washing") becomes the emphatic term. Throughout the remainder of the essay, these terms will never peaceably coexist but continually threaten to cancel each other out, with the nature-culture hierarchy obsessively reversing itself until the conclusive impasse in the "Idealism" section. As an echo of the introductory impasse, this concluding impasse makes "Spirit" necessary.

As a whole the essay reactivates, as its principle of composition, a double consciousness. Each time Emerson reformulates an earlier statement (a "foregoing generation") in a later one, it is as if he has silently spoken the first paragraph in the interval. So this opposition can be said to exist not in and for itself but in order to reveal the space between the ideas of the idealist and the demands of the child as the charged space distinguishing what has been said from what can be said.

That charged space is exactly what the opening passage turns out to be. For if we do not discharge the felt power of its discontent into mutually antagonistic subjectivities, we will find in it a force violently oscillating between the fathers and "us," as though this exchange of power were itself generative of a new will directing its regenerative power against the notion of a subjectivity knowable apart from this separative relation. Neither fathers nor "we" emerge as primary in this power struggle, but rather the relation effecting itself through both as an ever-renewed power.

In other words, the opening passage enacts the power of influence itself, an ever-oscillating energy which exceeds the identity of both fathers and sons, idealists and children. Never adequately embodied in any particular meaning or identity, this power turns out to be the ever-emergent yet always unrealizable character of regeneration. When it makes itself visible between successive generations, regeneration appears as the indefinite suspension between what has been and what will be. When discharged into subsequent generations it releases new possibilities; when undischarged, regeneration appears as the power of transition.

To put it paradoxically, this paragraph is not a beginning so much as an ever-renewed transition; and heard aright, this natural transiting power will fill in the space of the grammatical transitionals elided from Emerson's text.

A Sublime Transition

Two observations should follow from the foregoing analysis: we get a strong sense of ourselves only in opposition to others (which is why it is so difficult not to believe in the Declaration of Independence), and Emerson envisioned a force prior to or independent of even this seemingly fundamental opposition. But this force, although intimated in the opening passage, does not really emerge until after Emerson in effect begins *Nature* again in the "Nature" section, for here Emerson experiences a radical solitude free of any need for the image of another (even if that other be only the self-conscious self)[22] to reflect and thereby concretize the self. Let us put this experience in its most abstract terms: in "Nature" Emerson experiences independence, free of the self-other opposition, in the form of influence as such.

He does so twice. The first time is while under the stars: "But if a man would be alone, let him look at the stars. The rays that come from these heavenly bodies will separate between him and what he touches." Through the transparent atmosphere man can see "in the heavenly bodies the perpetual presence of the sublime, though always present they are inaccessible, but all natural spirits make a hundred impressions when the mind is open to their influence."

The words I want to dwell on are "the rays . . . will separate between him and what he touches." Hear them one way and these lines are indeed touching, for we need only recall how many relations Emerson has lost touch with—his first wife, father, two brothers—to know his wish *not* to be touched, to remain out of touch with all (possible, lost) relations. But Emerson clearly does not mourn here, and he does not quite wish not to be touched; rather he experiences the separation between the self and what it touches as the sublime. Unlike the Kantian negative sublime defined as an excess of signification simultaneously breaking down the capacity of the understanding and awakening the reason as the only possible agent of comprehension,[23] and unlike the use to which most American orators put the sublime, as an expression of their power over their audience, or nature, or both, the Emersonian sublime results from an intensification of the interval, an excess—paradoxically enough—of relation. Or rather the Emersonian sublime arises with the breakdown of a continuous "determinate" relation between self and other until only the connection between remains.

Once the connection between them asserts itself, the subject and object poles dissolve and what remains is the sublime influence, the natural regenerative force itself. Consequently, "influence" cannot be considered a "property" belonging to any identifiable subject or object. The universalization of its influence from "heavenly bodies" to "all natural objects" makes clear the independence of the sublime ray from any specific object. While influence can be known only through the relation between an influencer and an influenced, it can be localized in or appropriated by neither pole but only in the exchange of power, the regeneration taking place when the sublime influence lights up the *interval* or *transition between* terms. A man who experiences the sublime influence is disconnected from both himself and the world and quite literally occupies a state of self-reliance.

In its radical independence from the rest of the essay, a second yet intransitive beginning as well as a fresh start, the entire section entitled "Nature" becomes an extended exercise in the sublime. But its second rendition of the sublime is even more difficult to account for than the first. Immediately following the famous "crossing the bare common" sequence and after his transition to the woods,[24] Emerson exclaims, "all mean egotism vanishes. I become a transparent eye-ball. I am nothing, I see all; the currents of the Universal Being circulate through me." This time it is the startling declaration "I become a transparent eye-ball" which must give pause. The image stares out at us like a shock separated from its consoling recognition. It recalls the eyes of the fathers and the transparent sky, and anticipates the friends who will become transparent to their ideas. But it is also akin in its sphericity to the "embosoming" power of nature. Indeed the image threatens to open up no specific meaning but too many associations.

Idealism, sublimity, death, cognition, protection—these are some of the associations; yet none of them seems precisely appropriate to the absorptive power of the metaphor. Neither nature, the fathers, nor "I" seems adequate but a conversion of all three into "circulations of the Divine Being." But then it cannot be the Divine Being either, for that only circulates through the transparent eyeball. When we examine the metaphor itself for a clue to its meaning, the difficulties only multiply. A *transparent* eyeball is in essence an eye we look through to see something else; a transparent *eyeball* looks toward objects it dematerializes into "currents of the Universal Being." A transparent eyeball, then, would be, in the conflation of these two traits, a *seeing seen through*, as if Emerson wanted to provide an image for the impossible act of sight seeing itself. Further association can be teased out: the eyeball is trans-parent, trans-individual, trans-objective (in the sense that sight establishes the distance between self and object). Undefinable as either subject or object, God or nature, it seems more like a metaphor for the living glance resulting if God and nature should ever look face to face.

We might clarify these observations with another assertion, and a partial expansion of terms. Emerson's transparent eyeball is not a metaphor for another term; it is the original relation out of which metaphors can be made, which Emerson will later call the faculty of self-reliance. In *Nature,* Emerson provides, in the "transparent eyeball," an image of the relation existing prior to the differentiation of metaphoric tenor from vehicle. The "transparent eyeball" in this perspective cannot then refer to either God or nature, but both of these terms become fictions or ruses [25] necessary before we can imagine a relation as "original" as the one intimated here.

Partial justification for this description may be found in Emerson's journals where the line translated by "I become a transparent eye-ball" is "I am happy in my universal relations." But this "tenor" does not provide a referent for the image, but only underscores its inaccessibility. "Universal" relations, like original ones, can never be confined into particular referents precisely because they are always oscillating among an infinite number of terms.

As a literal reenactment of the sublime influence felt from the rays of the stars, this metaphor separates the idealist from the rest of his discourse, but separates him the way a metaphor does. If we define metaphor as that by means of which something is itself by becoming something else, the transparent eyeball, as the charged space something moves through to become something else, refers to the very activity of making metaphor, the transition of one term into another (a movement, by the way, which also makes all quests for meaning and purposes possible). Consequently one cannot call the transparent eyeball a metaphor; it is rather the metaphorizing power, the motive power or principle upon which metaphor works. No sooner does this power, or principle, appear in *Nature* than it threatens to make all the other sections metaphors for its activity.

No wonder the eyeball has been cited as a lapse in Emerson's taste. If in an earlier section of this discussion, we said that the eyeball could appear only in the gaps in Emerson's text, we now understand why: it is in itself a gap, a transition between what can be written and what can be "grasped" as meaningful. It literally surprises us out of our propriety and breaks us free of the closed circle of the discourse of idealism and its language authorized by the fathers. Not a meaningful expression but the imaged interval between words, the unthinkable transformative power or the genius of language that makes all significance possible, a "transparent eyeball" traverses the common sense of all words.

When we correlate the transparent eyeball with other elements in *Na-*

ture, we find it answered by "Spirit." As we have already seen, spirit appears less as a constituent aspect of this essay than as an exposition of what takes place in its breakdowns; spirit functions as a transition, as the afterthinking made necessary after the idealist has *over seen* nature, lost her for his ideas. After the idealist has seen through nature (as if by looking at her through the "transparent eyeball") into her ideas, he has *over* seen or rendered gratuitous the very subject giving purpose to his inquiry. In other words, he has made nature as much a mere transitional term as the transparent eyeball and spirit are. When we read *Nature,* then, we gradually find nature to occupy the same place in the discourse of idealism as that of spirit and the transparent eyeball: the space of the sublime, a charged interval finally unassimilable to the purpose of idealism. And although we cannot find spirit and the sublime within the context of the idealist's discourse, we read them, as it were, "between" the lines.

In the "transparent eyeball," the idealist recovers that "original relation" with the universe he wished for in the introduction. But he recovers it only outside the context of his discourse. In other words, in recovering this relation through an incomprehensible metaphor, he cannot really be said to have recovered it at all. If his two statements "I am nothing, I see all," when coupled with the declaration "I become a transparent eyeball," adequately describe the idealist's complete experience, that experience must be defined not as an actual event, but only as a virtual or possible experience. An experience in which no thing exists to be experienced, and no one exists to experience it, itself ceases to be an experience in other than a merely formal sense. And since such a fadeaway experience can never actually take place, but always remains possible, it can never be remembered but only commemorated in a subliminally sublime scene.

Moreover this subliminal scene—this transformation of the idealist into the transparent eyeball—"foresees" the death of the idealist; for "Discipline" will equate death with rendering a friend transparent before his essential ideas.

Such an "experience" of death is the ontological prerequisite for a discourse always in excess of its stated "ends." By incorporating the idealist's death (which is also on one level his own) into this pre-text, Emerson finds each repetition of this scene (in the lapses of the discourse of idealism) to be quite literal occasions for "being surprised out of his own propriety," which Emerson also envisions all "good" writing to be.[26]

The Crossing of the Eye

But now where do we find ourselves? Engaged in a discourse of idealism doomed to break down out of the excess of its original question, so stymied by its project that it must begin twice only to find that the second beginning can never take place.[27] Or to recompose this dilemma into its affirmative counterstatement: the entire discourse of idealism has produced, in its form, a reach in excess of its grasp, revealed to be man's "original relation" with the universe. Since, paradoxically enough, it is only through its self-defeat that the discourse can recover this original relation, we should explore the extent of this defeat as a means of acknowledging (but not quite comprehending) the dimensions of that achievement.

To begin at the beginning, we can say that in *Nature* the two beginnings work against each other to make the entire essay seem "in labor." The idealist develops a sequence leading from "Commodity" through "Beauty," "Language," and "Discipline" to culminate in "Idealism" as categories necessary and sufficient to answer the opening question "to what end nature?"; the "transparent eyeball," meanwhile, opens up a metaphoric level bound to exceed and transgress the limits of these categories. The authority of the idealist's sequence is grounded on a question whose answer results in the very separation from nature the question would avoid. Hence the idealist's categories finally subvert rather than serve the expectations of intelligibility implicit in his sequence.

The essay as a whole works by arousing a felt need to "trust" in the "order of things"; proceeds to translate that order into a sequence of categories based on a hierarchical (hence causal) paradigm; and then, in its transitional operations, violates the basis for that order.

According to the causal paradigm, each new category should build upon the preceding one, as its effect. but as if to violate its own ordering principle, the essay continually reactivates "commodity," the lowest rung on the hierarchical ladder. The "doctrine of use" appearing first in "Commodity" reappears as late as the "Spirit" section of the essay, where idealism, as if in a direct application of the proverb "Nothing in nature is exhausted in its first use," turns out to be "merely a useful introductory hypothesis."

Since the doctrine of use can be applied equally well to all of these categories, it signals in advance their merely provisional status. Each section ceases to be a definitive cognitive model, and instead becomes a commodity, valuable less as a definitive utterance than as a transitional force.

The contradictions, inconsistencies, sudden shifts in perspective, multiple rhetorical textures, and syntactic groupings in the essay all leave rents in its fabric and call attention to the distinctions between the ongoing argument and material unassimilable to it.

Predictably enough, these contradictions appear at the points of transition between levels of the essay. To give only one example: in the section entitled "Beauty," the idealist enjoins against looking for beauty from "the windows of diligence"; he then discovers in the culminating section the highest element of beauty to be available only in the contemplative "pursuit of the intellect." The intent here may be clear enough—the argument has shifted ground to distinguish between a material and an intellectual perspective—but the point to be made for our purposes is that Emerson has made this contradiction apparent in the transition between sections. He has not, as some commentators have maintained, subjected these contradictions to the dialectical principle of synthesis, nor has he validated a hierarchical paradigm.[28]

When they do not actively reveal them, the transitions between sections imply contradictions, which seem, therefore, to exist solely for the sake of making a transition. For example, in the "final" section of "Language," we find the adversative construction "But how great a language to cause such pepper corn information," where "pepper corn information" would apparently refer to all the assertions made in the previous section. But we need only mention one of the statements previously made to notice the mistake in the inference: "good writing . . . is the working of the Original Cause through the instruments he has already made." Obviously, if the section agreed to follow causal logic, this observation should have been reserved for the following section. As a result of this anticipation of its own subsequent developments, the essay seems to repeat itself, to "catch up with" what it has already said, thereby signaling in advance the provisional rather than the definitive status of all of its utterances. And the resulting multiple contradictions resist any attempt at a preterite order and release multiple possibilities in the transitions.

This is to say not that Emerson contradicts himself only at the points of transition, but that these nodal points underscore the transitional quality of all of his formulations: his capacity to restate yet unsay almost everything, to make all of his utterances seem tentative and provisional—mere preparations for what remains to be said, which in its turn seems to have been formulated already.

Or to see this situation from another perspective, the transitional contradictions are themselves aspects of a pervasive metaphoric design underpinning the entire text. In fact metaphor and contradiction have enough in common to make a distinction necessary. Both metaphor and contradiction state that something at once is and is not something else;[29] but whereas contradiction emphasizes the distinction, metaphor emphasizes the resemblance.

Having distinguished the two terms, however, we must subsume metaphor within contradiction before we can provide an insight into the peculiar status of the Emersonian metaphor, which asserts resemblance but without losing sense of the priority of the distinction. In other words, it is no longer a question, in Emerson's metaphors, of what is being compared with what, for the identity or self-givenness of the terms is exactly what becomes problematic in his use of metaphor. Unlike representational thought, Emerson's metaphorical thinking does not pretend to represent a self-present tenor in a vehicle, but illuminates the differences between each term. In *Nature*, there is no tenor or vehicle retrievable as the basic term, but only the "original relation" both tenor and vehicle serve to support.

For Emerson, words and things are metaphorical to begin with and so reveal their essence only by another metaphor. For example, in the observation "We say the heart to express emotion, the head to denote thought," we would expect "emotion" and "thought" to be the proper referents for "heart" and "head," but instead the passage proceeds, "and *thought* and *emotion* are words borrowed from sensible things, and now appropriated to spiritual nature," thereby catching up each word in an endless metaphoric play.

Emerson justifies the refusal to assign a single significance to either an object or a word by invoking the medieval model of correspondence, though not without also insisting upon his departure from it. Whereas correspondence theory posits a final relationship between a natural object and its spiritual counterpart, Emerson separates the "ray of relation" from the corresponding objects to effect a notion of correspondence without limits. Emersonian correspondence asserts the self-transcending, metaphorical—in short, relational—quality of all things. In his view, each existent must relate to another before it can "possess" its own significance. Since man's divisive fall into self-consciousness is the decisive model for such a relation, man becomes the central principle of this interrelation, as "a ray of relation passes from every other being to him. And neither can man be understood without these objects nor these objects without man."

So pervasive is this metaphorizing that neither ideas nor God (Emerson's apparent "god" terms) seems free of it. Emersonian ideas can reveal themselves only as qualities common to two objects and God himself serves only as the switch point where each "fossil metaphor" passes into a new relation: "In God every end is converted into new means." In other words, Emerson's style converts even its most fundamental terms into dominant metaphors rather than ontological entities. But if even "God" can be "grasped" only by becoming other than himself, we find not unity but relations at the origin of Emerson's ontology, and, in a remarkable reversal, all things become metaphors for this original relation.

When Emerson muses, in the section marked "Prospects," that "a dream lets us deeper into the secret of nature" than a "digested system," he provides still another perspective from which to view the action of nature. If, as we have already seen, the excess of demand placed on nature by the idealist's opening question leads to nature's exile in "Idealism," this same excessive demand necessitates the production of *Nature* itself as what is "projected into the unconscious," where, as in Freud's dreams, the wish for an "original relation" is fulfilled.

For the sake of a prospective vision, we might entertain the possibility that the metaphoric level of *Nature* constitutes an equivalent to the human unconscious, which, reveals its presence only through the lapses of logic, contradictions, and ellipses in the surface discourse.

But since even this perspective still affirms *Nature*'s recovery of an original relation, perhaps it would be better by way of a conclusion to this discussion of *Nature* to make a metaphor[30] and say that the entire text is an extended proverb. Like a proverb, *Nature* signifies not a specific meaning but too many possible applications; essentially incomplete, it defies placement in a fixed system but demands that it be placed in ever new contexts. It is a wandering figure of thought, a turn of the phrase always in the process of surpassing and rendering arbitrary every interpretation meant to grasp it. Translating what is known into what can be known, a force rather than a statement, it is a field of play where every conception approaches the inconceivable . . . *Nature* is the law of nature at work.

Proverbs

Having finally arrived at the point in our discussion where the essay produces a peculiar consciousness—a consciousness of an original relation rather than a subjective identity—we must ask whether or not the preterite line of *Nature,* even if it exists only for the sake of its disruptions, can be spoken by an individual subject. We can begin to answer this question by reexamining the relationship of the idealist to the materialistic child. These two subjects oppose yet fulfill each other. Earlier we treated their opposition as if it alone constituted the full range of subjectivity in *Nature.* But when the idealist and child speak together, their relationship seems to generate still another consciousness finally reducible to neither the idealist's nor the child's, but which nonetheless can say "I" only by speaking through their double disguise. Paradoxically, this new "I" can never be localized in the content of what "I" says.

Consider, for example, the passage at the end of "Idealism" wherein the idealist tries to explain his dematerialization of nature to the child: "I do not wish to fling stones at my beautiful mother nor soil my gentle next. I only wish to indicate the true position of nature in regard to man . . . and bring the mind to call that apparent which it uses to call real." The meaning of the passage reduces to I do and I do not wish to dematerialize nature; the propositions are at an equal distance from one another, so that it is impossible to affirm without denying or the reverse. No sooner do "I" speak from the locus of the child who would not throw stones at his mother than "I" am flung in the opposite direction by the very discourse "I" am speaking. With this chain of reversals in mind, we can maintain that the true "subject" of *Nature* is the practice of the transference of the self onto the position of other, and that the real force of this "subject" results from its successively occupying several discursive positions. When, as in this passage, the "I" who speaks (the idealist) is also an "I" spoken to (by the child), each "I" must be said to speak the discourse of the other. Consequently, the subject of the discourse is always in a skewed relation to the "I" who is speaking. Consequently, an interval appears between what is said and who says it.

But this is to reiterate, only this time through the concept of intersubjectivity, what we have been saying all along—spirit or the law of nature occupies the place of the subject in Emerson's essays, and each time Emerson writes, he impersonates this subjectivity. When he describes writing as an activity where "I gain my point, I gain all points, if I can reach my companion with any statement which teaches him his own worth," Emerson equates writing with the activity of transferring this spirit or natural genius, visible between his "point" and a companion's worth, from himself to a reader. Reducible neither to Emerson nor to his reader, this genius quickly universalizes itself into all points precisely because it cannot be limited to any single entity. We require the "transparent eyeball" to imagine[31] this spirit or genius, just as we need the law of nature to describe it.

The influence at work in *Nature* does not require a self-other opposition wherein Emerson would prove his originality by surpassing (or repressing) the worth of another writer (or reader). Influence charges the space between writer and reader with the power of nature's laws. The words in this space can be said to belong neither to Emerson nor to his readers but to the quotable proverbs in which nature has recorded its laws.

When a writer's words become proverbial, they no longer require attribution to him. For he is speaking in proverbs, and proverbs spontaneously belong to the public domain.[32] A proverb breaks free of any specific context almost as immediately as it separates from any single "author." The unusual status of the speaker of proverbs becomes clearer from another perspective. When "I" quote a proverb, then "I" am spoken by the applicability of this utterance to my situation. But we cannot confidently identify a proverb's authority with its author. He too has been impersonated by this proverbial authority by speaking as if he were repeating a proverb. We must instead relegate the subject of Emerson's proverbs to the movement of absolute interconnection we mentioned earlier.

We need go no further than the "Prospects" section of *Nature* to recognize how proverbial the entire essay has become. After reading Emerson's quotations of the orphic poet's proverbs in that section, however, we must pause long enough to realize that Emerson is quoting a poet who does not yet exist outside the context of *Nature*. Appearing as he does in the "Prospects" section, a section which, in its unresolved tension between possibility (or prospect) and fulfillment, recapitulates in miniature the structuring principle of *Nature,* this poet, like "Spirit," speaks his proverbs only after the discourse of idealism has reached its logical conclusion, in a context not assimilable to but fragmented from the rest of *Nature*.

Furthermore, the poet does not make original statements but repeats proverbs,[33] which are, however, like those in the "transparent eyeball" sequence, also outside the context of the rest of *Nature*. So in a double or even treble sense, the poet speaks not his own thoughts or even the idealist's, but the thoughts which remain unthinkable, the always possible though never actual afterthoughts of *Nature*.

By means of these proverbs at the end of *Nature,* the essay provides a literal equivalent to Emerson's description of his reading experience, for here as well his own unwritten thoughts return with a kind of "alienated majesty." If the orphic poet's proverbs are then by way of analogy the essay's way of reading its own unwritten thoughts, he may also be described as Emerson's "ideal" reader ("who heard" from Emerson what he "never spoke"), literally produced by what remains unassimilable to the rest of the discourse, the essay's potential rather than actualized utterances. He is the reader who has made something of the spirit of *Nature*—namely himself. Or rather, by speaking the unconscious, or the "dream text," of *Nature,* the orphic poet seems literally to be a figure rising out of the dream of *Nature,* its fulfilled wish. In him nature speaks as a "realized will, the double of man," and through this *Nature* humanized, the speaker can at last satisfy the wish which took him on his quest to begin with, for like the fathers he can enjoy an original relation with nature.

As the echo of the "secret" thoughts of nature, the orphic poet can finally be equated with neither the reader nor the writer of *Nature,* but with the sudden "sally of spirit," the power of natural genius in transition between the two. In him, neither Emerson nor the reader speaks, yet both are spoken by him. As was the case in Whitman's description of Emerson's influence, this genius disappears once it has inspired the reader with the power of his share in nature's law.

Chapter Seven

Melville and Cultural Persuasion

Be a man's intellectual superiority what it will, it can never assume the practical, available supremacy over other men, without the aid of some sort of external acts and entrenchments, always in themselves, more or less paltry at the base.

And, as in real life, the proprieties will not allow people to act out themselves with the unreserve permitted to the stage; so, in books of fiction, they look not only for more entertainment, but, at bottom, even for more reality, than real life itself can show. Thus, though they want novelty, they want nature, too; but nature unfettered, exhilarated, in effect transformed.

—*Herman Melville*

The broad topic of this book has been the loss, by the mid-nineteenth-century America public sphere, of one ruling cultural mythos and the efforts exerted by certain cultural figures to achieve another. There has also been an implicit topic, invoked previously only as an undersong: the way in which these works from the nineteenth century have been received as classics of the American Renaissance by the twentieth. In the preceding chapters I have kept these two topics separate, bringing in the latter topic only to underscore the differences between modern and post-Jacksonian America. But in this chapter, I will make the difference between *Moby-Dick* as a nineteenth-century social text and *Moby-Dick* as a modern classic an explicit topic of discussion. To make this difference explicit I will need to show how *Moby-Dick*, the nineteenth-century social text, resists the procedures involved in forming a modern canon, just as its subject matter resisted or more precisely disarticulated the ruling mythos in the nineteenth century.

This mythos formed a backdrop for our discussions of the visionary compacts negotiated in the works of Emerson, Hawthorne, Whitman, and Poe. Melville moved this mythos onto center stage in *Moby-Dick*. In that novel, he explored historical and cultural activities lacking anything other than a sheerly rhetorical relationship with the scene of the Revolution.

In this chapter I will refer to this mythic context as a scene of cultural persuasion. And throughout this chapter I am going to investigate the lack of real relationship between the motives sanctioned by the Revolutionary scene and actions which take place in a post-Revolutionary world. I begin with the quarterdeck scene.

The Quarterdeck as a Scene of Cultural Persuasion

Melville constructed the quarterdeck scene around an argument between Captain Ahab and Starbuck, his first mate. Starbuck was not persuaded to Ahab's course of action. In opposition to Ahab's revenge quest, Starbuck reminded Ahab of the contract everyone on board the *Pequod* signed. According to the terms of that contract, the Pequod's crew agreed to hunt whales for the Nantucket market, not to gratify the captain's need for revenge. Action taken against a dumb brute motivated only by the appetite for revenge, Starbuck concluded self-righteously, constituted a blasphemy—against the God of Christianity as well as Nantucket's marketplace.

Now, the grounds for Starbuck's dissent are well-founded. They are rooted in both a faith in God and a belief in American free enterprise. He underscored the religious dimension of his argument with his accusation of blasphemy. Had he added other terms usually reserved for religious controversies—like Ahab's heresy and infidelity and his own despair—he may have persuaded the crew of their moral duty to mutiny against Ahab. But he did not use these other terms, and the rest of the crew did not mutiny.

To understand why they did not we need to consider Ahab's response:

> "Hark ye yet again,—the little lower layer. All visible objects, man, are but as paste-board masks. But in each event—in the living act, the undoubted deed—there, some unknown but still reasoning thing puts forth the mouldings of its features from behind the unreasoning mask. If man will strike, strike through the mask! How can the prisoner reach outside except by thrusting through the wall? To me, the white whale is that wall, shoved near to me. Sometimes I think there's nought beyond. But 'tis enough. He tasks me; he heaps me; I see in him outrageous strength, with an inscrutable malice sinewing it. That inscrutable thing is chiefly what I hate; and be the white whale agent, or be the white whale principal, I will wreak that hate upon him. Talk not to me of blasphemy, man, I'd strike the sun if it insulted me. For could the sun

do that, then could I do the other; since there is ever a sort of free play herein, jealously presiding over all creations. But not my master, man, is even that fair play. Who's over me? Truth hath no confines. Take off thine eye! more intolerable than fiend's glarings is a doltish stare."[1]

In responding with these words, Ahab does not deny Starbuck's charges. Ahab agrees to the religious context Starbuck proposed as the basis for their argument. Starbuck spoke with righteous indignation, but Ahab's response intensifies Starbuck's indignation until it sounds more like a prophet's wrath. He justifies his own wrath by placing it in the prophetic frame of reference the Book of Revelation affords him. In thus taking Starbuck down a "little lower layer," Ahab takes rhetorical control of the situation leading up to Starbuck's indignation.

By diving for a deeper religious motive than Starbuck can command, however, Ahab implicitly chastens Starbuck for the comparatively shallow purposes to which he puts his indignation. If Starbuck is willing to kill whales only for the capital their oil will accrue back in Nantucket, he is not willing to see them as representative of any purpose deeper than the profit motive. His profit motive compels him to see whales as dumb brutes. Ahab, in informing the whale with purposes involving a cosmic *enantiodrama,* turns Starbuck into an implicit blasphemer. For in treating the whale as nothing but a "pasteboard mask" for his vainglorious profit motive, Starbuck confirms Ahab's moral judgment. As a Christian whose faith is equiprimordial with a profit motive, Starbuck can interpret whaling only in a market context. To remind Starbuck of a deeper motive, Ahab speaks with all the rage of a man who can no longer remain satisfied with a religion based on marketplace values. So instead of responding to Starbuck's charges, Ahab condemns Starbuck's context and does so with all the rage of a man who experiences Starbuck's marketplace religion as only an example of a further justification for his own revenge quest.

In other words, Ahab does not respond either in or to the terms of Starbuck's argument; rather, he displaces Starbuck as well as the terms of his argument onto another motivational scene. On this other scene, however, Starbuck cannot continue his argument with Ahab. For Ahab has recast the terms (the profit motive, the Nantucket market, the instrumental reason) informing Starbuck's argument into the role of an oppressor. Or rather he lets the terms share this role with Moby-Dick. When turned into a cosmic struggle Ahab alone can fathom, the public argument with Starbuck moves inward where it becomes Ahab's private argument with the cosmos. This internalization, in its turn, invalidates the terms of the public argument with Starbuck. Ahab does not remain a cruel captain whose exploitation of his crew could justify Starbuck's mutiny, but becomes an understandably enraged victim of a malicious cosmic design. In taking Starbuck down onto his personal lower layer, the psychological dimension where he confronts his motives, Ahab internalizes Starbuck's animus, thereby turning it into a version of his own motive for revenge: Ahab acts out Starbuck's motive for mutiny, then, but in a scene of apocalyptic wrath which leaves Starbuck with no motive of his own.

Having coopted the terms able to justify Starbuck's potential mutiny, Ahab then virtually eliminates any genuine motive for Starbuck to embody. In a series of stunning rhetorical maneuvers, Ahab idealizes Starbuck's impulse to mutiny. Then he elevates Starbuck's defiance to such an apocalyptic pitch that it appears utterly coincident with his own wrath. Whereupon Ahab, instead of needing to oppose Starbuck, gives Starbuck's defiance its most noble expression, as his quest for Moby-Dick.

In laying prior psychological claim to Starbuck's defiance, however, Ahab does not immediately lessen Starbuck's anger. But he does bring Starbuck into consciousness of the consequences of rage. By experiencing himself as an enraged man, Starbuck feels all the passion for revenge he formally identified with Ahab. Before Ahab's speech, Starbuck felt able to oppose Ahab precisely because of the clear distinction between Ahab's rage and his own ethical identity. But following Ahab's speech, Starbuck can only identify Ahab's rage with an impulse in his own inner life. Consequently Starbuck can no longer claim the character of a rational, Christian man.

After provoking Starbuck to "anger-glow," Ahab, in the most remarkable move in this extraordinary scene, does not, as might be expected, challenge Starbuck to match his rage against Ahab's. Surprisingly gentle in his response, Ahab chides Starbuck to let go of an anger Ahab alone has been chosen to embody.

> "So, so, thou reddenest and palest; my heat has melted thee to anger-glow. But look ye, Starbuck what is said in heat, that thing unsays itself. There are men from whom warm words are small indignity. I meant not to incense thee. Let it go. Look! I see yonder Turkish cheeks of spotted tawn—living, breathing pictures painted by the sun. The pagan leopards—the unrecking and unworshipping things, that live; and seek, and give no reasons for the torrid life they feel! The crew, man, the crew! Are they not one and all with Ahab, in this matter of the whale? See

Stubb! he laughs! See yonder Chilean! he snorts to think of it. Stand up amid the general hurricane thy one tost sapling cannot, Starbuck. And what is it? Reckon it. 'Tis but to help strike a fin; no wondrous feat for Starbuck. What is it more? From this one poor hunt, the best lance out of all Nantucket, surely he will not hang back, when every foremost-hand has clutched a whetstone? Ah! constrainings seize thee; I see! the billow lifts thee! Speak, but speak!—Aye, aye! thy silence, then, *that* voices thee."[2]

This passage completes Ahab's separation of Starbuck's person from Ahab's rage, thereby eliminating Starbuck from a scene of persuasion where Ahab alone can determine the motives for action. In an earlier address to the crew, Ahab provoked his own reaction to the universe, a defiance grown out of rage, in Starbuck. In this passage he recovers personal possession of that defiance—but as if it were an act of Christian self-sacrifice. Consequent to this speech, rage once again became his personal trial and not the burden of a man now free to recover his rightful place among the crew. Following this speech Starbuck need no longer trouble himself with the moral dilemmas in Ahab's world. Ahab has relieved him of that duty. He can let Ahab take care of the deeper questions.

In his encounter with Starbuck, Ahab elicited from Starbuck's inner life a rage against a potentially nihilistic universe which Starbuck must deny in order to remain himself. And Ahab acted out that inner life as a means of dominating Starbuck, who can free himself from this immoral rage only by finding it already thoroughly perfected in Ahab's extraordinary character.

Once transmuted onto his scene of persuasion, Ahab ceases to be a target for Starbuck's dissent; instead he elevates Starbuck's dissent into an apocalyptic plane where dissent and Ahab's wish for a final reckoning with the powers of the universe become indistinguishable from one another. In this elevation, however, Ahab also utterly separates the ideological motives for action—the struggle between an utterly self-reliant man and oppressive cosmic forces—from the set of actions possible for Starbuck. Once he has voiced his own rationale for hunting the whale, Ahab expects Starbuck not to hunt for the same reasons but to return to a scene more in keeping with Starbuck's career. In his revelation of the powerful forces at work in his inner world, Ahab does not invite Starbuck to share in the life of this inner world, but releases Starbuck from the need to "stand up amid the general hurricane," and enables him to return to his former position. Here instead of hunting whales for either cosmic revenge or the profit motive, he can be satisfied to "help strike a fin."

Having resituated the world of motives in a scene where he alone will have control over their resolution, Ahab places the crew in a second realm, one ideologically determined by the first. As is the case with the world of the pagan leopards who live and seek but without the need to understand, the crew cannot act and know the real motives for their actions. These motives subsist only in Ahab's realm where Ahab alone embodies them. His scene of persuasion collapses the space of argument, where dissent would otherwise be acknowledged, into an opposition—that between him and cosmic forces—whose terms carry their conclusion within the form of their organization.

That Ahab manages all this in cadences borrowed from Shakespeare only underscores the "scenic" character of his separation from the crew.[3] If he talks to the men at all, he talks to them in a language that immediately encloses him in a theatrical frame: a theatrical frame, moreover, claiming all the "unapproachable" cultural power that Melville, in his review of Hawthorne's "Mosses from the Old Manse," claimed Shakespeare wielded over the mob.[4] Thus Ahab not only "acts out" and "ideally resolves" the principle of rebellion he evokes in the crew, but does so in a language so invested with cultural power that they can only be inspired by the cultural heights to which Ahab elevates their will to rebel. In short, Ahab seems here to embody not only the crew's inner life but also the best means of articulating it.

The Jacksonian Persuasion

In *The Jacksonian Persuasion,* Marvin Meyers spells out some of the political factors contributing to the formation of this scene of persuasion. Meyers locates a basis for Ahab's persuasive power in the complex workings of American politics. Meyers argues that all post-Jacksonian Americans shared Starbuck's need to interpret their motives according to some higher purpose than economic profit. Like Starbuck most Americans could be described as shareholders in a national joint-stock company. But, again like Starbuck, most Americans needed to replace the acquisitive and speculative drives of nascent capitalism with some other explanatory framework.

To meet these needs, orators and politicians devised slogans like "manifest destiny" promising to elevate individuals' business enterprise into a historical destiny.[5] These high callings had unwanted side effects, however, resulting in a division of psychic labor between the activities of America's citizens and the official or accepted rationale for these activities. Following the example set by their leaders, most Americans wanted to "preserve the virtues of a simple agrarian republic."[6] But by 1850 the republic had become distinctly nonagrarian.

To preserve republican virtue, many Americans turned the agrarian ideal into a sanction for social discriminations. When interpreted in terms of the agrarian model, American life divided itself into fairly neat moral categories. The "common people" in America set their reverence for equality against aristocratic privilege, their love of liberty against the domination of the wealthy, their natural dignity against cultural status, their honest work against dishonest speculation.

When they applied this orientation to their own activities, however, Americans discovered that people did not divide up into such neat oppositions. The national economy turned many Americans into speculators, elevated many more into positions of privilege, and demanded a domineering attitude from more than a few. If they were unwilling to sacrifice their belief in the possibility of upward mobility (and most Americans were not), the "common people" often could not distinguish their own activities from those they opposed. Almost everyone, for example, aspired to those positions of economic privilege they felt compelled by the rhetoric of republican virtue to oppose.

No matter how inadequate it was as a description of their lives, most Americans needed to preserve this orientation as a structure of belief. So they preserved this model as a "persuasion." Marvin Meyers helpfully defines their "persuasion" in terms of what it is not. It is not "a consistent doctrine, not a finely articulated program . . . but a broad judgment of public affairs informed by common sentiments and beliefs about the good life in America."[7] Like the Revolutionary mythos, the persuasion worked best when confronted with contradictions.

As confused morally and politically as America was in 1850, to be of a persuasion held out the promise of coherence and consensus. Recovering one's "persuasion" meant recovering emotional commitment to beliefs, attitudes, and projected duties able to secure a life against dissension and doubt.

On the post-Jacksonian scene of persuasion, an orator could find himself born again out of a simple agrarian past. It did not matter whether a birth certificate could verify the terms of rebirth. All that truly mattered was the association of an actual person with the ideal, ancestral lineage known as the common people of America.[8]

Once transformed from his actual profession whether as laborer, entrepreneur, banker, politician, or whatever else into one of the "common people," an American entered what was quite literally another world. Here he could act as a "guardian of republican virtue." In carefully prepared speeches, he could replenish all the agrarian virtues: equality over privilege, honest work over idle exploitation, liberty over domination. And here he could resolve the division of loyalties between motive and act by making it appear as if he acted only from these ideal motives.

This resolution of the conflict between motive and act reestablished the power of the persuasion, then, but at something of a cultural cost. In resolving the conflict only in a specifically designated cultural location, the scene of persuasion permitted Americans to distinguish their other everyday activities from this scenic action. Since they were unable to be the "common people" and lead their everyday lives, Americans needed persons able to continue the life of the "common people." And they found these ideal persons in the orators whose words and deeds sustained the "persuasion."

In sustaining this persuasion but in a place apart from everything and everyone else, America's orators invested themselves as well as their persuasion with great cultural status. To take the most obvious example, after his elevation into one of the "common people," Andrew Jackson ceased to be one of the "common" Americans and became "King Andrew." Not just Andrew Jackson, but Van Buren, Polk, Tyler, and every other aspiring "guardian of republican virtue" acquired privileges more appropriate to a monarch or a prince of an empire than a leader of a democracy.

Worship was the price Americans were willing to pay to keep their ideals. Worship was the cost of a separation of their idealized motives from their actual lives. We watched as Starbuck paid this price when he let Ahab idealize his profit motive into a version of manifest destiny on the quarterdeck. Unlike other orators, however, Ahab was not content with the separation between his purposes and the crew's activities. He wanted to resolve the conflict between his purposes and their everyday activities—but at the cost of their actual lives.[9]

Cold War Commentary on a Survivor Text

Ahab, in transforming Starbuck's dissent into a demonstration of the force of his own character, silenced all other opposition. As if to supply the opposition to Ahab the crew could not, a lineage of commentators, from F. O. Matthiessen to the present, have found an alternative figure of dissent. They find freedom displayed not in Starbuck's argument but in Ishmael's narrative. And they set Ishmael's subversive narrative energies against the totalitarian will at work in Ahab's policy.[10] Now, I began this chapter by claiming the intention to resist the reading making *Moby-Dick* a canonical text. In this reading Ishmael proves his freedom by opposing Ahab's totalitarian will. In what follows I wish not to offer an alternative reading but to argue that the canonical reading appropriated *Moby-Dick* to a modern scene of cultural persuasion analogous to the one at work in Melville's age. This modern scene of persuasion is the global scenario popularly designated as the Cold War. While the Cold War may initially seem out of place in a discussion of *Moby-Dick,* I hope to demonstrate that it is crucial both for the canonical reading and for the ongoing placement of *Moby-Dick* within the national context F. O. Matthiessen called the American Renaissance.

Unlike other paradigms in the American sphere of political discussion (but like Ahab in his "dialogue" with Starbuck), the Cold War scenario does not mediate or adjudicate discussion. It is persuasive, that is to say, without either having resulted from discussion among individuals with differing opinions or having persuaded a liberal nation to any action other than the acceptance of the scenario. Instead of arguing its persuasion, the Cold War simply exemplifies it.

The best way to ascertain the compelling force of its persuasiveness is to attempt locating any geographical territory or political question that could not be accommodated by the Cold War frame. In portraying the globe as a super opposition between the two superpowers (the free world supervised by the United States and the totalitarian countries under Soviet domination), the Cold War can recast all conflicts, in any place in the world, and at any time, in the terms of this pervasive opposition. So inclusive is this frame and so pervasive is its control of the interpretation of world events that there appear to be no alternatives to it. Since this scenario coopts the universe of argumentation with a global opposition, there is no moving outside of its frame. As soon as we might believe we have moved outside this arena, we discover we still must use the terms organizing the Cold War scenario as well as its foregone conclusion.

Anyone wishing to question this frame rather than oppose the two superpowers composing it can witness, on the world stage, this opposition already acted out, as it were, in the international arena called the third world. For whatever the specifics of third-world conflicts, whether in El Salvador, Chile, or Chad, and however alien they may appear to first-world concerns, in fact they are assimilated to the ideological opposition between the United States and the Soviet Union.[11]

What we understand through this paradigm are not historical facts or specific historical events but a way of organizing their relationship. In positing the conclusion rather than arriving at it through argument, the Cold War scenario produces as implicit the resolution that never has to become explicit. And in translating explicit political argument into the implicit resolution of that argument,[12] the Cold War scenario silences dissent as effectively as did Ahab in the quarterdeck scene.

Now, in what follows I wish to use the term "scene of cultural persuasion" to designate the ideological work performed in two different cultural contexts: that of the publication of *Moby-Dick* and that of the elevation of *Moby-Dick* into a masterwork of the American canon. The recognition of the difference in the ideological work performed by these two different scenes will, I hope, produce a historical context sufficiently alienated from the Cold War to make *Moby-Dick* susceptible to another reading.

The Cold War and Consensus Formation

The scenes of cultural persuasion generated by the Cold War and Captain Ahab depend upon a radical form of displacement—one in which the specific terms of conflict or dissent are recast in other terms and on another scene. Captain Ahab, when confronted with Starbuck's commonsense argument against his revenge quest, converts the commonsense opposition into a scenario in which Ahab's belief in his right to utter self-reliance has been violated by cosmic design. Ahab in other words embodies nineteenth-century faith in the self-made, self-reliant man. And in embodying this faith—the ideological ground for Starbuck's right to dissent—Ahab must be perceived not as opposing Starbuck's right to dissent but as justifying it.

As the enabling ground for Starbuck's dissent, Ahab cannot be responsive to the specific terms of Starbuck's dissent; instead he provides Starbuck with an occasion to witness the visionary basis for this right to dissent: Ahab's embodiment of absolute freedom.

Moreover, Ahab's displacements of the terms of Starbuck's dissent onto another scene resolves the implicit contradiction between Starbuck's rights and Ahab's demands. Ahab's oratory elevates that contradiction into an ideal, revolutionary opposition between a free Ahab and a tyrannical universe. With an even greater display of efficiency, the Cold War scene can transform any objector to the scene itself into one of the agencies of the opposition. So when a political analyst as astute as, say, Noam Chomsky writes about the distortions of the Cold War frame, he can find himself pictured, in the reviews of his work, as the dupe of a totalitarian power.[13] In short, the Cold War scenario manages to control, in advance, all the positions objectors can occupy. And all the objectors—whether the Battista regime against Cuban rebels, the Israelis against the Palestinians, or Ishmael against Ahab—can be read in terms of "our" freedom versus their totalitarianism.

Both scenes of cultural persuasion put into words the same fundamental operation: the displacement of potentially disorienting political arguments onto a context where the unquestioned ground—the ideological subtext justifying political dissent—can empty them of their historical specificity and replace them with ideological principles: Ahab's absolute freedom in the case of *Moby-Dick,* America's freedom as opposed to Soviet totalitarianism in the case of the Cold War.

But a problem arises for critics who have assimilated *Moby-Dick* to a Cold War consensus. Their logic demands an Ahab whose totalitarian will is opposed by the freedom at work in Ishmael's narrative. But as we saw in our discussion of the quarterdeck scene, Ahab is not utterly identified with a totalitarian will. It is Ahab's belief in absolute freedom that constitutes the basis for any of his crew's—whether Starbuck's or Ishmael's—exercise of freedom. The Cold War frame flattens out the contradiction between absolute and individual freedom at work in Ahab's character into an opposition between two different characters.

In Melville's time, Ahab's need for absolute power over the crew was interpreted psychologically as monomania[14] rather than politically as totalitarianism. And, as I will suggest, it is not at all clear that for Melville Ishmael was any more immune to the contradictory pulls between individual and absolute freedom than was Ahab. While Ahab and Ishmael may have represented two different rhetorical traditions, neither these traditions nor the characters representing them quite contradicted so much as they complemented one another in the formation of a national character quite different from that of postwar America.

Moby-Dick and *American Renaissance*

In coming to terms with the difference between these two cultural periods, I can best begin with a document on the American Renaissance published in the year—1941—of America's entrance into a world war that would make the Cold War scenario necessary as a means of postwar containment.[15] I want to return, in other words, to F. O. Matthiessen, whose work on the cultural period in which Melville wrote *Moby-Dick* would establish American literature as a discipline and America as a culture, at a time America needed such a self-representation in order to acknowledge that it stood to lose a great tradition to a totalitarian power, as different from the Soviet Union as Nazism was from Communism.

Matthiessen wrote at a time when America needed to be educated to the global duties of Renaissance men. In writing of an American Renaissance, Matthiessen hoped to supply America with a national tradition great enough to enable it to take its place as a free nation among free nations. With the publication of *American Renaissance: Art and Expression in the Age of Emerson and Whitman,* Matthiessen tried to meet what he called the need of every great civilization, "like the Renaissance," to create "its own heritage out of everything in the past that helps it to transcend itself."[16] His choice of an age was timely, for those were the years when the United States, in confronting the issue of slavery, union, and expansionism, would decide to wage a just war destined to establish her identity as a nation among nations.

Curiously, however, as if not to threaten the coherence of the cultural space called the American Renaissance, Matthiessen, while he did not completely eliminate them, at least discounted such political questions informing his own earlier work as class inequality and the extension of democracy to economic as well as political levels. Moreover, as Jonathan Arac has pointed out, he reduced the political questions informing the age he called the American Renaissance to the opposition between what he called the Emersonian will to virtue and Ahab's will to power.[17]

Yet in 1941 Matthiessen could exclude certain political issues, for the political questions were as clearly defined then by the international arena as the Cold War claims to define them today: in both cases, as the struggle of the free world against a totalitarian power. What was needed was what *American Renaissance* provided: the designation of a cultural power morally superior to that of any totalitarian power with which the free world was then at war. And not the least sign of that cultural power was *American Renaissance's* claim for a canonical place among the American masterworks for a work that had only recently been discovered: a survivor from the period of greatness in America's past, and a text which in its plot seemingly enacted the survival by a free man of the destructive actions of a totalitarian figure. *Moby-Dick,* in getting into *American Renaissance,* seemed to prefigure America's power to get the free world through a war.

Acting as a means of consensus formation then, as well as canon definition, Matthiessen's *American Renaissance* displaced the need to acknowledge dissenting political opinions from the past onto the power to discover an unrecognized masterwork that guaranteed a future for a free world. Among the dissenting opinion *American Renaissance* silenced was Matthiessen's own, for, in restoring to the time of Whitman and Emerson his political aspirations for a democracy free of class division, Matthiessen's political aspirations could be treated as already achieved—in the past. But with the return, after World War II, of political opinions—most specifically the anticapitalism of *From the Heart of Europe*—to his literary work, the progenitor of the American Renaissance was designated a "fellow traveler"[18] rather than a cultural hero. This redesignation turned Matthiessen himself into the sign of the cultural power of another consensus formation. In reading Matthiessen's dissenting opinions as the discourse of the enemy within, the Cold War paradigm ironically turned him into one of its first opponents (and later one of its first victims).

As we have seen, Matthiessen anticipates this repressive activity in his own work of consensus formation. His great work of cultural consensus silenced not only his own potentially disruptive political opinions but those of the politicians and orators he simply excluded from the American Renaissance. More precisely, Matthiessen did not quite leave them out altogether but consigned them to a subordinate context, one easily assimilated by the cultural consensus he formulated through the "art and expression" of Emerson and Whitman. In the years after the war, with the disappearance of the need for a united cultural front, we might say that another F. O. Matthiessen, unpersuaded by the consensus formation underwritten by the American Renaissance, appeared. Before we can hear this other Matthiessen, however, we have to locate for him a context other than *American Renaissance* that, like the Cold War, silenced his dissent.

Writing as he did at a time when the international political arena was threatened by Nazi aggression, when national self-consciousness could not appear merely locally political, Matthiessen made cultural politics appear indistinguishable from consensus formation. But, writing in the years when the Vietnam War made national self-consciousness appear indistinguishable from the political rhetoric of the Cold War, Sacvan Bercovitch found the Cold War rhetoric supported by what he called the tradition of the American jeremiad.[19] And he found a broad-based locus for this form precisely in the rhetoric Emerson and Whitman shared with the orators and politicians of the American Renaissance. If for F. O. Matthiessen the American Renaissance proved its power as a cultural consensus by silencing dissenting political opinions, for Bercovitch the American jeremiad derived all its cultural force at precisely that moment in the nation's history when dissenting political opinions over such explosive issues as union, slavery, and expansionism would make a difference in the very form of the nation handed over from the past.

American Jeremiads

But, like the Cold War paradigm it prefigures, the American jeremiad did not quite come to terms with these explosive issues. Rather, it put them into other terms, making them sound indistinguishable from those surrounding the single event—the American Revolution—that, once resolved, seemed to have made up the nation's mind once and for all. Seeing issues in terms of the American Revolution, that is, precluded them from becoming disruptive political questions. For the Revolution, in its office as the fulfillment of the Puritan divine mission, lost its status as a historical event and turned into a perpetual national resource, a rhetorical means for making up the nation's mind over whatever issue presented itself. Displaying the same power to alienate opposition we found at work in the Cold War scenario, the jeremiad compels any listener intent on issuing his own dissenting opinion to discover that his dissent has, in the American Revolution, already achieved its ideal form. So dissent, the cultural locus for committed political discourse, turns into a national Revolutionary ideal which, Bercovitch argues, has in its turn become the ideological representation of the free enterprise system.

When translated into the form of the American jeremiad, political issues become occasions for scripture lessons like the one Theodore Parker attached to his 1848 "sermon" on the Mexican War. In this sermon, America's war with Mexico turned into the "lesson" of King Ahab, who coveted Naboth's Vineyard.[20] Now, whatever may be obscure in Parker's account of Ahab's lesson, what remains clear is that it did not provide an occasion for persuading a group of individuals to perform an action by presenting an argument about a complex issue. If the Mexican War embroiled the American people in an anxious political conjuncture involving debates over slavery and national identity, in Parker's lesson that war and all the anxiety surrounding the issues that gave rise to it gave way to another scene, a calm and secure one. On this scene Divine Writ seems to have already adjudicated these as well as all other matters.

Despite the clearly security-inducing effect of Parker's sermon, it nevertheless should serve as an occasion to complicate Bercovitch's model. For Parker does not directly discuss the Mexican War in terms of the American Revolution. He does, however, borrow on that power to discuss political events in religious terms that was authorized by the Revolutionary moment, in which God's will and the nation's will become one, secured by the American jeremiad. And Bercovitch needs some explanation for the willingness of the American public to cede him this power. Such an explanation cannot simply posit the power of the jeremiad to constrain public opinion but must demonstrate how, given the cultural variations and violent dislocations of American life, it could continue to attract public attention at all. Why, for example, given Bercovitch's terms, is not the very form of the American jeremiad, a form in which figures from the past reappear, an occasion for anxiety over the loss of relation with those figures?

A consideration of Parker's sermon in terms borrowed from our earlier discussion of the conditions overdetermining the acceptance of the Cold War paradigm could begin to provide an explanation. For in this oratorical scene Parker depends on his audience's anxiety and doubt over the issues surrounding the Mexican War for his authority to invoke his biblical scene. Once replaced by figures like King Ahab, these anxiety-provoking issues disappear, for such figures seem already to have acted out the present dilemma in the past, thereby relieving the American public of the need to let the issues enter its consciousness at all. Or they enter in the form of another scene, one, as is the case with the Cold War opposition, in which all the issues have, in their presentation within the language of Divine Writ, already received definitive judgment. In Parker's sermon, then, King Ahab, the figure designating the issue of the Mexican War, turns out to have already resolved it.

In such jeremiads as Parker's, political issues turn into great public occasions for the displacement of scenes of present troubles by scenes in which those troubles have already been solved. And the same figures who made up the public's mind for it in the past, in acting out potentially divisive public issues, can in the present separate the issue from the anxiety attending it. In place of the anxiety over political events in the present, these figures foreground a threat that seems to have a greater claim to public attention: the loss of a relation with a past. These same figures then allay that anxiety by returning from the past. The past then becomes all the more gratifying because of its claim to fulfill all present political aspirations.[21]

The "other scene" does not utterly displace any political issue, but works in the background to relieve explicit political questions of their attendant anxiety by presenting them as already resolved. The "mental energy" that might otherwise have been expended in the doubts, second thoughts, calculations, and judgments informing any political decision is released.[22] It gets released, moreover, in a discovery that, if it ever became conscious, might be called inspired—that the political issue troubling the mind has already been solved by the same rhetorical figures used to articulate the problem.

Perhaps we should pause over this discovery to register one more observation. The very wording of the political issue in the jeremiad excludes the question of individual freedom. More precisely, the jeremiad identifies individual freedom not with the freedom to perform an action, but with the freedom from the doubts, decisions, and judgments leading to action. Which is to say that this other scene depoliticizes freedom, exempts it from political questions. Since the very words used to articulate political questions have already resolved them, the individual's freedom moves elsewhere, into a realm emptied of pragmatic judgmental, determinate energies: but with the foreknowledge that the sheer freedom and sheer chanciness of this potentially "free" realm will be returned to security once the need for security overdetermines the need to return to the other scene.

Obviously, the "other scene" did not limit its power to the listeners. For the orators, in their abilities to transcribe everyday events into a form that interwove them with inspired words of the God of the Revolutionary father, turned into "figural" effects of these words. When perceived as the effects rather than the proponents of the words that seemed to utter them, such orators became indistinguishable from those rhetorical figures appearing within their orations. In their office as realized effects of the Revolutionary fathers, these orators gave the American people still another opportunity. For in their sermons, the American people did not quite hear whispered the word of God but witnessed the ways in which their own historical lives had become inspirations for God's words. And in their office as present occasions for divine inspiration, the American people felt compelled not so much to hear God's word as to conceive themselves as His means of representing it. Consequently, such scenes of public persuasion as that performed by Theodore Parker became occasions in which the public idealized the most basic form of social acknowledgment. Instead of turning a listener toward a neighbor, the need for mutual recognition turned him toward the orator, in whose "inspired" figure he was to recognize what he, in his everyday life, had become.

As an occasion for the prophetic fulfillment of both speaker and listener, the jeremiad does not really represent their differing positions but, like the scene of persuasion in the Cold War paradigm it might now be said to prefigure, it assimilates both speaker and listener into the means of articulating its form. Moreover, although, unlike the Cold War paradigm, the jeremiad represents its premediation of all positions as if it were an unmediated vision, nonetheless the effect of both paradigms remains the same. Either you come to your decision in their terms or you cannot decide. The same all-or-nothing logic was at work then as now: either you use the terms sanctioned by the form, or, as a person literally outside of the shared language of the American people, you lose the possibility for representation in the scene of public persuasion altogether.

A Crisis in Persuasion

While the concept of the American jeremiad is quite resourceful in disclosing the way in which the distinction between consensus and compulsion, always a difficult one to maintain, disappears altogether, nevertheless it cannot quite account for what we have identified as national crises in persuasion occasioned by those moments in American cultural history when identical figures in nearly identical forms of the jeremiad were used to represent opposing opinions on related questions. When scenes of cultural persuasion work, they are able to return all the potentially disruptive contradictions in political debate to their ideological ground, which, as we have seen, is capable of functioning as the ideal resolution for these contradictions. But when the scenes of cultural persuasion themselves become sources of contradiction, they threaten the nation's ideological ground. Such a threat clearly appeared when Theodore Parker speaking against slavery, John Calhoun speaking against union, and David Lee Childs speaking against expansionism could all use Ahab as the rhetorical figure capable of corroborating the validity of their position.[23] But when King Ahab could be put to similar usage in the construction of quite differently oriented political arguments, "King Ahab," the figure of jeremiadic persuasion, could not be said to have made up his mind on these matters. And with the recognition of Ahab's confusion, Americans lost their traditional way of feeling compelled about what to do.

Given our analysis of the unique cultural apparatus brought into existence by the different consensus formations we have called the American jeremiad and the Cold War, we cannot simply dismiss such moments as manifestations of cognitive dissonance on a massive scale. In the national economy of the representation of dissent we have been describing, the figures who idealized dissent into final, resolved form existed in a world we called the other scene, in which everyday dissenting opinions, doubts, and contradictions existed only in a fully resolved state. And the relation between the everyday world of indecision and the other scene of "the decision" was an overdetermined and compensatory one. This everyday world could function smoothly precisely because that other scene converted all of its irresolution into a resolved form. It is not simply that doubts and indecisions do exist in local, contingent forms, but they exist free from the need for decisive resolution precisely because this other scene exists as the locus for "the resolution."[24] Dissent exists free from the need for resolution in the everyday world because the jeremiad can absolve dissent of its indecision by wording it into an indubitable final reckoning on the other scene. Thus, the other scene not only permits indecision and doubts; it demands them as ongoing proof of its authoritative power to judge.

In the context of this relation between worlds, we can perform a thought experiment enabling us to understand the apocalyptic dimensions of this crisis in persuasion. Imagine one of the rhetorical figures used to free the individual of the consequences of doubt (that is, the need to decide on a course of action)—such as Ahab in Parker's sermon—himself become human enough to experience the indecision he could not discharge through persuasion. What results is a confusion of realms on an apocalyptic scale. When the Ahab who exists to absolve this world of its conflicts himself can be imagined as experiencing on that other scene the irresolvable doubts attending the secular world, the other scene reverses its relation to secular concerns. Whereas before, actual indecision over political issues could be discharged through its symbolic resolution on the other scene, now King Ahab, whose figure symbolically resolved indecision on the other scene, could be imagined as in need of the actualization of his indecision—but in the everyday world. Whereas before, "the decision" on the other scene was an overdetermined form of the indecisions of everyday life, following this confusion of realms everyday decisions would be invested with the overdetermined energy of "the decision."

Unless one were an orator who actually experienced himself as a figure brought into existence by the words uttered on that other scene, it would be difficult to imagine a rhetorical figure (like the Ahab used by different orators to justify expansionism, slavery, and union) who can come into the actual world full of those conflicting demands the other scene can no longer resolve. Melville brings just such a figure into existence in *Moby-Dick*. In this novel, the Ahab who formerly was used as an ideal figure of oratorical speech able to resolve conflicting demands in the public sphere now appears as an actual character, a sea captain, whose speech does not resolve but expresses some of the conflicting demands in that same public sphere. It might be said that Melville's Ahab has moved out of his usual domain, as a mere figure of speech helpful as a means of making up the mind of the public sphere, and has come into actual existence—but as the "character" of that mind. As the "lived experience" of its betrayed resolution, he expresses what we can call the "national character," but obsessed with a desperate need to convert conflicting demands back into a decisive form.

As the force released by the American jeremiad's loss of authority, Ahab, the embodiment of the conflicted national character, discloses the prior form of the American jeremiad's power. It generated and contained two different worlds. But the relation between these two worlds was not that of a "type" fulfilled by an "antitype" in the typological model Bercovitch offers. Instead, the one world (the other scene) definitively separated the doubts and indecisions of an other world (everyday life) from the need for resolution. Existing as a colossal estrangement effect, the other scene provided the occasion for individuals to reexperience their personal failures to decide as freedom from the need to decide.[25]

The other scene provided other "personal" benefits as well. As the source world of primary action, the other scene relegated authenticity not to the activities of individuals in the everyday world, but to the action performed by such gigantic rhetorical figures as Ahab in Parker's sermon. Consequently, those "persons" who sensed the disconnection between the individual as an effective cause and agent and the individual as an effect of forces beyond any individual's control could redefine the nature of freedom. With the relocation of "personal" authenticity to the "national character" acting on the other scene, they could interpret alienation from an authentic self as the freedom to perform a multiplicity of roles.[26]

The loss of Ahab's power on the other scene also brought about a reversal in the national relation to "act" and "action." And while I do not want to reduce the national motives for the Civil War to the terms of this reversal, I do want to note that this crisis in the nation's means of self-representation could no longer, as Kenneth Burke suggests rhetoric should, purify the motives that made war necessary. Instead of transposing them into a resolved form, the scene of cultural persuasion accompanied the critical economic and political issues awaiting the Civil War for resolution. When the form of the jeremiad could no longer contain national conflicts in the final reckoning acted out on the other scene, this undecided conflict demanded an actual rather than a symbolic war in order to become a decisive opposition once again. Without eliminating the political and economic issues, we might say that from a rhetorical perspective the Civil War became a means of recovering in the everyday world the stability and force of containment lost by the rhetorical figures in the other scene. If, before the war, staging the other scene was all the persuasion there need be, the Civil War resulted when that persuasion was exposed as merely staged. And this exposure encouraged individuals to actualize rather than act out those dissenting opinions the American jeremiad (in its ideal resolution of the "national character") had alienated from them.

The Ahab in Parker's sermon was the figure of the "national character" who impersonated the American jeremiad's force of containment and resolution. But the conflicting Ahabs in Calhoun's and Child's orations released a different Ahab, who could no longer feel persuaded by the form of the American jeremiad. If Sacvan Bercovitch feels, like the other Americans in his text, the need to recover the form of the American jeremiad at moments—like that immediately preceding the Civil War—when it loses all of its effective historical force, he recovers it at the expense of the conflicted character of the orators' figure of Ahab, who no longer feels persuaded by it. If, in the perhaps excessive characterization of our discussion, Ahab was earlier said to impersonate the power of the jeremiad to persuade, he may also be said to impersonate the felt loss of the authority of that power.

But the figure of Ahab, who feels the compulsive need to persuade utterly separated from the form sanctioning persuasion does not appear in anyone's jeremiad. He appears in Melville's novel *Moby-Dick*. Should we follow Melville's lead and remain attentive to the demands not of the American jeremiad but of the figure who is not persuaded by it, we can turn to another American Renaissance. This time, however, prepared by Melville's Ahab, we are guided not by the Matthiessen who organized the American Renaissance into an ideal consensus formation, but by that other F. O. Matthiessen, whose own dissenting opinions were silenced by what we can now recognize as the jeremiad of *American Renaissance: Art and Expression in the Age of Emerson and Whitman*.

When guided by those of Matthiessen's opinions in conflict with the consensus formed by *American Renaissance,* we can reconsider the use to which he put Emerson and Whitman. In using Coleridge's organicist aesthetic to distinguish the political rhetoric of such orators as Parker from what he called the "vitally" aesthetic writings of Emerson and Whitman, *American Renaissance* (as a consensus formed at the expense of Matthiessen's own dissenting position) strategically promotes Whitman's and Emerson's rhetoric, in which national self-consciousness becomes indistinguishable from personal self-consciousness, into a cultural asset.[27] Moreover, this act of promotion constituted the historical power of consensus formation in 1941. For in order to sanction America's national right to a free culture at a time when that right was threatened less by national than by international politics, *American Renaissance* locates a cultural past so united that even the political issues surrounding the Civil War seem petty.[28] When viewed in this context, Whitman and Emerson perform the same function for Matthiessen, in his politics of consensus formation, that they performed for the politicians who used the American jeremiad to form the consensus in their time. They silence the conflicting claims in that form by replacing the politicians' forensic motives with motives open to the more rarefied concerns of aesthetics. Seeming, then, to distinguish Emerson and Whitman from the politicians, *American Renaissance* in fact locates in their writings an organicist aesthetics which serves as a justification for the rhetoric of national individualism at precisely the moment when the politicians seem to be losing the divine justification for that rhetoric. As we have seen, this bracketing out of politics through a turn to aesthetic questions in fact served Matthiessen's "higher" political purpose—to devise a national consensus. Now we might best sense the cultural power of his "higher" purpose if we imagine F. O. Matthiessen coming after Sacvan Bercovitch to convert the "mere rhetoric" of the American jeremiad into the achieved art of the American Renaissance.

Matthiessen's *American Renaissance* on the Quarterdeck

When conceived in terms of this "higher" purpose, however, Emerson and Whitman lose their purely aesthetic characters and reveal the explicitly rhetorical use to which *American Renaissance* put them. Nowhere does Emerson lose this character and Matthiessen lose control of the working of his consensus formation more definitively than in the midst of the analysis of the quarterdeck scene in *Moby-Dick*. Curiously, Matthiessen presents this analysis in what we could call a scene of critical persuasion. but we do not discover the doctrine to which he would be persuaded until the conclusion of his analysis.

Matthiessen pays no attention to specific lines in the quarterdeck scene, but reads Ahab's compelling domination of the men as a "sign" of Shakespeare's "power over" Melville. Then, in a monodrama intended ultimately to reveal Melville's artistic power, he transcribes the lines exchanged by Ahab and Starbuck into blank-verse and observes that "the danger of such unconsciously compelled verse is always evident. As it wavers and breaks down into ejaculatory prose, it seems never to have belonged to the speakers but to have been at best a ventriloquist's trick." [29] The itinerary Matthiessen follows here needs a summary statement: having first posited Shakespeare's language as the rhetorical power informing Ahab's exchanges, Matthiessen then rediscovers this power in the spell Shakespeare cast over Melville's prose. This dramatic conflict ends only after Melville "masters" the power Shakespeare's rhetoric wields over him, by discovering the secret of his own dramatic power.

Of course the power in this drama inheres less in Melville's discovery than in the dramatic use to which Matthiessen puts it. Matthiessen's drama should have concluded with an example of Melville's triumphant "mastery" of Shakespeare's prose. But instead of revealing itself through one of Melville's own characters or representing one of Melville's own themes, Melville's "vital rhetoric" is said to "build up a defense of one of the chief doctrines of the age, the splendor of the single personality."[30] In other words, Melville's recovery from Shakespeare's rhetoric becomes a means for Emerson to defend his doctrine of self-reliance.

That Matthiessen sees the need for this defense gives pause. But the cause for the defense is implicit in the drama that builds up to it. Although he mentions Hitler only in his account of Chillingworth, the figure whose totalitarian position Matthiessen wrote *American Renaissance* to oppose is everywhere present in his discussion of Ahab. By staging the textual reappearance of the doctrine of self-reliance within the scene of Melville's recovery from a compulsive rhetorical principle, Matthiessen defends its rhetoric in advance from the charge that it may be as compelling in its excesses as Hitler's. When Matthiessen writes, "living in the age of Hitler, even the least religious can know and be terrified by what it is for a man to be possessed,"[31] it is clear that compulsive rhetoric, in all its forms, is what figures from Matthiessen's *American Renaissance* exist to oppose. Consequently, when Melville dramatically achieves independence from the compulsive hold of Shakespeare's rhetoric, he earns, in eyes trained to see by *American Renaissance,* the authenticity of the doctrine of self-reliance by literally realizing that doctrine as his defining aesthetic action.

The compelling logic of this dramatic sequence is clear. Matthiessen wants to see the doctrine of self-reliance at work, but by "hearing" this doctrine enunciated by Ahab, he loses all the benefits accrued by the rest of his drama. Matthiessen's own earlier treatment of Ahab posits Ahab as the principle of mere rhetoric rather than authentic art. And this earlier treatment releases troubling questions. If Ahab served as the dummy figure through whom Matthiessen could reveal Melville's act of "working through" his possession by Shakespeare's rhetoric, does he not, once Matthiessen hears him speaking Emerson's rhetoric of self-reliance, disclose Matthiessen's unstated fear that compulsion might be at work in the doctrine of self-reliance? In short, does not the quarterdeck scene become Matthiessen's pretext for the articulation of a felt need—not to defend Emerson's ideology of self-reliance, but to defend himself against it—which informs the consensus formation he called the American Renaissance?

Instead of revealing an instance of self-reliance at work, this scene releases (as two Matthiessens) the conflicts Matthiessen experienced in relation to the doctrine of self-reliance but which *American Renaissance* made it impossible for him to state. While Matthiessen wished to affirm Emerson's essays as liberating rather than disabling rhetoric, the moment Emerson appears within the context of *Moby-Dick* his doctrine appears least vital because most coercive. Moreover, the moment Matthiessen would defend self-reliance, he becomes, according to the logic of his own dramatic metaphor, less himself than an occasion for self-division in which—through the figure of Ahab—one Matthiessen doubts what the other Matthiessen affirms: that is, the liberating power of Emerson's rhetoric.

As we have seen, Melville's Ahab discloses the conflicts the American jeremiad could no longer silence. When Matthiessen attempts to speak the doctrine of his jeremiad through the figure of Ahab, the other Matthiessen, the Matthiessen whose dissenting opinions *American Renaissance* existed to silence, the Matthiessen who fears the doctrine of individualism may deny rights to "all the people," begins to speak instead. This doubling is crucial. For it indicates not only Matthiessen's understanding of the conflict between absolute freedom and individual rights and duties in Melville's time; it also articulates the presence within Ahab of the principle of freedom, or the "Ishmael figure" the Cold War scenario sets in opposition to Ahab. *American Renaissance,* in its most telling moment, acts out the different crises in consensus formation in Melville's as well as Matthiessen's time.

Matthiessen not only found self-reliance to be the chief ethical doctrine of the age he was writing about but made it the ethical principle of the work he was writing, earning for that age a cultural power that, in organizing the American canon, has itself become canonical. But, despite *Moby-Dick*'s power to reduce the doctrine of self-reliance—and the canon of *American Renaissance* which it informs—to the status of a ventriloquist's figure, I should consider the persuasive power of this doctrine before turning again to *Moby-Dick,* the book that I will argue is not of the same persuasion.

Self-Reliance and National Compulsion

In earlier chapters on Whitman and Emerson, I argued that the transcendentalists' doctrine of self-reliance be considered within a political and historical context. Writing at a time when politicians compromised the principles within the nation's covenant, Emerson urged that Americans renew the bond by turning within. Here they could rediscover the nation's founding principles in their uncompromised state, or so the doctrine of self-reliance claimed.

Whitman's notion of the "man-en-masse" also depended on the equivalence of the nation's founding covenant and what is more usually defined, when found in an individual, as a soul. Like Emerson, Whitman believed a nation could lose its soul when it lost its principles. Unlike Emerson, Whitman believed the nation's soul could be recovered only through relations with the whole mass of Americans rather than within a single self. He believed mankind was spoken into existence by nature's oration, in the endless apostrophe more commonly known as the evolutionary process. But both Whitman and Emerson followed essentially the same political program. Both wished to return the nation's founding principles to their place within the unconscious, where they could be acted upon as unquestionable truths rather than argued over, as political beliefs.

Of course you could follow these doctrines only if you already believed the nation had a soul to lose, or that these doctrines were fundamentally different from a politician's. Melville was unpersuaded of the difference between Emerson's doctrine of self-reliance and Whitman's belief in nature's oratory, on the one hand, and the scene politicians claimed when they addressed their constituents, on the other. Emerson's claim to the scene of the nation's founding was no different from a politician's. Whitman's idealization of nature itself into an orator only elevated, in Melville's view, the political orators. The politicians and Emerson believed they spoke from the place of America's origin; Whitman believed nature continued to regenerate this place of origin. In Melville's mind these claims were false, indicative more of the speaker's hubris than his truth. When Melville described to his publisher, the prominent literary figure E. A. Duyckinck, his experience as a member of an audience held spellbound by Emerson's oratory, he places Emerson and his oratory in the same "otherworldly" context as he does Ahab's rhetoric. Emerson revealed his hubris, Melville wrote, with the "insinuation that had he lived in those days when the world was made, he might have offered some valuable suggestions."[32]

Melville's description of Emerson urges quite a different interpretation of Emerson's doctrine of self-reliance. For Melville, the attempt to translate founding principles to the level of unconscious motives could not be distinguished from a program of psychological compulsion.[33] Emerson's doctrine certainly lends Melville's interpretation credibility. Emerson states the doctrine with a simplicity that almost conceals its power: "Self-reliance is precisely that secret, to make your supposed deficiency redundancy. If I am true, the theory is, the very want of action, my very impotency, shall become a greater excellency than all skill and toil."[34] When revealed, the secret is as simple as the doctrine; it makes a promise to convert powerlessness into a form of power. Before the listener can wish to find this doctrine appealing, however, he needs, in his previous experience, to feel powerless. The doctrine, in other words, presupposes a disproportion between a secret inner man and an outer world that the doctrine maintains. Actually, the doctrine of self-reliance does not simply presuppose such a disproportion between inner man and inner world but demands it as the context for its display of power.

By definition, a self-reliant man must rely not on an outer world but only on an inner self, experienced as superior to the external world. But he can create this inner self only by first reducing the outer world to the level of an abstract externality, as arbitrary as it is merely contingent. Such a reduction cuts two ways. A world that is viewed as at best arbitrary allows for a retreat from it without too much regret. And this separation from the mere contingencies of the external world can, out of sheer contrast, be experienced from within as the first authentic choice in an otherwise arbitrary world.

But at least two problems attend the appearance of this inner self. If its authenticity is derived from a prior experience of contingency, then the inner self has not replaced but only internalized the contingency of an outer world. What results, moreover, is what Ishmael, at the beginning of *Moby-Dick,* calls a bad case of the "hypos": that is, a wish for intense action but, given the contingency of internal as well as external worlds, without any incitement to act. The self-reliant man, then, feels empowered to act but has disconnected himself from any world that can acknowledge his action.

In addressing these two problems, Emerson devised two distinct roles for self-reliance to perform. In its role as a doctrine, self-reliance encouraged a sense of withdrawal from the world; but in its role as an address, self-reliance converted this withdrawal into the appearance of a power. In this second role, self-reliance acts less like a doctrine corroborating any particular inner self and more like one of those rhetorical figures of will we saw at work on the other scene of the American jeremiad, capable of providing the private person with the freedom in relation to the external world denied him by the doctrine. We begin to understand the power inherent in this division better when we discover what happens when Emerson declares this doctrine in an address. As a product of the self-reliance he evokes, Emerson can presume to speak not from a position external to his auditors but with all the power of that "secret" inner life to which each self-reliant individual aspires. And so effective is this power to speak the inner life that such public figures as John Jay Chapman, James Garfield, and Moncure Conway will declare after listening that Emerson's words have become their "secret character."[35]

When speaking *as* what we might call the sovereign figure of the will released by the doctrine of self-reliance, however, Emerson does not encourage the individual either to act in the world or to will action. Instead he encourages the individual to discover his power in his inability to act: "If I am true, . . . my very impotency shall secure a greater excellency than all skill and toil." In what we could call a compensatory unconscious, the inability to perform any particular action recovers the sovereign capability to perform all actions. And through this remarkable turn, the sovereign will can recover the motivation lost after the devaluation of the external world. The individual will recovers its motivation, however, not by bridging the gap between motive and action but by enlarging it to the point where the motivating power, the sheer impulse to action, assumes priority over any particular action.

Thus the doctrine of self-reliance fulfilled the private will, but only through an address by a figure effected by a sovereign will, who relocates within the abstract capability of the alienated individual the other scene of final reckoning we discovered in the form of the American jeremiad. If the jeremiad separated the individual from the need to decide political issues by providing the scene upon which everything had already been decided, self-reliance alienated individual action from an individual's motives for action by providing an internal sovereign will whose abstract capability to do what "might be done" was all the action there could ever be. When addressed by a spokesman, like Emerson, for this sovereign, the private man could feel persuaded not to perform any particular action but to experi-

ence the sheer force of the motivation to act—resounding in such imperatives as "trust thyself, every heart vibrates to that iron string"—as if it were
already the only fulfillment needed.

If the doctrine of self-reliance justified the individual's alienation from a
world of action, the power of address it made possible justified the separation of self-reliant individuals from one another. In replacing the merely
private will with the "sovereign will," self-reliance also allowed for a great
economy of discussion in the public sphere. For it eliminated first and third
persons altogether and turned everyone into representations of what we
could call a national second person, an empty discursive slot to be filled in
by a figure addressing the nation. While this second person seems to address "you," he derives all of his power by presuming to speak as "your"
inner life. thus, in listening to him, "you" can believe you are investing
yourself with executive power. But some pathos should return when "you,"
perhaps as a "second thought," recognize that this second person alone
possesses the only self-reliant inner life in the nation.

Thus, the status of this national and sovereign second person must give
pause. For not only is he composed of, and as "compensation" for, the
powerlessness of first persons, but he is empowered, as it were, out of a
sensed disconnection between persons. In a nation of second persons, individuals do not discuss matters with other individuals but "address"—or,
better, "move"—one another with inspirational apostrophes and imperatives. They need not listen to or even recognize one another but can, in
moving one another, look forward to being unmoved in return; or, if
moved at all, be moved by that sheer power of motivation politicians identify as the sovereign will of the people. And here again we see not consensus but a kind of compulsion in its place. The work of compulsion performed by the figure we have called the sovereign will of the self-reliant
man faces none of the conflicts that tore apart the form of the American
jeremiad. There, as we saw in the person of Ahab, the conflicting claims
the form of the jeremiad was used to sanction internalized rather than silenced the conflicts. But since the figure of sovereign will can perform any
action, no particular position can lay claim to his power to sanction. Without the possibility for conflict, the sovereign will need not negotiate conflicts among separate individuals. Instead, its only appropriate effect is the
separation of individuals.

While it is everywhere present in Emerson's theory of friendship, Thoreau elevates disconnection into a national ideological value when he

writes, "When they say farewell then indeed we begin to keep them company . . . [For just as] I always assign to him a nobler employment in my absence than I ever find him engaged in, so I value and trust those who love and praise my aspiration rather than my performance."[36] In these lines Thoreau etherealizes friendship to the point of mutual evanescence, as the sheer potential to be an inspiring friend replaces the need for any actual friendship, or as sheer motivation replaces action.

But an even clearer sense of the cultural value of this doctrine of friendship arises when we juxtapose it with the doctrine of self-reliance. That doctrine, as we recall, separated the inner self from a devalued because external world. But the address of the sovereign will to the internal world from a position external to it revalued, if not the external world, at least an external field of force: a second person capable of addressing private individuals with all the force of their inner life. This second person—less a person than an abstract addressee—in belonging to nobody in particular provided a platform of address for everyone in general. And as the sheer capability of address, belonging to everybody in general and no one in particular, this sovereign will, through Thoreau's doctrine of the friend, could be the means of mutual inspiration and function as the very principle of community. In other words, this sovereign will could, despite its origin in the sensed disconnection of self-reliant individuals from one another, represent itself, in its capacity to speak for everybody and nobody, as the general will of the people. When speaking from this position, an individual could, through the fiction of the sovereign will, claim to address the people from the position not of their will or his will but (with all the force of a second person) *thy* will.

As was the case with the witnesses of the scene of persuasion in the American jeremiad, however, the "general will" of the people did not originate from discussions among themselves. Instead, the people could hearken to their inner life only as it addressed them from the position of that irresistible field of force resulting from the sensed disconnection of individuals both from the world and from each other: a force we have called the national second person.

In its role as the spokesman for the sovereign will of the people, Emerson's doctrine of self-reliance obviously provided politicians and orators with a tremendous practical advantage, in what we would call a rhetoric of pure persuasion. For, in self-reliance, the public found a way to be inspired by the felt sense of the motive to act but purified of any need for a specific action. In valuing motive over action, listeners need not question the acts to which orators would persuade them. Perhaps here we have the reason such public figures as Garfield, Conway, and Chapman felt so empowered by Emerson. Aspiring as they did to speak for the will of the people, they found in Emerson's self-reliant or sovereign will the people's consent. In listening to an orator, a self-reliant man need not question what was said, for he was not being addressed as a figure other than the figure addressing him. In a relentlessly closed communication circuit, self-reliance addressed that figure of will Emerson called self-reliance. On these occasions, the individual could witness his own independence coming to him, as it were, in the person of the nation's second person. Most important, however, Emerson's conversion of the politician's purposive rhetoric into pure persuasion had the effect of purifying that rhetoric of the confusions we saw at work when King Ahab was used to sanction three conflicting attitudes toward national politics. Since pure persuasion turned purpose into a "purposiveness without purpose," it became a means of preserving the inspirational power of political rhetoric in the face of conflicting political demands.

Tall Tales

When observing what he called the resultant American "pleniloquence" from the detached position of a third rather than second person, Alexis de Tocqueville did not, as did Matthiessen and Bercovitch, use it as an occasion either to describe or engage in consensus formation. Instead he recovered the first-person privileges of the humorist:

> Debating clubs in America are to a certain extent a substitute for theatrical entertainment: [for] an American *cannot converse* . . . [instead] his talk falls into a dissertation. He speaks to you as if he were addressing a meeting, and if he should chance to become warm in the discussion, he will say "Gentlemen" to the person with whom he is conversing.[37]

Since Tocqueville, in his outsider's account, seems to have achieved a position enabling him to discover a first person capable of poking fun at what I have called the scene of cultural persuasion, I want to take this opportunity to distinguish his outsider's narrative not only from the forms of address called the jeremiad and the sovereign will but also from those insiders' nar-

ratives—the legends and tall tales—written by Americans as means of remaining within the address of the national second person.

In order to understand how this inside narrative works, we need to return to the scene of pure persuasion to emphasize its crucial distinction
from the American jeremiad. In privileging motive over act, the scene of
pure persuasion does not recall agents from the nation's past but demands
that agents as well as their actions imitate inspiring motives. The second
person does not commemorate the heroic deeds performed by characters
from the nation's past. Instead, he calls individuals to aspire to actions indistinguishable from the motivational power of the orator's figures of will.
In Emerson's remarkable turn, the Revolutionary fathers, instead of remaining ideals to be imitated, became effects of the self-reliant man's inspiring words, embodiments of the motivating power of his speech. As a
result of the claims implicit in Emerson's rhetoric, the people were able to
internalize within the sovereign will not only the idealized Revolutionary
fathers but also the biblical figures who in the form of the American
jeremiad provided the fathers with their divine rights. Which is to say that
in Emerson's rhetoric even God's word became indistinguishable from the
sovereign will of the nation's second person.

This same absorptive power—the ability of the sovereign will seemingly
to claim every preexisting cultural authority as an effect of its power—introduces another dimension in the relationship between sovereign will and
action. For although, as we stated, there was no connection between any
particular action and the infinite capability of the sovereign will, that same
sovereign will could claim any action as an effect of its motivating power.
In this context, heroic deeds did not need to be conceived as motives that
became actions (which would threaten the superiority of motive in relation
to deed) but could be considered as actions that were indistinguishable
from the motivating power to act. Orators secured this equivalence by converting certain actions in the world into tropes of pure persuasion. So
whenever an individual "acted out" the inspiring power of the orator's motives, he became a figure of will indistinguishable from the inner life of the
self-reliant man and earned, as was the case with Ahab, the right to speak
as the national second person he, in his personal life, had already become.
He could motivate others, in short, because he had already equated their
inner motivation with his public action.[38]

Such national second persons as Ahab were the subject not only of legends which assimilated the excesses of the orator's rhetoric to a human

shape but also of tall tales that, like Tocqueville's "humorous" observations, toppled these legendary figures by exposing their apparently heroic deeds as mere "stretchers." Here the distinction that needs to be made is between demystifying a rhetorical position and telling a tall tale. For the latter displaces the need to do the former. Instead of wishing to acknowledge the rhetorical status of a tall tale, the teller never wants to get outside its format. For if he did he would not have the pleasure of "taking in" a third person. This third person, in his turn, does not recognize what it is that has taken him in, but simply experiences the pleasure of "taking in" another third person with another tall tale. The legend and the tall tale, then, establish what we might (in keeping with the figure of the national second person) call a "second first" and a "second third" person who never become skeptical or even self-conscious about the rhetoric of pure persuasion but who wish instead to claim their second-person privileges and remain in the position of persons addressed by the nation's second person.

But when narratives facilitate inclusion within the form of address of the nation's second person, reading narratives became an occasion to locate the power of this will to address. Reading, in other words, offered an occasion to turn what is read—that is, words as motive forces—into what does the reading. Or, what is the same thing, reading became a means of internalizing and so—following the logic we found at work in the doctrine of self-reliance—of making sovereign what we have called the nation's second person.[39]

The interrelationship between the activities of listening, speaking, arguing, and reading—activities valued most, on at least one cultural level, when most indicative of a certain independence of mind—and what we have called the sovereign will triggers an alarming recognition. When accompanying the "democratic" operations acclaimed as proof of the power of individual Americans to make up their own minds, the sovereign will turns these operations into expressions of a national compulsion.[40] Individual Americans did not make up their own minds but experienced having their minds made up for them on the national scene as an exercise of self-reliance.

Perhaps this recognition will have its greatest value if we imagine it stated by the F. O. Matthiessen who led us to it:[41] not the one who used Emerson's doctrine of self-reliance to form the consensus he called the American Renaissance but the one whose dissenting political opinions were silenced by *Art and Expression in the Age of Emerson and Whitman*.

Since it was in his reading of the quarterdeck scene of *Moby-Dick* that we began to hear this Matthiessen who was not persuaded by the scene of cultural persuasion, perhaps we can use this scene as an oppositional one. And since the narrative of *Moby-Dick* offers an occasion for Matthiessen to signal opinions in conflict, we should expand the context of this oppositional scene by differentiating Melville's narrative vision from *American Renaissance: Art and Expression in the Age of Emerson and Whitman.*

Melville and Hawthorne in Dialogue

At around the time of the composition of *Moby-Dick,* Melville imagined a reading experience utterly at odds with what we have described as the internalization of the sovereign will. Moreover, he discovered what he called the "will of the people" by reading not Emerson or Thoreau but a figure Matthiessen included as another (subsidiary) voice in *American Renaissance*. Reviewing Hawthorne's *Mosses from an Old Manse,* a work attentive enough to the value of different opinions to provoke in the reader a series of conflicting attitudes, Melville devised a way to release these conflicting reactions rather than resolve them in a consensus. Recorded over a two-day period by a Virginian vacationing in Vermont, his review reverses the prerogatives of what we have called a scene of cultural persuasion. Instead of finding his mind already made up, this Southerner vacationing in the heart of the abolitionist Northeast discovers in himself a whole range of conflicting reactions to these tales: with each reaction possessed of sufficient self-consciousness to organize itself into an articulate opinion and each opinion accompanied by a second thought—the shocking recognition of the limits of that single opinion. In an intricate series of moves, Melville reads neither as an individual nor quite as a general will but as the conflicting opinions within a reading public—not a ready-made consensus but a consensus in the process of formulation, or what Melville calls a "plurality of men of genius."[42]

In other words, Melville, at the time of his composition of *Moby-Dick,* imagined the release of the reading public from the sovereign will of the national second person. Moreover, he released that public by giving multiple voices, each with the possibility of "parity," to the conflicts silenced by that sovereign will. We got some indication of the dimensions of those conflicts when we analyzed how Ahab was used as a rhetorical figure to voice opposed political views in the nineteenth century. But as Alan Heimert and Michael Paul Rogin have pointed out, the other two principals in *Moby-Dick*—Ishmael and the Leviathan—were also deployed in Melville's time, in all their rich biblical allusiveness, to voice contrary political positions on the issues of abolitionism, secession, and manifest destiny in the form of the American jeremiad.[43] Indeed, Ahab, Ishmael, and Leviathan were popular figures in politicians' speeches as well as ministers' sermons.

In our previous discussion we suggested that the loss by these rhetorical figures of the power to contain conflict in the jeremiad form resulted in the public's need to actualize this conflict. Melville turns the rhetorical figures of Ahab, Ishmael, and the Leviathan—the second-person powers through whom the American public was persuaded to make up its mind—into actual characters and then lets them act out their felt separation from the power legitimately to secure consent. Moreover, since Ahab and Ishmael share, as it were, the privileges of the second person, Melville revokes those privileges by exposing the compulsion at work in their rhetoric.

If we can imagine, in the broad context of a scene of cultural persuasion, the political conjuncture of the issues of slavery, secession, and expansionism, and then if we imagine the three Ahabs, Ishmaels, and Leviathans used to word these issues into jeremiads, we can see how conflicted the space that was used to achieve consensus had become. If such cultural forms as the jeremiad, pure persuasion, the legend, and the tall tale had been used to "work through" the conflicts in the general will, Melville, in emphasizing the contradictions these forms could not resolve, restored the American people to a sense of the conflicts produced by their rhetoric.

Emerson in Ahab

The "great tradition" of American literature founded by the *American Renaissance* silenced these contradictory relations by converting all of them into the opposition between Ishmael's freedom and Ahab's totalitarian will. And this opposition resolves the felt force of the contradiction by converting it into an "ideal conflict," a (Cold) war whose appropriate outcome has already been determined. In his analysis of the quarterdeck scene, however, Matthiessen displays a contradictory relation, a contradictory attitude unresolvable by the ideal opposition between Ahab and Ishmael. In his analysis, Matthiessen identifies Ahab as both a totalitarian will and the freedom a self-reliant man must use to oppose it. Put another way, through the figure of Ahab Matthiessen reads the feared compulsion at work in what he formerly regarded as the sovereign freedom of the self-reliant man.

He reads the compulsion, but, as we have already seen, he reads it in terms of Shakespeare's blank verse.[44] And whereas Melville represented Ahab's use of Shakespearean language as a sign of his power over the crew, Matthiessen treats this language as a sign of Shakespeare's power over Melville. By reading Ahab's silencing of Starbuck's dissent as a disclosure of the power Shakespeare wielded over Melville's prose, Matthiessen of course acknowledges the political power of Shakespeare's language. (Shakespeare, in the politics of canon formation, had, after all, functioned as Matthiessen's means of securing English Renaissance validity for American Renaissance figures.) But he displaces the context for the display of this power, moving it from the relation between Ahab and the crew to the relation between Melville and Shakespeare. And in doing so, Matthiessen simultaneously praises (through his mastery of Shakespeare's language) the Ahab he condemns (as the proponent of a totalitarian will). More specifically, Matthiessen in his one-dimensional reading of Ahab's totalitarian will also reenacts Starbuck's scenario. For Ahab performs for Matthiessen the same function he performs for Starbuck: because his inner life is an embodiment of compulsion, he releases Matthiessen from the need to find compulsion at work in the doctrine of self-reliance, the Emersonian will to virtue informing the body of his work.

We might say that the contradictory attitudes released by Matthiessen's reading disclose his doubts about Emerson's will to virtue rather than about the effectiveness of both scenes of cultural persuasion—Ahab's with Starbuck and Ahab's with Matthiessen. Earlier we suggested that the scene of cultural persuasion displaced political dissent experienced in the public sphere, making the contradiction disappear into the ground terms, or replacing the specific terms of dissent by the principles sanctioning the right to dissent. In Matthiessen's reading, the political contradictions existing at the time Melville wrote (between democratic ideals and the principle of self-reliance) turn into the opposition (between the totalitarian will and individual freedom) sanctioned by the Cold War. But Matthiessen's discovery of the agency of individual freedom (Emerson's "will to virtue") within Ahab's totalitarian will indicates only the failure of the scene of persuasion to resolve the contradiction.

But the contradictions released by Matthiessen's reading do not simply point up his conflicting responses to the character of Ahab. Since these contradictions appear at the point at which Matthiessen fails to remain persuaded in the scene he used to appropriate nineteenth-century America—that is, *American Renaissance*—these same contradictions open up a cultural space corresponding to none of the scenes of persuasion operative in Melville's, Matthiessen's (or, by extension, our own) time. Since these contradictions are released within the character of Ahab's totalitarian will and are concerned by extension with his canonical opposition to Ishmael's "freedom," perhaps we should conclude with a consideration of that relation.

We can begin with an observation missing from Matthiessen's concentration on Ahab's totalitarian will. Ahab's very power to silence dissent also causes him to reexperience his sense of loss. Unlike the spokesmen for the American jeremiad, Ahab cannot depend on Divine Writ to sanction his words. Consequently, a dual recognition accompanies his every act of persuasion: the terrible doubt that it may be without foundation, and the "experience" of his separation from another. Both recognitions remind him of the loss of his leg. And it is Ahab's need to justify this sense of loss—to make it his, rather than God's or fate's—that leads him to turn his will, which in each act of persuasion repeats that separation of his body from his leg, into the ground for his existence.[45]

Indeed, all of Ahab's actions—his dependence on omens, black magic, thaumaturgy—work as regressions to a more fundamental power of the human will. They constitute his efforts to provide a basis in the human will for a rhetoric that has lost all other sanction. Ahab, in short, attempts to turn the coercion at work in his rhetoric into fate, a principle of order in a universe without it. But since this will is grounded in the sense of loss, it is fated to perfect that loss in an act of total destruction.

Ishmael and Ahab

That final cataclysmic image of total destruction motivated Matthiessen and forty years of Cold War critics to turn to Ishmael, who in surviving *must,* the logic would have it, have survived as the principle of America's freedom who hands over to us our surviving heritage. When juxtaposed with Ahab, Ishmael is said to recover freedom in the midst of fixation; a sense of the present in a world in which Ahab's revenge makes the future indistinguishable from the past; and the free play of indeterminate possibility in a world forced to reflect Ahab's fixed meanings.[46]

Given this juxtaposition, we should take the occasion to notice that if Ahab was a figure who ambivalently recalled the scene of persuasion in the American jeremiad, Ishmael recalls nothing if not the pure persuasion at work in Emerson's rhetoric. Like Emerson, Ishmael uncouples the actions that occur from the motives giving rise to them, thereby turning virtually all events in the narrative into an opportunity to display the powers of eloquence capable of taking possession of them.[47] Indeed, nothing and no one resist Ishmael's power to convert the world that he sees into the forms of rhetoric that he wants. The question remains, however, whether Ishmael, in his need to convert all the facts in his world and all the events in his life into a persuasive power capable of recoining them as the money of his mind, is possessed of a will any less totalizing than Ahab's. Is a will capable of moving from one intellectual model to another—to seize each, to invest each with the subjunctive power of his personality, then, in a display of restlessness no eloquence can arrest, to turn away from each model as if it existed only for this ever-unsatisfied movement of attention—is such a will any less totalitarian, however indeterminate its local exertions, than a will to convert all the world into a single struggle? As it happens, Matthiessen opposed Emersonian doctrine to Ahab's will because he wished to remain persuaded of that doctrine. That's also why Ishmael opposes his rhetoric to Ahab's. Both Ishmael and Emerson want to keep their rhetoric of motives separate from their actions; Ahab is Ishmael's way of maintaining this separation.

Since, in a certain sense, Ishmael puts his will to work by converting Ahab's terrifying legend into cadences familiar from the tall tales, we might take this occasion to differentiate Ishmael's tall tale from those we analyzed earlier. In telling his tale, the Ishmael who was taken in by Ahab's rhetoric does not, as was the case with other narrators of the tall tales, use the tale to work through the excesses in Ahab's rhetoric. Instead, the extraordinary nature of Ahab's words and deeds legitimizes elements of Ishmael's narratives that might otherwise seem inflationary. As the figure whose excesses in word and deed cause him literally to be read out of Ishmael's narrative, Ahab enables the reader to rule out the charge of excess in Ishmael's rhetoric. Ishmael occupies three different spaces in his narrative. As the victim of Ahab's narrative, he exists as a third person. As the narrator of his own tale, he is a first person. And as the subject of such urgent addresses as "Call me Ishmael," a second person. But since, as a first-person narrator, he turns Ahab into the figure who has victimized Ishmael, Ishmael does not have to be perceived as taking anyone else in. Ishmael turns Ahab into both the definitive third-person victim and the perfect first-person victimizer. In perfecting both roles, Ahab becomes Ishmael's means of exempting his narrative in advance of the charge of trying to victimize anyone. Moreover, since, in Ishmael's case, first-person narratives always turn into pretexts for second-person sermons, Ahab, the locus for all false rhetoric, also becomes Ishmael's means of redeeming his own second person by exempting it in advance from all charges of mystification.

Ahab is Ishmael's means of purifying his individual acts of persuasion. In his conflation of victim and agent, motive and deed, Ahab turns out to be Ishmael's "second person." For he is the figure of will who performs actions absolutely indistinguishable from the motive powers within Ishmael's rhetorical exercises. In Ishmael's rhetoric each individual act of perception turns into an occasion for an exercise of persuasive power. Through Ahab's death, Ishmael exempts these occasions from any charge of coercion (which has already been perfected, so the narrative logic would have it, by Ahab).

The sensed loss of Ahab, however, results in another, less desirable state of affairs. In Ahab, Ishmael finds the one figure in his narrative capable of realizing inspired words in matching deed.[48] Buried within Ishmael's display of remarkable oratorical power is his reiterated demand that the world be indistinguishable from the will of words; also buried within Ishmael's narrative is the one figure capable of making these words consequential— Ahab. In reaction to the fate befalling Ahab, Ishmael retreats into endless local performances of rhetorical exercises, with each performance invested with the desperate complaint that the world is not consequential enough. Each of these performances—these momentary indulgences in a sense of power superior to the given structures of the world—becomes Ishmael's means to make the force if not the person of Ahab reappear.

In speaking with the force of Ahab's demand for a world indistinguishable from his human will, but free of the consequences of that will, Ishmael can discover pleasure not quite in another world but in a prior world, in which the endless proliferation of possible deeds displaces the need for any definitive action. The pleasure in this prior world results from the endless delay of a conclusion to the pleasure-inducing activity. The capacity to experience this delay as pleasure (rather than frustration) also derives from

Ahab. The fate befalling Ahab's decisive conversion of words into deed determines Ishmael's need for a realm in which the indeterminate play of endless possible actions overdetermines his indecision.

We can understand the dynamics of this relationship better when we turn to the crucial distinctions which critics during the Cold War have drawn between Ishmael and Ahab. In their view, Ishmael, in his rhetoric, frees us from Ahab's fixation by returning all things to their status as pure possibilities. What we now must add is that Ishmael has also invested all the rest of the world of fact with possibility, then invests possibility with the voice of conviction.[49] And when all the world turns out to be invested with the indeterminate interplay of possibility, it does not seem free but replicates what we call boredom (the need for intense action without any action to perform), and what Ishmael called the hypos, the "drizzly November in his soul" that made him feel attracted to Ahab in the first place. This interpolation of an excess of indeterminacy between motive and act displaces Ahab's fixation, but in doing so causes Ishmael to develop a need for Ahab. In short, Ishmael's form of freedom does not oppose Ahab but compels him to need Ahab—not only as the purification of his style, but as the cure for a boredom verging on despair. Only in Ahab's final act can the Ishmael who has in his rhetoric converted the external world into an exact replica of the restless displacements of endlessly mobile energies of attention find a means to give all these energies a final, fatal discharge. Ahab's fatal, decisive deed permits Ishmael to feel the excessive force of Ahab's decision overdetermine his exercises in indecision. Put more simply, Ahab's compulsion to decide compels Ishmael not to decide.

At this point, however, Ishmael cannot be said to oppose Ahab as freedom would totalitarianism. But the form of his narrative does anticipate the totalizing logic we saw at work in the Cold War scenario. For in identifying all coercion as the work of Ahab's totalitarian will, and not his own boredom, Ishmael is free to multiply his scenes of persuasion with the knowledge that all of them will be free in advance of the charge of coercion. Since in Ishmael's rendition it is Ahab alone who controls us against our will, we are "free" to read Ishmael's own obsessive multiplication of occasions to compel our attention as the work of Ahab.

Thus *Moby-Dick* does not expose only the scene of cultural persuasion in its own time. Ever since Matthiessen's reading of it as the sign of the power of the freedom of figures in the American Renaissance to oppose totalitarianism, *Moby-Dick* has been a Cold War text, one that secures in Ishmael's survival a sign of the free world's triumph over a totalitarian power. But Melville, in his exposure of Ahab and Ishmael's narrative relation as a single self-conflicted will, instead of letting Ishmael remain in opposition to Ahab, reveals the way in which Ishmael's obsession depends on Ahab's compulsion. Nor does he alienate opposition by positioning all opinions within the conflict between Ishmael and Ahab. Instead he "works through" the vicious circularity informing the conflicted will at work in both Ishmael and Ahab. If the Cold War consensus would turn *Moby-Dick* into a figure through which it could read the free world's survival in the future struggle with totalitarianism, Melville, as it were, speaks back through the same figure, asking us if we can survive the free world Ishmael has handed down to us.

Afterword

I have ended this discussion of *Moby-Dick* with an analysis of the mutually self-destructive nature of the bond Ishmael shared with Ahab. In Ahab Melville condemned the self-interest at work in the oratory of the nation's politicians. In Ishmael he condemned the cultural despair at work in the counterrhetoric of the nation's transcendentalists. Ishmael and Ahab share not a visionary compact but a social contract in which each agreed to justify the other's self-interest.

To end this book with an analysis of the breakdown in the nation's bonds of associations would violate its spirit. Such an ending would also violate the spirit with which *Moby-Dick* was written. In the process of writing that book Melville remained in correspondence with Nathaniel Hawthorne, the one figure in America's republic of letters who Melville believed wrote with a strong sense of the civil covenant in which all Americans participated.

In dedicating *Moby-Dick* to Hawthorne, Melville established a visionary bond quite different from the contract joining Ahab to Ishmael. Throughout his tales and romances, Hawthorne reminded his readers of their continuing relationship with the ancestral agreements upon which the nation was founded. He broke the spells cast by self-interested leaders, exposing the basis for their oratory in the will rather than the nation's covenant. His writing set Hawthorne in dramatic contrast to Ahab, who invoked the nation's founding compact, but only the better to impose his will on the crew.

Without this covenant with which every American citizen could agree, the bonds of association citizens share could have disappeared as well. In his writings, Hawthorne called forth unrealized purposes, ideals, and aspirations from the past that present generations could inherit, as bonds of national fellow feeling. Without shared purposes, a nation's individuals can ground their actions in nothing more permanent than self-interest. Ahab charges the self-interested motives for his actions with an apocalyptic energy, then borrows tropes from the Bible, Webster, and Shakespeare to socialize his self-interest.

When Ishmael reflects on Ahab's actions, he does not participate in the deliberative process he shares with the rest of the crew. Instead of reactivating a scene of communal deliberation, as Hawthorne did in *The Scarlet Letter*, Ishmael indulges in flights of imagination as willful as Ahab's revenge.

In a way, Ishmael underscores the fundamental problem for a society which has lost sight of a shared covenant. Without a common basis for their judgments, a nation's citizens have nothing more enduring than their self-interests with which to reflect. In our analysis of *Pym*, we pointed to the home feelings secreted within the adventurer's consciousness as the basis for his later reflections. But Ishmael is a man without home feelings. In his consciousness he does not preserve a set of shared political and philosophical symbols with which he can reflect upon his experiences. He simply moves distractedly from one observation to another, with no basis for any of his observations more enduring than his need for exciting self-expression.

Unlike Ishmael, Melville, in his correspondence with Hawthorne, preserved the civil covenant he believed bound them together. Melville's correspondence with Hawthorne provided him with a visionary bond enabling him to oppose Ishmael's obsessive-compulsive attraction to Ahab with a friendship grounded in genuine fellow feeling. Since his letter of November 17, 1851, indicates the depth of his need for a visionary compact with Hawthorne, I will quote from it to end this book.

> Whence came you, Hawthorne? By what right do you drink from my flagon of life? And when I put it to my lips—lo, they are yours and not mine. I feel that the Godhead is broken up like the bread at the Supper, and we are the pieces. Hence this infinite fraternity of feeling. . . .

Notes

Index

Notes

Chapter 1: Visionary Compacts and the Cold War Consensus

1. D. H. Lawrence, *Studies in Classic American Literature* (New York: Viking, 1923), p. 12.

2. Ibid., p. 14.

3. Ibid., p. 17.

4. The finest study in the crisis of legitimation remains Jürgen Habermas, *Legitimation Crisis*, trans. Thomas McCarthy (Boston: Beacon Press, 1975).

5. The definitive statement of the mythos can be found in Sacvan Bercovitch, *American Jeremiad* (Madison: University of Wisconsin Press, 1978).

6. On liberalism as a distortion of early American notions of freedom, see Louis Hartz, *The Liberal Tradition in America: An Interpretation of American Political Thought since the Revolution* (New York: Harcourt and Brace, 1955).

7. Charles Feidelson, *Symbolism and American Literature* (New Haven: Yale University Press, 1959).

8. Leslie Fiedler, *Love and Death in the American Novel* (New York: Stein and Day, 1975), p. 341.

9. For a discussion of the conflict between the general will, the public good, and American democracy, see Robert N. Bellah, *The Broken Covenant* (New York: Seabury Press, 1975), pp. 1–136.

10. Allen Grossman, "Criticism, Consciousness and the Sources of Life," in Monroe Engel, ed., *Uses of Literature* (Cambridge: Harvard University Press, 1973), p. 45.

11. Garry Wills, *Cincinnatus: George Washington and the Enlightenment* (Garden City, N.Y.: Doubleday, 1984).

12. Ibid., p. 305.

13. Ibid.

14. On the founding families, see John P. Diggins, *The Lost Soul of American Politics: Virtue, Self-Interest, and the Foundation of Liberalism* (New York: Basic Books, 1984), pp. 64–100.

15. These quotes appear in Michael Davitt Bell's *The Development of American Romance: The Sacrifice of Relation* (Chicago: University of Chicago Press, 1980), pp. 16–18.

16. Richard Chase, *The American Novel and Its Tradition* (New York: Doubleday, 1957), p. 82.

17. Ibid., p. 14.

18. Paul de Man, *Blindness and Insight* (New York: Oxford University Press, 1971), p. 162.

19. Frank Lentricchia, *Criticism and Social Change* (Chicago: University of Chicago Press, 1983), p. 119. Throughout this study Lentricchia calls attention to the conflict between meaningful social change and the temporality of modernity.

20. Terry Eagleton, *The Function of Criticism: From "The Spectator" to Post-Structuralism* (Minneapolis: University of Minnesota Press, 1984).

Chapter 2: Hawthorne's Discovery of a Pre-Revolutionary Past

1. For a further discussion of the Puritans' communal and social orientation, see Michael Zuckerman, "The Fabrication of Identity in Early America," *William and Mary Quarterly,* 34 (1977), 184–185.

2. For a fine discussion of the role legend played in creating a public identity for Washington, see Garry Wills, *Cincinnatus: George Washington and the Enlightenment* (Garden City, N.Y.: Doubleday, 1984).

3. In "My Kinsman Major Molineux," Hawthorne complicates the strategy somewhat. Their common Puritan ancestor would have permitted Robin to address Major Molineux as a kinsman. But the patriotic feelings he shared with the townspeople made it necessary for him to condemn the royalist in his kinsman. Here political fellowship takes precedence over blood kinship, and does so in a way that Hawthorne pointedly questions.

4. Michel Chevalier, *Society, Manners and Politics in the United States,* trans. from the 3d Paris ed. (Boston: Weeks, Jordan, 1839), pp. 298–299.

5. Nathaniel Hawthorne, *The Scarlet Letter,* ed. Sculley Bradley, Richmond Croom Bradley, and E. Hudson Long (New York: W. W. Norton, 1962), pp. 35, 16. Future reference will be in parentheses in the text.

6. For the best formulation of America's cultivation of the mythos of the Revolution, see Sacvan Bercovitch, "The Rites of Assent: Rhetoric, Ritual and the Ideology of American Consensus," in Sam B. Girgus, ed. *The American Self: Myth, Ideology, and Popular Culture* (Albuquerque: University of New Mexico Press, 1981), pp. 5–43.

7. Roy Harvey Pearce, in "Hawthorne and the Sense of the Past" (*Historicism Once More* [Princeton: Princeton University Press, 1969]), makes the strongest case for Hawthorne's romance as a metaphysical philosophy of history intended to give us a strong sense of the totality of the events with which we have to deal. According to Pearce the historical romance provides the means whereby "the past can be conceived, even celebrated, precisely as it has had necessarily to give way to the present" (166). But such a "giving way" would only have given further sanction to a present age Hawthorne deplored.

8. For a view of partisan politics as a loss of civic commitment, see Edward L. Mayo, "Republicanism, Antipartyism, and Jacksonian Party Politics: A View from the Nation's Capital," *American Quarterly,* 31 (Spring 1979), 3–21.

9. Hawthorne thus serves as a revelation or what I have called a future memory for the Puritans, who projected him into the future as a way of reminding themselves of the cultural duty they owed to time.

10. Here Hawthorne discovers his own answering debt to temporality, his means of discovering what temporal duties his age has not yet fulfilled from the past. For a

fine discussion of the historical criteria of the modern concept of revolution, see Reinhart Kosselleck, *Futures Past: On the Semantics of Historical Time* (Cambridge: M.I.T. Press, 1985), pp. 39–55.

11. Stephen Greenblatt, *Renaissance Self-Fashioning from More to Shakespeare* (Chicago: University of Chicago Press, 1980), p. 227.

12. Ibid., p. 224.

13. This freedom from constraints is only another formulation of the demands liberalism makes on its proponents. For a fine critique, see Roberto Mangabeira Unger, *Knowledge and Politics* (New York: Free Press, 1975), pp. 29–100.

14. Walter Benjamin, "On Some Motifs in Baudelaire," *Illuminations,* trans. Harry Zohn, ed. Hannah Arendt (New York: Schocken Books, 1969), p. 158. Cited by Geoffrey Hartman in his fine essay, "The Sacred Jungle 2: Walter Benjamin," *Criticism in the Wilderness: The Study of Literature Today* (New Haven: Yale University Press, 1980), pp. 63–85.

15. An aura is really the palpable presence of the residues, the traces, of the work of collective memory in persons and things.

16. For the notion of an unprogressive temporality, see Hartman's discussion of Benjamin, "The Sacred Jungle 2."

17. Retelling the tale creates a republic of storytellers.

18. Hawthorne was not alone in his sense of the need to sustain a romance with history. For a cogent discussion of this relationship, see David Levin, *History as Romantic Art: Bancroft, Prescott, Motley and Parkman* (New York: Harcourt, Brace and World, 1963), particularly the first two chapters.

19. For a further discussion of the cultural reserve, see Geoffrey Hartman, *The Fate of Reading and Other Essays* (Chicago: University of Chicago Press, 1975), pp. 106–109.

20. Hartman, *Fate of Reading,* p. 107.

21. For an excellent discussion of the instantaneous in opposition to the enduring, and the relationship of both forms of time to ghosts, see Kosselleck, *Futures Past,* pp. 213–260.

22. For a fine study of the concept of the general welfare and its place in a public philosophy, see William M. Sullivan, *Reconstructing Public Philosophy* (Los Angeles: University of California Press, 1982), pp. 25–51.

23. For a study of the separation during the nineteenth century of civic duty from republican virtue, see Joyce Appleby, *Capitalism and a New Social Order* (New York: New York University Press, 1984), pp. 25–51.

24. Once again I am trading on my central contention: that Hawthorne while in the Custom House experiences the return of a repressed general will—but in the form of a reactivated collective memory.

25. Maurice Halbwachs, in *The Collective Memory,* trans. Francis J. Ditter, Jr., and Vida Yazdi Ditter (New York: Harper and Row, 1980), emphasizes the relationship between collective memory and deliberative social processes (78–87).

26. For the origin of the general welfare in the Whig tradition, see J. G. A. Pocock, *The Machiavellian Moment: Florentine Political Thought and the Atlantic Republican Tradition* (Princeton: Princeton University Press, 1975), pp. 333–361.

27. For a discussion of the unusual relationship between privilege and the common people produced by the spoils system, see John William Ward, "Jacksonian Democratic Thought: A Natural Charter of Privilege," in Stanley Coben and Lorman Ratner, eds., *The Development of an American Culture* (Englewood Cliffs, N.J.: Prentice Hall, 1970), pp. 44–64.

28. Arthur O. Lovejoy, *Reflections on Human Nature* (Baltimore: Johns Hopkins University Press, 1961), pp. 61–62.

29. For further discussion of the relationship between the fear of secession and the erosion of civic virtue, see John P. Diggins, *The Lost Soul of American Politics: Virtue, Self-Interest, and the Foundation of Liberalism* (New York: Basic Books, 1984), pp. 134–141.

30. Michael Davitt Bell turns social exclusion into a psychological principle giving rise to the form of the romance. See *The Development of American Romance* (Chicago: University of Chicago Press, 1980).

31. For a polemical reinterpretation of the Puritans, see Michael Walzer, *The Revolution of the Saints* (Cambridge: Harvard University Press, 1965).

32. It also differs from what David Levin and a long tradition of scholars have called romantic histories.

33. Fredric Jameson, "Magical Narrative: Romance as Genre," *New Literary History,* 7 (1975), 158.

34. Ibid., p. 145.

35. The point I need to emphasize here is the loss of the relation of desire to civic situations, which is to say that the Revolutionary mythos itself eroded civic virtue.

36. Nathaniel Hawthorne, *The House of the Seven Gables,* ed. Seymour L. Gross (New York: W. W. Norton, 1967), p. 1.

Chapter 3: A Romance with the Public Will

1. Alexis de Tocqueville, *Democracy in America,* trans. Henry Reeve (New York: Vintage, 1945), 2:76.

2. Michael Davitt Bell, in *The Development of American Romance* (Chicago: University of Chicago Press, 1980), argues this point most cogently by describing the romance form as the private compensation for a "sacrifice of relations" with the public world.

3. Rufus Choate, "The Importance of Illustrating New England History by a Series of Romances like the Waverly Novels," *Works,* ed. Samuel Gilman Brown (Boston: Little Brown, 1862), p. 319.

4. Ibid., p. 323.

5. Nathaniel Hawthorne, *The Scarlet Letter,* ed. Sculley Bradley, Richmond Croom Beatty, and E. Hudson Long (New York: W. W. Norton, 1962), p. 49. Further references will be in parentheses in the text.

6. On the history of this notion of the family as a "haven in a heartless world" and its sociological implications, see Christopher Lasch, *The Culture of Narcissism: American Life in an Age of Diminishing Expectations* (New York: W. W. Norton, 1978), pp. 154–187.

7. For a fine discussion of this aspect of *The Scarlet Letter,* see James M. Cox,

"Emerson and Hawthorne: Truth and Doubt," *Virginia Quarterly Review,* 45 (Winter 1966), 89–107, and "*The Scarlet Letter:* Through the Old Manse and the Custom House," *Virginia Quarterly Review,* 51 (Summer 1975), 432–447.

8. This position on the function of Hawthorne's prose is stated most cogently, I believe, by Richard Chase in *The American Novel and Its Tradition* (New York: Doubleday, 1957), pp. 12–13 and 67–80.

9. For a strong presentation of Hawthorne's efforts to enter into relation with his present age by way of a developed historical consciousness, see Roy Harvey Pearce, *Historicism Once More* (Princeton: Princeton University Press, 1969), pp. 137–175.

10. For this aspect of the social basis of the unpardonable sin, see Quentin Anderson, *The Imperial Self: An Essay in American Literary and Cultural History* (New York: Random House, 1971), p. 14.

11. Kenneth Dauber begins to acknowledge the communal orientation of Hawthorne's allegory in *Rediscovering Hawthorne* (Princeton: Princeton University Press, 1977), pp. 87–99. But for a clear statement of the relationship between an individual's repentance and communal intimacy, see *Soloveitchik on Repentance,* trans. Pinchas H. Peli (Ramsey, N.J.: Paulist Press, 1984), pp. 97–102.

12. This recovery of utterly private relations, which Hawthorne associates with the "unpardonable sin," has been defined as Hawthorne's purpose for writing the romance by most critics.

13. See Georg Lukacs, "The Ideology of Modernism," rpt. in David Lodge, ed. *Twentieth Century Literary Criticism: A Reader* (London: Longman, 1972), pp. 474–489, for an analysis of the function of psychoanalysis as a producer of privacy in the modern world.

14. Chase, *American Novel and Its Tradition,* pp. 67–80.

15. Dimmesdale's final sermon elaborates this surplus of private relations into a form of public discourse.

16. Throughout *The Scarlet Letter,* the community has responded to the repressed, or unspoken, material in Dimmesdale's sermons, as if the unspoken discourse were the true subject of the sermons.

Chapter 4: Walt Whitman and the Vox Populi of the American Masses

1. In this chapter I follow the line of Roy Harvey Pearce, whose fine study of Whitman in *Historicism Once More* (Princeton: Princeton University Press, 1969) called attention to the democratic qualities in the poetry. But I choose the 1855 rather than the 1860 edition to make the point. My reasons for the choice are complex but involve a wish to recognize Whitman's change of attitude from journalist to politician to poet.

2. Quentin Anderson recognizes this quality—Hawthorne's love for communal organization and distrust of mobs—but uses it in his analysis of Hester and Arthur to affirm privacy as the pertinent sphere of social relationships in Hawthorne. See *The Imperial Self* (New York: Random House, 1971).

3. For an elaboration of this point see Michael Zuckerman, "The Fabrication of Identity in Early America," *William and Mary Quarterly,* 34 (1977), 179–185.

4. On the nature of repentance and cultural intimacy, see Walter Benjamin, "The

Storyteller," *Illuminations,* trans. Harry Zohn, ed. Hannah Arendt (New York: Schocken Books, 1969), pp. 83–92.

5. Zuckerman, "Fabrication of Identity in Early America," p. 83.

6. For a fine distinction between the way a people live their myths and the way historians interpret them, see James Henretta, "Social History as Lived and Written," *American Historical Review,* 84, no. 5 (1979), 1293–1322.

7. For Hawthorne, collective judgment was the community's way of transmuting its impulses into a covenant, which was the heart of a community.

8. I know this notion of "body electric" was not fully elaborated until the editions following that of 1860. But Whitman anticipated this elaboration in the 1858 preface.

9. Walt Whitman, *Prose Works,* ed. Floyd Stovall, 2 vols. (New York: New York University Press, 1965), pp. 308–309.

10. For the historic relation between the masses and the western territories, see Robert H. Wiebe, *The Opening of American Society from the Adoption of the Constitution to the Eve of Disunion* (New York: Random House, 1985), pp. 131–143.

11. For a discussion of Whitman's attitude toward secessionism, see Justin Kaplan, *Walt Whitman: A Life* (New York: Simon and Schuster, 1980), pp. 158–162.

12. Paul Zweig, in *Walt Whitman: The Making of the Poet* (New York: Basic Books, 1984), is acute in his discussion of Whitman's politics (3–58).

13. For the difficulties in the relation between the notion of the people and popular votes, see Dorothy Ross, "The Liberal Tradition Revisited and the Republican Tradition Addressed," in John Higham, ed., *New Directions in American Intellectual History* (Baltimore: Johns Hopkins University Press, 1976), pp. 116–130.

14. For further discussion of Jackson's elevation of the people into a privileged voting bloc, see John William Ward, "Jacksonian Democratic Thought: A Natural Charter of Privilege," in Stanley Coben and Lorman Ratner, eds., *The Development of an American Culture* (Englewood Cliffs, N.J.: Prentice Hall, 1970), pp. 44–64.

15. For more on the forging of mass parties in America, see Ronald P. Formisano, *The Birth of Mass Political Culture: Massachusetts Parties, 1790–1840* (New York: New York University Press, 1983). The classic study in western expansionism remains Albert K. Weinberg's *Manifest Destiny: A Study in Nationalist Expansionism in American History* (Baltimore: Johns Hopkins University Press, 1935).

16. The best study of the nature of association in nineteenth-century America is Wilson Casey McWilliams' *The Idea of Fraternity in America* (Los Angeles: University of California Press, 1973), particularly pp. 9–33 and 224–239.

17. See Ward, "Jacksonian Democratic Thought," pp. 50–60.

18. As a people whose association was based on the principle of equality, Americans had difficulty finding a principle for adjudicating differences. See Allen Grossman, "The Poetics of Union in Whitman and Lincoln," in Walter Benn Michaels and Donald E. Pease, eds., *The American Renaissance Reconsidered: Selected Papers from the English Institute* (Baltimore: Johns Hopkins University Press, 1985), pp. 183–209.

19. Walter Benn Michaels interprets "romance" as the literary result of this alien-

ation of the individual from his freedom in "Romance and Real Estate," in Michaels and Pease, *American Renaissance Reconsidered,* pp. 156–182.

20. For a discussion of Hawthorne's sense of the Puritan community he envisioned through his experience at Brook Farm, see James R. Mellow, *Nathaniel Hawthorne in His Times* (Boston: Houghton Mifflin, 1980), pp. 178–192.

21. For a discussion of the place of holidays and civil religion, see Robert N. Bellah, "Civil Religion in America," *Daedalus,* 96, no. 1 (1967), 1–19.

22. These unconscious motives are related to what we have called the spirit of place.

23. For the status of the "self-evident" in American philosophy, see Morton White, *The Philosophy of the American Revolution* (New York: Oxford University Press, 1978), pp. 61–97.

24. This term comes from Cornelius Castoriadis, "The Imaginary Institution of Society," in John Fekete, ed., *The Structural Allegory* (Minneapolis: University of Minnesota Press, 1984), pp. 6–46.

25. See Kaplan, *Walt Whitman: A Life.* For Whitman's attitude toward manifest destiny, see Weinberg, *Manifest Destiny.*

26. Georg Simmel provides the classic notion of association among strangers. See "The Stranger as Insider," in Richard Sennett, ed., *The Psychology of Society* (New York: Vintage, 1977), pp. 150–154.

27. For the implications on American character of a nation of strangers, see Edward Pessen, *Jacksonian America: Society, Personality, and Politics* (Homewood, Ill.: Dorsey Press, 1978).

28. Zweig (*Walt Whitman*) discusses Whitman's momentary anti-abolitionism, pp. 79–83.

29. For more on the 1842 riot, see Kaplan, *Walt Whitman: A Life,* pp. 95–114.

30. Michael Paul Rogin has compiled some of the contradictory rhetorical formations in *Subversive Genealogy: The Politics and Art of Herman Melville* (New York: Knopf, 1983), pp. 102–187.

31. Zweig (*Walt Whitman*) is particularly acute in his analysis of Whitman's turn from politics to poetry, pp. 111–143.

32. James Miller, *Rousseau: Dreamer of Democracy* (New Haven: Yale University Press, 1984), pp. 36–37.

33. The magisterial study of this subject is Marvin Meyers' *The Jacksonian Persuasion: Politics and Belief* (Stanford: Stanford University Press, 1960).

34. Ideology of course has other cultural functions than this one. For a succinct description of them, see Jonathan Dollimore, *Radical Tragedy: Religion, Ideology, and Power in the Drama of Shakespeare and His Contemporaries* (Chicago: University of Chicago Press, 1984), pp. 9–17.

35. Of course this may be only another way of saying they are ideological, but I want to suggest this attribute is correlated with what Castoriadis ("Imaginary Institution of Society") calls the cultural imaginary and Whitman the soul.

36. For natural law as the basis for democracy, see White, *Philosophy of the American Revolution,* pp. 142–187.

37. For a good discussion of Webster's choice of union over liberty, see Eric Sundquist, "Slavery, Revolution and the American Renaissance," in Michaels and Pease, *American Renaissance Reconsidered,* pp. 3–5.

38. On Whitman's losing his job over the slavery question, see Kaplan, *Walt Whitman: A Life,* pp. 114–124.

39. Cited ibid., p. 97.

40. Throughout his poetry Whitman refers to his cultural task as one of realizing liberty.

41. Roger Scruton, *Dictionary of Political Thought* (New York: Harper and Row, 1982), p. 213.

42. For a brief summary of the debate over natural law, see White, *Philosophy of the American Revolution.*

43. Daniel Boorstin, *The Lost World of Thomas Jefferson* (Boston: Beacon Press, 1948), p. 254, n. 3.

44. Cited by Catherine Albanese in *Sons of the Fathers: The Civil Religion of the American Revolution* (Philadelphia: Temple University Press, 1976), p. 120.

45. See Cushing Strout, *The New Heavens and New Earth: Political Religion in America* (New York: Harper and Row, 1973), p. 153.

46. Walter Benn Michaels ("Romance and Real Estate") recapitulates the legal debate over the related issues of property and freedom, pp. 157–170.

47. For a discussion of the relationship of nature's laws and American culture, see Emerson's *Nature.*

48. Richard Slotkin, *Regeneration through Violence: The Mythology of the American Frontier, 1600–1860* (Middletown, Conn.: Wesleyan University Press, 1973).

49. Again, Michael Paul Rogin's *Subversive Genealogy* abounds with examples of these rhetorical reversals.

50. Cited by Joseph Jay Rubin in *The Historic Whitman* (University Park: Pennsylvania State University Press, 1973), p. 80.

51. From *Walt Whitman: Complete Poetry and Collected Prose,* ed. Justin Kaplan (New York: Library of America, 1982), p. 5.

52. Ibid.

53. On the relationship between Hobbesian nature and the British Civil War, see J. G. A. Pocock, *The Machiavellian Moment: Florentine Political Thought and the Atlantic Republican Tradition* (Princeton: Princeton University Press, 1975), pp. 333–365.

54. This idea of the return to nature for a second time has been around at least since Schiller and is discussed by Geoffrey Hartman in "Romanticism and Anti-Self-Consciousness," *Beyond Formalism: Literary Essays 1958–1970* (New Haven: Yale University Press, 1970), pp. 298–310. For a fine discussion of the role nature plays as the "scapegoat muse" of critical theory, see Daniel T. O'Hara, *The Romance of Interpretation: Visionary Criticism from Pater to de Man* (New York: Columbia University Press, 1985).

55. For a moving discussion of the ways in which Americans conceived of themselves as realizations of aspirations of the past when confronted by the return of General Lafayette, see Fred Somkin, *Unquiet Eagle: Memory and Desire in the*

Idea of American Freedom, 1815–1860 (Ithaca: Cornell University Press, 1967), pp. 145–195.

56. Robert N. Bellah insists on the relationship between revolution and covenant in *The Broken Covenant* (New York: Seabury Press, 1975), pp. 1–36. Without the covenant to render stability, the nation remains the victim of a permanent revolution.

57. See *Complete Poetry and Selected Prose by Walt Whitman,* ed. James E. Miller, Jr. (Boston: Riverside, 1959), p. 411.

58. Ibid., p. 416.

59. Ibid., p. 414.

60. The more usual conception of metaphor is that through it we recognize the difference. But in Whitman the possibility that one can become *all* demotes the role that difference plays.

61. *Complete Poetry,* ed. Miller, p. 412.

62. Walt Whitman, *The Uncollected Poetry and Prose of Walt Whitman,* ed. Emory Holloway, 2 vols. (Garden City, N.Y.: Doubleday, 1921), pp. 64–65.

63. I have deliberately included a variation of Kierkegaard's definition of eternity as "recollection of the future" because it offers the best understanding of what Whitman means by regeneration.

64. In this way nature's laws follow the lead of Emerson's description of spiritual laws.

65. *Complete Poetry,* ed. Miller, p. 417.

66. Ibid., p. 416.

67. Ibid., p. 417.

68. Throughout *Leaves of Grass* Whitman will address "savages" on equal terms rather than with "hauteur."

69. Here Whitman offered a vision of nature different from that supported by the frontier myth.

70. Whitman's America was an endless revelation, not the completion of someone else's dream.

71. Tzvetan Todorov, *The Conquest of America: The Question of the Other,* trans. Richard Howard (New York: Harper and Row, 1984).

72. Ibid., p. 153.

73. Ibid.

74. This explanation of language origin is the one Freud invoked in his story of the "Fort-da" game played by his grandchild in *Beyond the Pleasure Principle,* trans. James Strachey (New York: W. W. Norton, 1955).

75. Todorov, *Conquest of America,* pp. 157, 158.

76. With a difference: the Aztecs never possessed any sense of individuality, while Whitman's men-en-masse do.

77. The 1855 edition had no sections.

78. *Complete Poetry,* ed. Kaplan, p. 58.

79. Ibid., p. 59.

80. Ibid., p. 58.

81. See, for example, *Complete Poetry,* ed. Kaplan, p. 80, where he describes his evolution: "All forces have been steadily employed to complete and delight me."

82. In *Themis* (Cleveland: World Publishing, 1962), Jane Harrison refers to such word floods as holophrastic devices and correlates them with the collective soul. See pp. 181–253.

83. *Complete Poetry,* ed. Kaplan, p. 39.

84. *Complete Poetry,* ed. Miller, p. 441.

85. Mikhail Bakhtin, in *The Dialogic Imagination: Four Essays,* ed. Michael Holquist, trans. Caryl Emerson and Michael Holquist (Austin: University of Texas Press, 1981), p. 37.

86. Whitman intended this introduction of a kinship surplus to the masses as a way of preventing the Civil War.

87. *Complete Poetry,* ed. Miller, p. 423.

88. *Complete Poetry,* ed. Kaplan, p. 38.

89. Grossman, "Poetics of Union in Whitman and Lincoln," pp. 186–187.

90. Again I cannot overemphasize the importance for Whitman of a bond capable of uniting the nation.

91. Kaplan, *Walt Whitman: A Life,* p. 246.

92. *Walt Whitman's Workshop,* ed. Clifton Furness (New York: Columbia University Press, 1964), p. 197.

93. Ibid., p. 198.

94. The best discussion of national oratory can be found in F. O. Matthiessen, *The American Renaissance: Art and Expression in the Age of Whitman and Emerson* (New York: Oxford University Press, 1941), pp. 420–435.

95. *Complete Poetry,* ed. Kaplan, p. 80.

96. Whitman always emphasized the relationship he found between the masses and natural processes.

97. Emile Benveniste, *Problems in General Linguistics* (Coral Gables, Fla.: University of Miami Press, 1971), p. 148.

98. *Complete Poetry,* ed. Kaplan, p. 70.

99. Ibid.

100. Ibid., p. 71.

101. Ibid., p. 41.

102. Again, the Freudian "Fort-da" game is the psycholinguistic notion in operation here.

103. Whitman has again borrowed on a reversal of the usual functions of memory.

104. That there can be no end to these associations is Whitman's hope.

105. In an interesting new book, *The Needs of Strangers* (New York: Viking, 1984), David Ignatieff suggests the relationship between a psychology of unfulfilled needs and a welfare society.

106. *Complete Poetry,* ed. Kaplan, p. 29.

107. Ibid., p. 36.

Chapter 5: Edgar A. Poe: The Lost Soul of America's Tradition

1. The context for this dream is itself like an interesting dream. Whitman recounted his dream of Poe to reporters at Poe's reburial in Baltimore on November 16, 1878. He asked the reporters to accept this dream of Poe in place of a "speech":

"In a dream I once had, I saw a vessel on the sea, at midnight in a storm. It was no great full-rigg'd ship, nor majestic steamer, but seem'd one of those superb little schooner yachts . . . now flying uncontroll'd with torn sails and broken spars through the wild sleet and winds and waves of the night. On the deck was a slender, slight, beautiful figure, a dim man, apparently enjoying all the terror, the murk, and the dislocation of which he was the centre and the victim. That figure of my lurid dreams might stand for Edgar Poe, his spirit, his fortunes and his poems—themselves all lurid dreams." See *Walt Whitman: Complete Poetry and Collected Prose,* ed. Justin Kaplan (New York: Library of America, 1982), p. 874.

2. For a brief discussion of the debate between Derrida and Lacan as well as Barbara Johnson's discussion of it, see Donald Pease, "Marginal Politics and 'The Purloined Letter': A Review Essay," *Poe Studies,* 16, no. 4 (June 1983), 18–23. Joseph Riddel's account of Poe can be found in "The Crypt of Edgar Poe," *boundary 2,* 7, no. 3 (Spring 1979), 118–144. John Carlos Rowe's account is in *Through the Custom House: Nineteenth-Century American Fiction and Modern Theory* (Baltimore: Johns Hopkins University Press, 1982), pp. 91–110. Louis Renza's essay is "Poe's Secret Autobiography," in Walter Benn Michaels and Donald E. Pease, eds., *The American Renaissance Reconsidered: Selected Papers from the English Institute* (Baltimore: Johns Hopkins University Press, 1985), pp. 58–90.

3. For a further discussion of the French appropriation, see Patrick Quinn, *The French Face of Edgar Allan Poe* (Carbondale: Southern Illinois University Press, 1957). Quinn is remarkably acute on the relationship between deceiver and deceived in Poe.

4. Quinn takes up this point briefly in *The French Face of Edgar Allan Poe,* but the subject is worth much further discussion. As is the question of the role America played for postrevolutionary governments generally.

5. For further discussion of the French use of America as a screen memory for a lost world, see Bruce James Smith, *Politics and Remembrance: Republican Themes in Machiavelli, Burke and Tocqueville* (Princeton: Princeton University Press, 1985), pp. 155–225.

6. Ibid., pp. 218–238.

7. Ibid., p. 173. Smith also quotes another telling remark from *Journey to America:* "The immigrants in coming over brought what was most democratic in Europe. They arrived having left on the other side of the Atlantic most of the national prejudices in which they had been raised" (173).

8. See also in Smith this quote from Tocqueville: "Those who would like to imitate us—the French in America—should remember there are no precedents for our history" (170).

9. For further elaboration of this point, see François Furet, "The Conceptual System of Democracy in America," *In the Workshop of History,* trans. Jonathan Mandelbaum (Chicago: University of Chicago Press, 1984), pp. 167–197.

10. For further discussion of this aspect of the language of deconstruction, see Wlad Godzich, "The Domestication of Derrida," in Jonathan Arac, Wlad Godzich, and Wallace Martin, eds., *The Yale Critics: Deconstruction in America* (Minneapolis: University of Minnesota Press, 1983), pp. 20–43.

11. Cited in Smith, *Politics and Remembrance,* p. 168.

12. For a more general account of Poe and his readership, see Jonathan Auerbach, "Poe's Other: The Reader in His Fiction," *Criticism* (Fall 1982), especially pp. 343–360.

13. From *The Complete Works of Edgar Allan Poe,* ed. James A. Harrison, 17 vols. (New York: Crowell, 1902), 11 : 43. Further citations will be in the text.

14. Paul de Man, "The Rhetoric of Temporality," in Charles S. Singleton, ed., *Interpretation: Theory and Practice* (Baltimore: Johns Hopkins University Press, 1969), p. 191.

15. Ibid.

16. William C. Spengemann, *The Adventurous Muse: The Poetics of American Fiction, 1789–1900* (New Haven: Yale University Press, 1977), p. 2.

17. *Selected Writings of Edgar Allan Poe,* ed. Edward H. Davidson (Boston: Houghton Mifflin, 1956). Further citations will be in the text.

18. Washington Irving, *Works,* 11 vols. (New York: 1887), 1 : 11–12.

19. *The Journal of Henry Dana, Jr.,* ed. Robert F. Lucid (Cambridge: Harvard University Press, 1968), p. 8.

20. The term "absolute irrelation" appears in Poe's "Eureka," *Works,* 16 : 241.

21. Geoffrey H. Hartman, "Toward Literary History," *Beyond Formalism: Literary Essays, 1958–1970* (New Haven: Yale University Press, 1970), p. 375.

22. Paul John Eakin, in "Poe's Sense of an Ending," *American Literature,* 45 (1973), also notices the desire on the part of Poe's narrators at once to see and to identify with death. But he does not implicate this desire in the sense of being disconnected from an appropriate form of temporality.

23. Larzer Ziff cites this passage in *Literary Democracy: The Declaration of Cultural Independence in America* (New York: Viking Press, 1981) and also notes Poe's self-division and correlates it, as I do, with the great disconnection he experienced in a modern world. But Ziff believes Poe wrote as a way of imagining an alternative world rather than as a way of being remembered by one. See Ziff, pp. 67–84.

24. For further discussion of Poe's reputation, see Donald Pease, "The Rendered and the Surrendered Pose of Edgar Allan Poe," *Cithara,* 20 (November 1980), 26.

25. For a discussion of this relationship in greater detail, see James M. Cox, "Edgar Poe: Style as Pose," *Virginia Quarterly Review,* 44 (1968), 65–77.

26. On Poe's writing as a way of forgetting the present surroundings and entering into relation with an unwritten and unknowable secret reserve, see Renza, "Poe's Secret Autobiography," pp. 65–70.

27. In being the raven, the speaker need not understand or recognize the situation as a mournful one.

28. Joseph J. Moldenhauer provides a fine interpretation of murder in his comprehensive and insightful discussion "Murder as a Fine Art: Basic Connections between Poe's Aesthetics, Psychology and Moral Vision," *PMLA,* 83 (1968), 283–297. Moldenhauer argues that "the inseparability or even identity, for Poe, of the condition of art and death—suggests a center of meaning or a unified design underlying these polar modes of imagination." By choosing death as his focus, Moldenhauer equates beauty with the eternal rest of death and maintains that Poe empties the world of its content in order to arrive at the unified vision of emp-

tiness. But Poe does not reduce beauty or unity to the status of an impoverished point; physical death begins a spiritual life in which all of the partially related earthly forms reach fulfillment in a moment alive with presence and not absence. The artist does not murder himself through the act of creation; he loses his self with the apprehension of a supersensuous world that restores his soul.

29. Poe uses the reader to produce a dream state in himself. In *Marginalia,* he describes his attempt to retrieve images from the dream world: "I have proceeded so far . . . as to prevent the lapse from the point . . . of blending between wakefulness and sleep . . . Not that I can continue the condition . . . but that I can startle myself from that point into wakefulness—and *thus transfer the point itself into the realm of Memory*" (16:90).

30. It seems noteworthy that Poe, in transmuting the unified point into the lost parent, has not so much returned to his parents—as psychological critics are fond of pointing out—as abandoned them for their principle.

31. Charles O'Donnell incisively perceives two opposed tendencies in Poe's art in "From Earth to Ether: Poe's Flight into Space," *PMLA,* 77 (1962), 85–91. O'Donnell separates an infolding embrace of self coupled with a fear of annihilation from an unfolding quest for union with the cosmic identity; and, predictably, he locates Poe's value in the exploration of the psychological tension that persists in the cleavage between inner reality and outer world. But he divides what Poe saw as a single action in which disintegration of ego is an inevitable outcome of the will to sensation—this disintegration working as a means of integrating the individual with the divine. The whirlwind, whirlpool, and vortex are all functional metaphors for a dynamic activity which exposes the fear of annihilation as a longing for union with God.

32. The objective correlative for Poe's universe might be found in the decaying body of a once beautiful lady whose deterioration demands that those who love her see through the decomposition into her original beauty as each progressive stage of deterioration activates a perception of her original ideal form.

33. For a concise discussion of primary repression, see J. Laplanche and J.-B. Pontalis, *The Language of Psycho-Analysis* (New York: W. W. Norton, 1973), pp. 390–394.

34. See the debate between Lacan and Derrida recounted in Pease, "Marginal Politics and 'The Purloined Letter.'"

35. Jacques Derrida, *Speech and Phenomena and Other Essays on Husserl's Theory of Signs,* trans. David B. Allison (Evanston, Ill.: Northwestern University Press, 1973), pp. 151–152.

36. Jean Starobinski provides a brilliant discussion of the relationship between sensation and private enterprise in *The Invention of Liberty* (Switzerland: 1964), pp. 53–74.

37. See Cox, "Edgar Poe," for more on Poe's style as his pose.

38. In "Le Tombeau d'Edgar Poe," *Esprit,* 12 (December 1974), 924, Maurice Mounier sees Edgar Poe spelled out A. G. Pym in the hieroglyphs on Tsalal.

39. Edward H. Davidson, in his groundbreaking *Poe: A Critical Study* (Cambridge: Harvard University Press, 1957), provides an example of the supernatural

reading, while Cox, in "Edgar Poe: Style as Pose," provides a persuasive reading of the white figure as "the ghostly identity of riddling perversity itself, which Poe's persistent self-consciousness has disclosed." In a reading which points up the ambivalence in the ending, Eakin, in "Poe's Sense of an Ending," argues that Pym has been on a "Lazarus quest" and has returned from the vision of the spirit's outer world to reenact it obsessively in each episode of his narrative. But in affirming Pym's experience of the ineffable, Eakin favors Poe's "posthumous experience" over his natural existence. In the narrative, however, Poe does not reenact the final scene so much as repeat the first scene, which is itself either a repression of the ending or an image of it.

Chapter 6: Emerson and the Law of Nature

1. Edgar Allan Poe, "The Man of the Crowd," in *Selected Writings of Edgar Allan Poe*, ed. Edward H. Davidson (Boston: Houghton Mifflin, 1956), p. 139.

2. Ralph Waldo Emerson, *Emerson in His Journals*, ed. Joel Porte (Cambridge: Harvard University Press, 1982), p. 200.

3. Harold Bloom, Review Article, *New York Review of Books*, 31, no. 15 (1984), 23.

4. Ibid., p. 24.

5. Harold Bloom, *A Map of Misreading* (New York: Oxford University Press, 1975), p. 167.

6. Bloom reads Freud's theory of primary repression in the same way as he reads Emerson's theory of self-reliance, as a wish personally to forget a cultural inheritance. When we read Freud through Bloom we recover that inheritance, which Freud had to consign to his unconscious in an anti-Semitic Vienna.

7. Walt Whitman, *Walt Whitman: Complete Poetry and Collected Prose*, ed. Justin Kaplan (New York: Library of America, 1982), p. 1054.

8. Richard Poirier, "Emerson and the Question of Genius," a talk delivered at Dartmouth College, November 11, 1984.

9. Ibid.

10. Whitman, *Complete Poetry*, p. 1053.

11. Throughout his journal Emerson describes Webster's power as originating from nature; and on February 7, 1843, he addresses him as "earth spirit, living, a black river like that swarthy stream which rushes through the human body is thy nature, demoniacal, warm, fruitful, sad, nocturnal." See *Emerson in His Journals*, p. 300.

12. Daniel Webster, *The Works of Daniel Webster*, 5 vols. (Boston: Little, Brown, 1851), 1:59–60, 72–73.

13. *Martin Buber and the Theater*, ed. Maurice Freedman (New York: Funk and Wagnalls, 1969), p. 66.

14. Bloom makes his strongest case for the relationship between poetry and repression in *Poetry and Repression: Revisionism from Blake to Stevens* (New Haven: Yale University Press, 1976).

15. Freud's notes on the work of mourning as the internalization of the lost object appear in the essay "Mourning and Melancholia." For a sustained analysis of

the character and work of a poet as a refinding of a lost object, see Richard J. Onorato, *The Character of the Poet: Wordsworth in "The Prelude"* (Princeton: Princeton University Press, 1971). It should also be noted, however, that Emerson uses the death scene as a "natural" transition from "Nature" to "Commodity," from "Discipline" to "Idealism," and from "Idealism" to "Spirit."

16. By converting compensation into an ethical principle as well, Emerson chose defeat as a means of achieving self-reliance. But this conversion leads to the question of whether he therefore *needs* defeat as a means of self-recovery. Compensation, in its double prepositional register of *for* and *by*, opens up, particularly in the case of the death of Ellen Tucker and Emerson's compensatory refusal to perform the communion ritual, a series of provocative questions. Does he displace the communion ritual with the transubstantiation of Ellen into the body of nature? If the deaths of Ellen and Christ are at all associated, does Emerson refuse to commemorate the communion ritual as a way of forgetting Ellen's death? Does he sacrifice Ellen as the body of nature to recover his idealism? Does he sacrifice nature to his idealism as his way of "getting even" (another connotation of compensation) with God for the death of Ellen?

17. In order to find the continued presence of the child in the idealist, we could correlate his abstract and abstractive language with the "Fort-da" game of the child, for in this game the child controls his anxiety over the disappearance of his mother by commanding and predicting it. What is more important in *Nature,* though, is the child's presence throughout the idealist's discourse. From the beginning, the child enjoys a relation with nature favored enough for the voice of nature to say, "He is my creature and maugre all his impatient griefs, he shall be happy with me."

18. This useful formulation appears in Geoffrey Hartman's tribute to I. A. Richards in *The Fate of Reading* (Chicago: University of Chicago Press, 1975), pp. 36–38. We should also attend to his suggestion here that excessively demanding wishes must descend into a dream text for their fulfillment.

19. I say *post*reflexive because no self remains as the reflecting agent and no world remains to be reflected upon. Both world and self get bracketed out by an intentionality which intends itself—with a resultant consciousness, so to speak, of consciousness.

20. All quotes from *Nature* are taken from *Selections from Ralph Waldo Emerson* ed. Stephen Whicher (Boston: Houghton Mifflin, 1960).

21. Although I will give a much more sustained analysis of Emerson's use of quotation later on, for now we can say that the idealist's use of quotation to corroborate his points evidences a rhetoric of defensive reaction, both assertive of independence from, yet demanding subservience to, the fathers. For such corroborative quotes advocate a concern not to surpass but to succeed the fathers. To justify their use, Emerson must modify his offensive rhetoric (whereby quoting would be groping among "dead bones of the past") with accommodating qualifications (such as "even the corpse has its own beauty").

22. Emerson clearly differentiates this experience of radical solitude from those experiences in his "chamber" when his very individuality made him feel as if he

were another person. Emerson refers to an identity prior to the self-other, reflecting-reflected antinomy at the end of "Spirit," when the poet finds something ridiculous in his delight until "he is out of the sight of men."

23. Kant's views on the sublime appear in the essay "Analytic of the Sublime," collected in *Critique of Aesthetic Judgment* (Oxford: Oxford University Press, 1911). For the best recent treatment of the sublime, see Thomas Weiskel's *The Romantic Sublime: Studies in the Structure and Psychology of Transcendence* (Baltimore: Johns Hopkins University Press, 1976). Weiskel acutely correlates the discontinuity of the sublime with the gap appearing between sign and referent consequent to the arbitrariness of any lexical definition. The sublime then "authorizes" and legitimizes the discontinuity (in the same way that the "transparent eyeball" may be said to authorize the gap in *Nature*).

24. This entire scene, in which winter becomes spring, cloudy skies turn to blue, thinking becomes thoughtfree, and gladness verges on fear, constitutes a condensed image of transition ("crossing the bare common" is also a literal translation of the transitional "to the contrary notwithstanding").

25. The term comes from Weiskel, *Romantic Sublime,* p. 46, and refers to the ruses necessary before the sublime can appear at all.

26. Though I will not make much of the point here, I could argue that the "transparent eyeball" constitutes Emerson's scene of writing.

27. Perhaps the more accurate, though perhaps too paradoxical, way of putting this is that Emerson begins *Nature* twice, and the second beginning (which never takes place as such) provides the space for the first beginning really to begin. Such a phrasing allows us to see the transitive and intransitive beginnings in *Nature*.

28. Kenneth Burke provides the most cogent defense of a dialectical interpretation in "I, Eye, Ay—Concerning Emerson's Early Essay on 'Nature' and the Machinery of Transcendence," in *Language as Symbolic Action: Essays on Life, Literature and Method* (Berkeley: University of California Press, 1968), pp. 186, 299. Burke argues that *Nature* contains bridging words (transcendental operators) effecting the elevation from a lower consideration to a higher (moral) contemplation of nature. But to realize this "coherent" dialectical reading, Burke does not take into account either the repeated violations of "beyonding" through the revaluation of "commodity" or the contradictions at the transitions of the principle of hierarchy Burke must privilege. *Nature* does not refer to a dialectical synthesis of opposing terms but means its disruptions and discontinuities.

29. Paul Ricoeur has made such a correlation of contradiction and metaphor in "Metaphor and the Main Problem of Hermeneutics," *New Literary History,* 1 (1974), 95–110. But to give the idea its metaphysical expanse, we should recall the "paradox of substance" whereby a ground term (such as pure unmanifest substance) can be itself only by becoming something else (manifest existence).

30. The "circle," Emerson's central image, provides another possible metaphor for metaphoricity, for the circle is a point always differing from itself, a decentering center condemned to trace a periphery as its means of describing its content. A circle like *Nature* means its process of transferring.

31. Emerson elsewhere describes the writing experience as "I be and I see myself

be." But in the transparent eyeball, the writing and the written self (usually in- volved in a reflecting/reflected polarity as if the writer were looking at his own back) turn to gaze upon each other and intersect in a locus independent of either reflecting or reflected selves.

32. Alain Cohen, in "Proust and the President Schreber: A Theory of Primal Quotation or For a Psychoanalytics of (desire-in) Philosophy," *Yale French Studies,* 22 (1977), 189–205, includes a long analysis of the quotations as signifiers of quotability. But he carries his analysis into a Lacanian perspective I find irrelevant to *Nature.*

33. To offer but one example, the entire "As when the summer comes from the South" passage recalls the "crossing the bare common" scene.

Chapter 7: Melville and Cultural Persuasion

1. Herman Melville, *Moby-Dick,* ed. Harrison Hayford and Hershel Parker (New York: W. W. Norton, 1967), p. 144. Subsequent references are to this edition.

2. Ibid.

3. For a concise discussion of Melville's indebtedness to Shakespeare's influence on nineteenth-century American culture, see Larzer Ziff's *Literary Democracy: The Declaration of Cultural Independence in America* (New York: Viking Press, 1981), pp. 287–289.

4. See "Hawthorne and His Mosses" in the *Literary World,* August 17 and 20, 1850.

5. For a discussion of the political duties performed by the fiction of manifest destiny, see Thomas R. Hietala, *Manifest Design: Anxious Aggrandizement in Late Jacksonian America* (Ithaca: Cornell University Press, 1985), pp. 1–10, 173–215.

6. Marvin Meyers, *The Jacksonian Persuasion: Politics and Belief* (Stanford: Stan- ford University Press, 1960), p. vii.

7. Ibid.

8. Herman Melville's brother Gansevoort Melville capitalized on his double Revolutionary descent to devise a persuasive political rhetoric. He wrote speeches for Polk that approached Ahab's rhetoric in intensity. See Michael Paul Rogin's *Subversive Genealogy: The Politics and Art of Herman Melville* (New York: Knopf, 1983) for a moving account of Gansevoort becoming a victim of his own rhetoric (42–77).

9. Ahab allowed the crew one ideological formation (social democracy) to de- scribe what they were doing and another (absolute freedom) to describe what he was doing. Only the pursuit of Moby-Dick could resolve the contradiction in these two conflicting ideologies. And that pursuit cost the crew their lives.

10. For the clearest formulation of the opposition between Ahab's totalitarian constraints and Ishmael's freedom, see Walter E. Benzanson, "*Moby Dick:* Work of Art," in Tyrus Hillway and Luther S. Mansfield, eds., *Moby Dick: Centennial Essays* (Dallas: Southern Methodist University Press, 1953), pp. 31–58.

11. In its capacity to bring about—through the intersection of a variety of differ- ent lines of intellectual, emotional, and psychological force—consensus, this Cold War logic may recall what Gramsci called hegemony. But what differentiates it is the

Cold War drama's ability to empty out any thematic value. The Cold War releases what we might call the *force* of persuasion, a force which, like prejudice, works best by economizing on the work of choosing. When within the Cold War arena, we feel "chosen" as a result of the choices we (do not need to) make.

12. The progress followed here is interesting: the Cold War appears first as a mode of structuring an otherwise chaotic world, but the neutral binary opposition informing the structure becomes charged, and the victory of one side in relation to the other promises itself as the outcome—but the outcome *within* the opposition. What we call deconstruction depends on the prior reduction of the world into this superopposition. But the inverting, displacing operations of deconstruction do not dislodge this structure so much as rationalize it. In acting out the logic of this opposition as if it were a revolutionary activity, deconstruction only maintains its cultural power. For a pointed discussion of the self-interest at work in many oppositional theories of criticism, see Paul Bové, *Intellectuals at War* (New York: Columbia University Press, 1986).

13. For an excellent discussion of these procedures, see Henry Pachter's "When the Government Is Lying," rpt. in Robert Boyers and Peggy Boyers, eds., *The Salmagundi Reader* (Bloomington: Indiana University Press, 1983), pp. 58–71.

14. See, for example, the review "Cause for a Writ de Lunatico," *Southern Quarterly Review,* 5 (January 1852), 262; or William Harrison Ainsworth, "Maniacal Style and Furibund Story," *New Monthly Magazine* (July 1853), pp. 307–308.

15. I realize that Matthiessen was not writing during the time of the Cold War, but I wish to argue that his *American Renaissance* helped to create the postwar consensus on American literature as Cold War texts.

16. F. O. Matthiessen, *American Renaissance: Art and Expression in the Age of Emerson and Whitman* (New York: Oxford University Press, 1941), p. 656.

17. For an intriguing discussion of the tension between Matthiessen's need to "authorize" the Renaissance of American culture and his own political views, see Jonathan Arac, "F. O. Matthiessen: Authorizing an American Renaissance," in *The American Renaissance Reconsidered: Selected Papers from the English Institute,* ed. Walter Benn Michaels and Donald E. Pease (Baltimore: Johns Hopkins University Press, 1985), pp. 113–156.

18. See, for example, Irving Howe, "The Sentimental Fellow Travelling of F. O. Matthiessen," *Partisan Review,* 15 (1948), 1125–1129.

19. See Sacvan Bercovitch, *The American Jeremiad* (Madison: University of Wisconsin Press, 1978).

20. Theodore Parker, *A Sermon on the Mexican War: Preached . . . June 25th, 1848* (Boston, 1848), p. 1.

21. The American people were given a literal representation of the return of the past to the present in General Lafayette's processional march throughout the nation in 1824. For a discussion of the relationship between Lafayette's return from the past and America's sense of destiny, see Fred Somkin, *Unquiet Eagle: Memory and Desire in the Idea of American Freedom, 1815–1860* (Ithaca: Cornell University Press, 1967), pp. 131–174.

22. Here we begin to acknowledge the "absolute" power of the paradigm: having already made all the decisions, it enables the individual to conceive the state of being deprived of choice as the freedom from the need to choose.

23. For a compilation of these and many other jeremiads authorized by the Ahab figure, see Alan Heimert, "*Moby Dick* and American Political Symbolism," *American Quarterly,* 15 (Winter 1963), 498–534. Heimert compiles this information with a remarkable sense of the interrelationship, but he does not, I think, have much sensitivity to the conflicts at work in the material he compiles.

24. The use of the "dramatic stage" as a context in which to discuss social and cultural issues presupposes the relation between social life and theatrical distraction, a relationship that may in itself serve certain political interests. We begin to sense the power of this context when we notice how an individual can, through the dramatic metaphor, reexperience the alienation from self that he feels in society as an opportunity to perform a variety of roles. The metaphor, however, cannot address the dramatic actor's distress over the number of roles inviting performance.

25. Here my emphasis differs from Bercovitch's. He calls attention to the inherent similarity between the ideology of free enterprise and the rhetoric in the jeremiad. I want to call attention to the indecision preserved by the form of the jeremiad.

26. This multiplicity of roles permitted Americans to work through any anxieties released in an upwardly mobile society. The reduction of social identity to the status of role made it possible for Americans to move among a variety of jobs—without anxiety.

27. Again see Arac, "F. O. Matthiessen," pp. 98–107.

28. In this case the nation's united past became a mirror image of the "united front" in pre–World War II America.

29. See Matthiessen, *American Renaissance,* p. 426.

30. Ibid., p. 430.

31. Ibid., p. 307. While this appears in Matthiessen's discussion of Hawthorne, I would argue that Melville and Hawthorne serve as locations for Matthiessen's dissent from the "vital doctrines" of Emerson and Whitman.

32. Cited in Ziff, *Literary Democracy,* p. 284.

33. For a discussion of the relationship between unconscious motives, compulsion, and literary forms, see Angus Fletcher, *Allegory: The Theory of a Symbolic Mode* (Ithaca: Cornell University Press, 1964), particularly pp. 221–236.

34. See *Selections from Ralph Waldo Emerson,* ed. Stephen Whicher (Boston: Houghton Mifflin, 1960), p. 146.

35. Garfield's account is cited in Ralph Leslie Rusk's *The Life of Ralph Waldo Emerson* (New York: Scribners, 1949), p. 385. Conway's account can be found in his *Remembrances of Emerson* (New York: Cooke, 1903), and John Jay Chapman's in "Emerson," in Edmund Wilson, ed., *The Shock of Recognition* (New York: Doubleday, 1943), p. 615.

36. *Walden and Other Writings of Henry David Thoreau,* ed. B. Atkinson (New York: Modern Library, 1937), pp. 357, 380, 386.

37. Matthiessen, *American Renaissance*, p. 20.

38. The difficulty with this separation of the inner life from any possible relation to action is the compensatory fantasy system which the need to make the connection produces.

39. I am suggesting, in other words, a strong causal relationship between the formation of an inner, private life and the activity of reading.

40. The compulsion, however, is directed not toward the performance of any action but toward the acceptance of the orators' rhetoric.

41. Of course Emerson also permits a series of conflicting voices to speak in his essays. But in effectively depriving them of a context in which they can appear as anything other than modulations in voice, he effectively converts them back into the motive powers of pure persuasion.

42. Throughout his writing of *Moby-Dick*, Melville engaged in a lengthy, intense correspondence with Hawthorne. Their dialogue allowed Melville a counter-example to the relationship between Ahab and Ishmael.

43. See Heimert, "*Moby Dick* and American Political Symbolism," and Michael Paul Rogin in *Subversive Genealogy* for examples of the various and conflicting uses to which these figures were put. Rogin needs to generate a Freudian-Marxist context in which to ensnare Melville, but this context reveals more of Rogin's nostalgia for the reappearance of that context (in something other than his father's political period) than it reveals about either the politics or the art of Melville.

44. To find out why Matthiessen needed to free Melville from Shakespeare's influence we must remember Matthiessen's association of Shakespeare's prose with the validity of American Renaissance texts. By opposing Shakespeare's prose, Melville became American.

45. For a discussion of the relationship between Ahab's missing leg and his ungratified need for wholeness, see Sharon Cameron, *The Corporeal Self: Allegories of the Body in Melville and Hawthorne* (Baltimore: Johns Hopkins University Press, 1981), pp. 35–51.

46. For a brilliant discussion of the relationship between Ishmael's processual identity and Ahab's compulsion, see Warwick Wadlington, *The Confidence Man in American Literature* (Princeton: Princeton University Press, 1975), pp. 73–104.

47. E. A. Duyckinck makes clear the relationship between Emerson's rhetoric and Ishmael's when he deplores traces in Ishmael of the "indifferentism of Emerson." Cited in Merton M. Sealts, Jr., *Pursuing Melville, 1940–1980* (Madison: University of Wisconsin Press, 1982), p. 383.

48. Ishmael makes clear the connection when he evokes Ahab as his ideal addressee: "Oh, Ahab! What shall be grand in thee, it must needs be plucked at from the skies, and dived for in the deep, and featured in the unbodied air."

49. For a discussion of the ways in which Melville drew inspiration from this confusion, see John Seelye, *Melville: The Ironic Diagram* (Evanston, Ill.: Northwestern University Press, 1966).

Index

Adventure narratives: Poe's *Pym* as, 168–75, 195–202; cultural function of, 168–70, 174–75, 194–95, 195–96

Allegory: Hawthorne's use of, 37–39, 64–65, 101–2, 167–68; as communal narrative, 37–39, 101; Chase on, 39–40; and freedom, 41, 101; and cultural reserve, 64–65; and individual identity, 101–2; Poe's of the instant, 166–68, 186, 189; de Man on, 168

Allen, Ethan, 120, 124

Arac, Jonathan, 246

Bakhtin, Mikhail, 140

Benjamin, Walter, 60, 62, 63

Bercovitch, Sacvan, 36, 248–49, 254, 255, 256, 297*n25*

Bloom, Harold, 9, 209–10, 211, 212–13

Boone, Daniel, 20, 23

Boorstin, Daniel, 120

Brown, Charles Brockden, 18–20, 22, 24, 31

Brownson, Orestes, 114

Buber, Martin, 209, 216

Burke, Kenneth, 254

Calhoun, John, 114, 252, 255

Campbell, Thomas, 36

Chapman, John Jay, 261, 264

Chase, Richard, 9, 10, 39–40

Chevalier, Michel, 51

Childs, David Lee, 252, 255

Choate, Rufus, 82

Chomsky, Noam, 245

Clay, Henry, 18, 146

Cold War: its effects on literary criticism, 11–12, 14, 24, 244–48, 270–71, 273–74; and cultural division, 40–41, 44; its ideology, 243–44, 245, 247–48, 296*n12*; its scene of cultural persuasion, 243–46, 295–96*n11*

Coleridge, Samuel Taylor, 190, 255

Collective memory: legend as, 31–32; Hawthorne's sense of, 46–47, 50, 58–60, 66–73, 79–80, 100–101, 206–7, 208, 210, 213, 274–75; Melville's sense of, 46–47, 274–75; distinguished from personal memory, 66–70; and civic duty, 49–50, 70–72; distinguished from mob rule, 72; as democratic process, 73; as cultural process, 79–80; and Romance, 81–82; and the literary canon, 164; violated in Poe's fiction, 164–66, 167, 173–75, 176–78, 179–80, 201–2, 275. *See also* Cultural reserve

Conway, Moncure, 261, 264

Cooper, James Fenimore, 20–23

Crocket, Davy, 20, 22, 23

Cultural persuasion: its use in the revolutionary mythos, 235–36; its scene in *Moby-Dick,* 236–40, 242–43, 244–46, 271–74; in Jacksonian politics, 240–42, 268; its scene in the Cold War, 243–46; in the American jeremiad, 248–55, 261; its use of doctrine of self-reliance, 261–64; as pure persuasion, 263–64, 265–67, 271. *See also* Oratory

Cultural reserve: as collective memory, 46, 47, 48; in Hawthorne's work, 46–47, 64, 65–66; visionary compacts as, 48; and allegory, 64–65; located in the unconscious, 100, 113, 192; rendered useless by Poe, 191, 192; as the logocentric tradition, 193; adventures as part of, 194–95. *See also* Collective memory

Dana, Charles Henry, 174

Deconstruction: of Poe, 158–59, 162, 163; as revolutionary project, 162–63, 296*n12*

De Man, Paul, 42, 168

Derrida, Jacques, 158, 162, 193

Duyckinck, E. A., 259

DESIGNED BY JOANNA HILL
COMPOSED BY G&S TYPESETTERS, INC., AUSTIN, TEXAS
MANUFACTURED BY EDWARDS BROTHERS, INC., ANN ARBOR, MICHIGAN
TEXT AND DISPLAY LINES ARE SET IN GALLIARD

Library of Congress Cataloging-in-Publication Data
Pease, Donald E.
Visionary compacts.
(The Wisconsin project on American writers)
Includes bibliographical references and index.
1. American literature—19th century—History and
criticism.   2. Authors, American—19th century—
Biography.   3. Alienation (Social psychology) in
literature—United States.   4. United States—
Intellectual life—1783–1865.   I. Title.   II. Series.
PS211.P38   1987   810'.9'003   86-23371
ISBN 0-299-11000-1